TRIUMPH
BOOKS

Praise for Angelo Cataldi and *LOUD*

"For decades, Angelo Cataldi was ringleader of the brashest, funniest, most popular radio show in Philadelphia. As a regular guest, I was often asked 'What's Angelo like?' Finally, in this book, we discover the intelligent, witty, and caring man behind the microphone. Spoiler alert: you'll like him even more once you've read it."

—Mitch Albom, author of *Tuesdays With Morrie* and 11 other bestsellers

"Thirty years ago, a very close friend of mine, Tom Brookshier, told me he was going to hire a sportswriter named Angelo Cataldi and see how he would do as a sports announcer.... I don't think Tom realized how well that decision would work out. I doubt anyone has ever done it any better."

—Dick Vermeil, Hall of Fame NFL coach

"Raucous. Rambunctious. Riveting. Cataldi's memoir is both a front-row seat to the last three decades of Philly sports and a revealing look at how an old school master of talk radio plied his trade in a tough town. *LOUD* is a master class for his alma mater, the Columbia Graduate School of Journalism, assuming they can stomach the political incorrectness inherent in his success."

—Michael Smerconish, bestselling author and host at CNN and Sirius XM

"In 33 years on the radio in Philadelphia, Angelo Cataldi became the most popular and influential sports commentator in the country. He did it by making 'sports talk' fun and outrageous, and by involving his listeners in a way that has never been done before. It made for 'can't miss' radio. This book tells the story of how he did it, and is as wildly entertaining as it was hearing it every morning!"

—Ed Rendell, former Pennsylvania governor and Philadelphia mayor

"I once booked for the *WIP Morning Show* the Eagles GM, the Phillies GM, and the Sixers GM all on the same day. We had our post-show meeting and Angelo said to me: 'Who ya got for us tomorrow?' That was his expectation. Excellence was expected every day. *LOUD* perfectly reflects what we did, and how we did it, for all those years."

—Rhea Hughes, co-host on the *WIP Morning Show* for 27 years

"Read this book before I do."

—Al Morganti, co-host of the *WIP Morning Show* for 31 years

"Legendary broadcaster Howard Cosell once said, 'If we see it, we have to say it,' and for the past 33 years Angelo Cataldi has followed that advice, loudly engaging the city of Philadelphia each morning. *LOUD* is an intimate story of the making of a radio man that created a sports-radio revolution in a city famous for revolutions. Cataldi is a great storyteller, and like his morning show, his writing is genuine, passionate, and most of all authentic. *LOUD* is a classic for those who seek the truth, and for those who want to learn how to say the truth. A must read for any sports fan or anyone entering the field of journalism."

—Mike Lombardi, longtime NFL executive and author of *Gridiron Genius*

"When I came to town in 1997 as the Sixers GM. I soon learned there was one voice that mattered in sports media, and that was Angelo Cataldi. When I would go on the air as the Sixers GM, he gave me the opportunity to give our view even if he disagreed with our view—which was most of the time. Listening to his show prepared me for the questions I was going to get from the media before a press event. For 33 years he set the sports media agenda in Philadelphia every morning. I never realized how hard he worked to prepare for every show until I joined him as a co-host. The stories and memories in this book are electrifying and gives you a glimpse into what he really thinks of some of the sports personalities he encountered in his long, legendary career."

—Billy King, former GM of the Philadelphia 76ers and Brooklyn Nets

"People always asked me, 'Did you hear what Angelo said this morning?!' Of course I did. Nobody knew Philly fans better than Angelo. Nobody held teams more accountable. Nobody made me laugh more. *LOUD* is just as honest, thought-provoking, entertaining, and funny as Angelo was on the air. A truly wonderful look back at his iconic career."

—Todd Zolecki, author of *Doc* and Phillies beat writer for MLB.com

"Angelo is a brilliant maniac and a supremely gifted storyteller. As a former WIP intern, I can confirm he was the greatest teacher of all time. As soon as I learn to read, this book will be so enjoyable!"

—Colleen Wolfe, host of the NFL Network

"The morning after a game, regardless of when I got home, my alarm was always set for 6:00 AM. I couldn't miss Angelo's opening Eagles rant. Nobody was ever more compelling. This is a book I couldn't put down."

—Merrill Reese, voice of the Philadelphia Eagles for half a century

"For as long as I can remember, Angelo Cataldi has been the indisputable voice of Philly sports fans, a pied piper with a loyal following of (mostly) lovable idiots who couldn't help but get emotional about their teams. That's not always a good thing, but with Angelo, it was always entertaining. *LOUD* is the outrageous story of a man who became a sports media legend in an adopted town and, in the end, earned the highest possible praise: he's a Philly guy."

—John Gonzalez, NBA beat writer for the Ringer

LOUD

How a Shy Nerd Came to Philadelphia and Turned Up the Volume in the Most Passionate Sports City in America

Angelo Cataldi

TRIUMPH
BOOKS

Library of Congress Cataloging-in-Publication Data

Names: Cataldi, Angelo, author.
Title: Loud : how a shy nerd from Rhode Island turned up the volume in the most passionate sports city in America / Angelo Cataldi.
Description: Chicago, Illinois : Triumph Books LLC, [2023]
Identifiers: LCCN 2023027975 | ISBN 9781637273548 (cloth)
Subjects: LCSH: Cataldi, Angelo. | Sportscasters—Pennsylvania—Philadelphia—History. | Sports journalism—Pennsylvania—Philadelphia—History. | Philadelphia Eagles (Football team)—Anecdotes. | Sports spectators—Pennsylvania—Philadelphia—Anecdotes. | BISAC: SPORTS & RECREATION / General | SPORTS & RECREATION / Football
Classification: LCC GV742.42.C42 C35 2023 | DDC 070.4/497963—dc23/eng/20230725
LC record available at https://lccn.loc.gov/2023027975

This book is available in quantity at special discounts for your group or organization. For further information, contact:

Triumph Books LLC
814 North Franklin Street
Chicago, Illinois 60610
(312) 337-0747
www.triumphbooks.com

Printed in U.S.A.
ISBN: 978-1-63727-354-8
Design by Patricia Frey

To the loud, proud Philadelphia sports fans
who welcomed me into their world for 33 magical years.

Contents

Foreword

We were settling into our chairs in the NBC Sports Philadelphia studio, clipping on our microphones and preparing for another edition of *Eagles Post-Game Live*. We were watching the monitor as quarterback Carson Wentz was slammed to the turf and fumbled the football, ensuring both an Eagles loss and a dispiriting postgame show.

No one could believe what we had just seen. The Eagles lost the 2020 regular season opener to a motley Washington Football Team, 27–17. The Eagles were expected to win easily and when they breezed to a 17–0 second quarter lead, we felt sure the issue was settled. Then somehow it all unraveled.

Wentz threw a pair of interceptions and he was sacked eight times as Washington, projected to be a hapless bottom feeder in the NFC East, scored 27 unanswered points to win the game. As we prepared to go on the air, a despondent Ed Rendell said, "I can't wait to hear what Angelo has to say tomorrow."

Here was the former mayor of Philadelphia and former governor of the Commonwealth, a man who literally could dial up the president of the United States on his cell phone, yet in his new role as a TV football analyst, the only voice he wanted to hear, the only voice he trusted to bring clarity to this gut punch of a game, was a radio talk show host.

Angelo.

No one asked, "Angelo who?" We all knew, everyone in Philadelphia knew, and at that moment most of them were thinking the same thing: What is Angelo going to say when he opens the microphone on tomorrow's *94WIP Morning Show*?

It would be a primal scream that reflected the shock and anger of the city's fan base, a bellowing monologue that would rattle coffee cups and car windows from Manayunk to Mayfair. All the frustration, all the anger, all the "what the hell were they doing?" exasperation the fans were feeling as they sat in traffic on the Schuylkill Expressway was there in the host's bullhorn voice.

Angelo.

Like Cher, Sting, and Prince, no second name is necessary. There is no shortage of Angelos in Philadelphia. Stand in the Italian Market and shout "Yo, Angelo" and you're likely to cause a six-car pileup. But if you are talking sports anywhere in the city, there is only one Angelo and it is Angelo Cataldi. That has been true across three decades and it will remain so even though he retired from radio after the Eagles' latest heartbreaking loss in the Super Bowl.

Angelo Cataldi was born in Rhode Island and grew up a Yankees fan, but he became the embodiment of a Philly guy, which is remarkable considering the provincial nature of Philadelphia. If you grow up there—and I did—it is easier to gain acceptance. Ray? He is one of us. He gets it. The Mummers, the cheesesteaks, the booing, the funny accent. Look, he still has the scars from the '64 Phillies collapse. He belongs.

It is much harder if you come from somewhere else as Angelo Cataldi did. But once he got behind the WIP microphone, he became not just part of the city's sports community, he became its Pied Piper, its conscience, its B.S. detector and, most of all, its voice.

In a sports town that is all passion and outrage, Angelo brought it every morning. He said what the straphangers on the Broad Street subway and

Market-Frankford El were thinking. He was both their advocate and their validation, that's why they listened and kept listening for 33 years.

He got the city's sports conversation started every morning. He set the agenda. Sports talk went around the clock on 94WIP, other hosts followed and fanned the flames, but it was Angelo who lit the fire.

There was a time when Philadelphia sports fans ran to the newsstand in the morning, plunked down their quarters, and picked up a newspaper to see what Larry Merchant, Stan Hochman, and Sandy Grady had to say about the big game. The columnists—the guys with their pictures on the side of the delivery trucks—were the opinion shapers. They drove the conversation in the diners and the taprooms.

But times have changed and newspapers are withering and the voices on radio and TV have become what the newspapers used to be: the pot stirrers. And in Philadelphia, no one stirred the pot quite like Angelo.

It is a distant memory now, but sports talk radio didn't always exist in Philadelphia. For years, WIP was a music station. My parents tuned in every morning to hear an affable DJ named Joe McCauley—he called himself "the Morning Mayor"—spin records by Frank Sinatra and Patti Page. It was easy listening at its easiest.

In 1988, Flyers owner Ed Snider and former Eagles star Tom Brookshier bought the station and introduced the all-sports format. Brookshier enlisted local sportswriters to host some shows. Angelo was one of them, I was another. We had no radio experience, we didn't even know how to turn on the microphone, but we figured what the heck, let's have some fun.

I thought the all-sports format would fizzle out in a year or two and WIP would move on to country music or politics, but instead the station became a huge success. Today it is one of the top stations in the market and a leader in sports talk radio nationwide, and it is largely because Angelo Cataldi made it so. He was the Springsteen of morning drive. He owned it.

The *WIP Morning Show* succeeded for many reasons. There was the customary morning-radio craziness. It was irreverent and ridiculous at times. The callers were loud and quirky. There were the laughs provided by comedian Joe Conklin, whose gift for mimicking voices—his Charles Barkley is pure gold—and creating song parodies could bring a smile to the face of even the most emotionally battered Philly fan.

The show was full of surprises, even for the guest. One morning, actor Ray Liotta came in the studio to promote his latest film. At one point the conversation got around to *Field of Dreams*, the 1989 baseball film in which Liotta played Shoeless Joe Jackson. *Field of Dreams* has many admirers, but Al Morganti, the *Morning Show*'s co-host, is not among them. Asked his opinion of the film, Al said he found it corny and manipulative. Liotta, the *Goodfellas* tough guy, was speechless.

It was Al who came up with the idea for Wing Bowl, the annual wing-eating contest that featured Sumo-sized gluttons, scantily clad women recruited from various strip clubs, and drunken spectators smashing beer cans on their foreheads, all of it at 7:00 AM. It was so outrageous that it became national news. It filled the Wells Fargo Center every Super Bowl eve and many years overshadowed the game itself.

The *Morning Show* was a frat house—no one would say otherwise—and that was part of its appeal. But there was more to it than that. Angelo, in his previous professional life as a reporter for the *Philadelphia Inquirer*, was a Pulitzer Prize finalist. Beneath the belly laughs, there was a savvy journalist and he brought that to the radio, too.

Angelo knew how to conduct an interview and he wasn't afraid to ask tough questions. When he pressed Eagles president Joe Banner on the team's rule prohibiting fans from bringing their own food into the stadium, you could almost hear Banner squirming in his chair. The Eagles ultimately rescinded the rule—WIP referred to it as "Hoagie-Gate"—and Angelo's persistent grilling of Banner had a lot to do with it.

The Philly fans always knew Angelo was on their side, and I think that was the biggest reason for his success. He understood the fans and genuinely liked them, referring to them as "the most misunderstood fan base in the country." He stood up for them when out-of-town writers criticized them. He asked Chip Kelly the questions the fans wanted asked on the morning after an Eagles loss.

Angelo didn't pander to the coaches, players, and owners of the local teams. He didn't care if they liked him. He was more interested in the fans, his listeners. They were the ones he talked to every morning. They were the ones who sat in their cars listening to his rants even if it meant sometimes being late for work.

Philly sports will go on without Angelo Cataldi. It will just be quieter.

And duller.

***Ray Didinger** has chronicled the Philadelphia sports scene for more than half a century, including 17 years as a columnist for the* Philadelphia Daily News, *a generation as a football analyst on NBC Sports Philadelphia and 12 years as a six-time Emmy winner with NFL Films. He has written a highly acclaimed play,* Tommy & Me, *and a dozen successful books, including* One Last Read, Finished Business, *and* The Eagles Encyclopedia. *In 1995, he won the Bill Nunn Memorial Award for long and distinguished coverage of pro football, and his name was added to the writers' honor roll in the Pro Football Hall of Fame in Canton, Ohio.*

Chapter 1

Maestro of the Mania

"Booooooo! Booooooo! Booooooo!"

Until the moment when that groundswell of rage shook the Felt Forum at the 1999 NFL Draft, it hadn't occurred to me that this whole idea was incredibly stupid.

I gathered together 30 of the loudest, grungiest fans of the Philadelphia Eagles—a team known for its loud, grungy fans—to welcome Ricky Williams to Philadelphia when he was claimed with the second pick in the first round.

Okay, genius. What happens if the Eagles choose someone else?

None of us at the draft had ever considered that possibility until commissioner Paul Tagliabue announced, "With the second pick, the Philadelphia Eagles select...Donovan McNabb, quarterback, Syracuse University."

Oops. The response was organic, and perplexing. To this day, a quarter-century later, it ranks among the loudest outbursts in draft history.

Of course, the person most perplexed was McNabb himself, who had labored most of his life for this moment. His brutal and unexpected introduction to the NFL that day in New York left a wound that has never fully healed.

At the time, I was able to rationalize those boos by handing most of the blame to the dynamic and sports-obsessed mayor of Philadelphia, Ed Rendell. After all, he started the ball rolling (right over McNabb) when he called into my sports-radio show on WIP a month before the draft and began the campaign for Williams, a gifted running back with a social anxiety disorder which he managed with frequent use of marijuana.

Rendell helped to get us the 30 tickets to the draft at a time when it was just beginning to grow into a TV event on ESPN. The mayor called our show every week or so to fan the flames of the populace as we carefully chose the 30 social outcasts who would represent our proud sports city.

Many years later, Rendell confided to me that he realized a day or two before the draft that the plan could go haywire if the Eagles chose someone else, but by then it was too late. There is no stopping Philadelphia sports fans once they get started. Ask the patrons who pelted J.D. Drew in center field with batteries after he shunned Philadelphia for St. Louis, or ask the wacko who shot a flare gun across the field and into the stands during a *Monday Night Football* game at Veterans Stadium, or, yes, ask the zealots who infamously pelted Santa Claus with snowballs.

In retrospect, the entire adventure was doomed before the bus rolled out from our studios at 5th and Callowhill Streets for the 90-mile mission on that cloudy day in late April. When we did the final count, we were missing our 30th day-tripper. "Dirty 29" just doesn't have the same ring to it, so we recruited a grubby homeless man on the corner a block from the station with the promise of free food and drink. It was clearly the best offer he got that week. He ate and drank like a king.

Meanwhile, the other 29 sports enthusiasts became increasingly, er, enthusiastic as we made our way up the New Jersey Turnpike. No alcohol was provided on the bus—by order of the WIP lawyers—but it's a safe bet that many of the fans smuggled in their favorite beverages. As I recall, most appeared to be legally drunk before we even crossed the New York state line.

A bulbous traveler appropriately named "Doughboy"—easily 350 pounds, maybe 400—saw an opportunity to shock a bus of senior citizens that pulled up next to us as we approached the tolls at the Lincoln Tunnel. Without notice, he yanked down his jeans, pressed his massive bare rump against the window in the emergency aisle, and mooned the old-timers.

Doughboy didn't make much of an impression on the senior citizens, but he made a big one on the window, which instantly cracked into a spiderweb of jagged crevices. In the end—since WIP had to pay for the damage—I was far more shocked by what he did than the intended audience. Most of the old-timers were oblivious.

Undaunted, we arrived at the draft in the damaged bus, waited two hours in line before the doors opened, and were placed in ideal seats to see all the action. ESPN must have had an inkling something might happen with these Philadelphia nitwits that would spike interest in the draft.

The ensuing boo has echoed through all these years—a staple for decades as the best advertisement on ESPN for the unpredictable nature of the event. It began another round of national debates about how uncivilized Philadelphia sports fans were, and we were depicted—accurately—as a collection of classless boobs.

As you probably know, even the goal of our mission was misguided. McNabb became the best quarterback in Eagles history, and Williams walked away in a cloud of pot smoke after a good, but not great, NFL career.

At the same time, we learned something about McNabb that predicted his failure to win a Super Bowl. He holds a grudge about that draft day even today, and it illustrated how unaccepting he would always be of adversity. He had magical feet, a powerful arm, and a sensitive soul—far too sensitive for a demanding city like Philadelphia.

In his only Super Bowl appearance, he vomited during a drive in the fourth quarter that consumed too much of the clock in a devastating three-point loss to the New England Patriots.

He choked. Literally.

McNabb still won't admit to that moment of weakness, despite the eyewitness reports of teammates. Since then, he ran out of time in Philly, bombed in Washington and Minnesota, and ended his career with no rings and no bigger regret than how we treated him on his first day as an Eagle.

A few years after the debacle in New York, he agreed to appear as a guest on my TV show, *Angelo and Company*, on Comcast SportsNet—a regional network that featured the games of the Phillies, Flyers, and 76ers. Since he had boycotted my radio show, I was stunned when he actually arrived at the TV studio.

We shook hands briefly, he took his place at the broadcast desk, and graciously answered questions. Early in the interview, I apologized for my stupidity, and he accepted my words of solace with a pained smile. Then we went to break. His tepid grin vanished. Despite my efforts to engage in small talk—never one of my strengths—he didn't utter another word until we went back on the air.

He hated me then.

He still hates me now.

Hey, you can't win 'em all.

For 33 outrageous, insane years, I was the maestro of the mania, the conductor of the symphony of vitriol that blares through the car radios every morning in the most passionate sports city in America. How could a shy nerd from Providence, Rhode Island, end up with this huge responsibility? I'll try my best to explain my evolution from a totally untrained radio performer to the first member (with my early partner, the far more accomplished Tom Brookshier) of the WIP Hall of Fame. It was the second-best honor of my career.

The best was simply being associated with the most endearing and misunderstood fan base in the country. I went on the air every day with a simple mission: talk about what the city is talking about, in the same tone. In other words, I screamed a lot, complained most of the time, and tried never to forget to laugh about it all, too. Our four major sports teams won two championships in 132 tries while I was in front of a microphone, so, for sanity's sake, laughter seemed a better option than tears.

When I finally retired in 2023, after the Eagles blew a 10-point halftime lead and lost the Super Bowl, I was a 71-year-old journalist/radio host with 50 years in the media and enough stories to fill a book (I hope).

For example, I hosted for 26 years arguably the craziest radio promotion in history, Wing Bowl, which annually attracted 20,000 fans at 6:00 AM to watch fat men eat chicken wings. I dealt with clinical depression that led to the end of my 24-year marriage. I was physically attacked twice by people I was covering. I watched a devoted fan die right across the street from Veterans Stadium. I got a clause in my contract that prevented my boss from talking to me.

And then there are the heroes I got to meet and interview, some of the most important people in the world. They included two presidents (before they were elected), Barack Obama and Donald Trump. I sat, one on one, with the most famous athlete in our lifetime, Muhammad Ali; my childhood sports hero, Wilt Chamberlain; the most controversial baseball player in history, Pete Rose; the basketball legend Larry Bird; and entertainment stars like Mark Wahlberg, Dennis Quaid, Joe Piscopo, Janet Leigh, Cliff Robertson, Debbie Gibson, Tippi Hedren, and Ray Liotta. I even got pelted one day with golf balls thrown by Arnold Palmer.

The interview that will remain etched in my brain forever is the hour-long visit we had with boxing great Sugar Ray Leonard just minutes before the planes crashed into the World Trade Center on September 11, 2001. How did he know to write out, in full, the date on the gloves he signed for me that day?

Yes, I definitely have some stories.

My résumé may surprise those who knew me only by my abrasive work on the radio. I attended the best journalism school in the world, Columbia Graduate School of Journalism in New York City, where I made a promise to ask the toughest questions and make no friends among the sports stars I covered. That message must have stuck because I was a finalist for the Pulitzer Prize in 1986 after exposing the lies Buddy Ryan told in his first year as Eagles head coach.

Then I threw it all away, at 38, to try sports radio during its infancy. I never lost the critical eye I developed at Columbia, but I added enough humor to survive in a radio world dominated by icons like Howard Stern and Rush Limbaugh. Eventually, I made a lot of money for the only station where I ever worked, and for myself. None of this would have happened without brilliant co-hosts like Tom Brookshier, Al Morganti, Rhea Hughes, Tony Bruno, and Keith Jones; a gifted impressionist, Joe Conklin; and a fantastic producer, Joe Weachter.

If I learned anything during that incredible run, it was to embrace the fan base, with all of its imperfections. I never gave a damn about the owners, the coaches, the managers, or the players. Oh, they didn't like what I had to say? Too bad. I outlasted all of them. Not a single owner, coach, manager, or player made it through all 33 years I was on the air. The fans were the only constant. They were also the only ones I could count on to be honest and genuine in good times and bad. They were the only ones *there* the whole time.

And they were a fantastic source of entertainment. Whenever I am asked to name the single most outrageous act by a fan I ever saw, I choose a day with two of them. It was October 5, 1992, in the final hour of a 15-hour pregame show before *Monday Night Football* that I hosted (along with many others), a bacchanal that featured sports passion bordering on lunacy.

It was my brilliant idea—in my first football season without Brookshier—to start our show at its usual time of 6:00 AM from a massive tent outside Veterans Stadium that I would occupy later in the day for our pregame show from 6:00 to 9:00 PM. Back then, I did seven hours of radio in one day without hesitation. In fact, if you count the four hours the next morning, I was on the air for 11 hours over a 28-hour period.

Those were the days, my friend. To gain a little extra attention for the annual visit of the despised Dallas Cowboys, I got the approval of WIP's management to move the entire station lineup to the tent that day and to bill the event as the longest pregame show in sports history. (This claim went unchallenged; we did no research to confirm it.)

What none of us calculated was that fans would start drinking in our tent 15 hours before the game and lose control long before kickoff. Especially in that era, the fan base used every Eagles game as an excuse to overindulge, and night games were often a license to get crocked. Unwittingly, we were inviting a new level of misbehavior.

Security removed frenzied fans from the tent throughout the day, but the crowd got so big that, as game time approached, the private police were powerless to restore order.

At one point, fans started throwing eggs and other debris at a Styrofoam tombstone with the words: HERE LIES A BIG MESS. DALLAS COWBOYS. DEFEATED AND DIED. OCT. 2, 1992. (We were not emphasizing our rapier wit back then.)

Unfortunately for our promotion director Dave Helfrich, he was holding a live mic right behind the tombstone, trying to get the sound of the assault, when a booze-inspired fan hurdled a barrier in our tent and threw his body, at full speed, into both the Styrofoam and Dave. The tent shook violently as the drunk slammed through a black curtain and into a barrier behind the display. He rose unscathed, wobbly more from alcohol than from the impact of his attack. Dave was shaken, but he had a story about the insanity of Eagles fans to tell for the rest of his life.

Later that same night, the main event unfolded. An odd fellow who went by the name “Chainsaw” arrived with a posse of morons, and he was determined to make his mark before the crowd made the trek across the street to the Vet. Fat and unkempt, Chainsaw brought with him two items—an inflatable doll with a Troy Aikman jersey on it, and a fully-functional chainsaw.

Much like the ill-advised boo at the draft, Chainsaw clearly had not thought through the plan, which was to sever the head of the Dallas quarterback with the chainsaw. Either because he was also plastered or maybe just really stupid, Chainsaw never calculated what would happen the instant the blade hit the air-filled doll.

“This is what the Eagles are going to do to Troy Aikman,” Chainsaw announced before sliding the blade under the doll’s throat.

It exploded, shards of plastic doll flying over the heads of hundreds of crazed fans. Then the chainsaw flew out of the Chainsaw’s hand and clipped the right wrist of his cousin, a limo driver named Dominic Yanni, before crashing to the ground. Yanni’s wrist was saved only because the chainsaw jammed before it could sever the bone.

The crowd filling every corner of the tent that night exploded in cheers, initially not noticing that Dominic was bleeding profusely. Even more remarkable was the victim’s reaction. He held up his bloody appendage seeking more approval—which inspired an even bigger roar. I strongly urged him to seek medical help, but my advice fell on deaf ears. He wrapped the wrist in a makeshift tourniquet and pranced triumphantly across the street with his equally impaired cousin.

The Eagles fulfilled our dreams that night, crushing the evil Cowboys, 31–7, but ultimately would disappoint the fans that season like so many other talented Philadelphia teams in that era.

As for Chainsaw, he became a regular caller, delighting in telling, over and over, the story about how his cousin got that big, ugly scar on his wrist.

Chainsaw's injury was not the worst thing that happened before an Eagles game, unfortunately. On one occasion, the tent went from fun and games to life and death. Even today, 27 years later, the fans who were there shudder at the memory of that awful day.

As the Eagles approached the home opener of the 1996 season, I started a quest to determine the patron with the longest consecutive-game streak, and what emerged from that on-air experiment was a 62-year-old Langhorne, Pennsylvania, loyalist who was about to cross the turnstiles for the 200th consecutive time. We called him "the Iron Man of Veterans Stadium."

John Zitter was right from central casting—a heavy-set working man with a deep commitment to family and a lifelong love of the Eagles. We talked a couple of times on the air before we honored him that Sunday in the tent. And when he arrived, John was the recipient of cheers for the first time in his long life as a sports fan.

As he approached the microphone right in front of our broadcast table, I could tell right away that he didn't look comfortable—a common reaction for someone who isn't accustomed to speaking in public. But then his condition worsened. We could all see as I introduced him that he was in distress. That was just before he fell backwards and appeared to lose consciousness, his head slamming against the concrete walkway.

In that moment, I didn't know what to say or do: Should I abandon the broadcast to help our fallen hero, or should I just keep reporting what was happening and hope someone else would rush to his rescue? Fortunately, several people more equipped to handle the emergency jumped in, as I wrestled with how much to report to our listeners, many of whom were stuck in traffic on the roadways surrounding Veterans Stadium.

Before long, it was clear that John Zitter was fighting a losing battle for his life. His lips were turning blue as a trained professional was administering CPR, to no avail. Soon, an ambulance arrived and whisked John off to a nearby hospital. It was too late by then. The Iron Man had suffered a massive heart attack. He was gone.

We didn't get the official word on John's status as game time approached, but we all knew what we saw. You never forget the first time you see someone's lips turn blue.

Before we left the air for the game broadcast at 1:00 PM, John's son, Jeff, arrived at the tent to find out what had happened. He said his family was stuck in traffic on the nearby Walt Whitman Bridge when they heard on our show about the emergency. Off the air, the only thing I could tell Jeff was that it looked serious, and that all of us were praying for his father.

Jeff made several appearances on our show in the next few years to honor the memory of his dad, but I can't help feeling embarrassed that we moved on so quickly from that nightmare. The end of a life at the beginning of a season.

Often, I remind myself that I chose sports as a career to escape the real world, but who was I kidding? As we learned many years later with the COVID crisis, there is no actual escape.

The John Zitter story is powerful and painful proof of that.

Through all of those early days, and then into the bulk of my time at WIP, I was just a loud voice in the din of Philadelphia sports. Okay, maybe the loudest voice. After all, I was the one with the microphone. But the response to my relentlessly obnoxious radio persona was mixed, at best.

I can remember attending a horse race in my early days at the long-forgotten Garden State Park Racetrack in Cherry Hill, New Jersey, and recoiling when the crowd booed at the PA announcement of my name.

In a way, this was a preview of what McNabb would receive later that decade, though his assault was much louder and nastier. In those days before the internet became a thing, I got letters all the time from people trashing me for an opinion they didn't like or for the way I expressed it. At best, I had an approval rate of maybe 20 or 25 percent.

In my final few years, though, something happened that I had never anticipated. Somewhere around year 30, people started calling me "a legend," a term which I joked was synonymous with "old." For the final five years of my career, I gave out my email address and answered every one myself. Believe me, the first words out of many mouths did not include "legend." Early in those email days, fans expressed their dislike of me with a blistering passion that, frankly, frightened me at times.

When you make comments for more than three decades that hold nothing back, when you call sports figures "gutless," or "moronic," or—my favorite—"weasels," you make enemies. Lots and lots of enemies, even among the many listeners who kept tuning in just to get aggravated all over again.

Then something happened that is hard for me to comprehend even now. After the worst of the COVID pandemic, I announced my retirement. From that day on—16 months before I actually left—I was loved by many and hated by few, or so it seemed. (McNabb being one exception, of course.) I felt the warm embrace of the most passionate sports city in America in a way I didn't really expect and, frankly, didn't really deserve.

At the very end, I agreed to attend a pep rally at the most popular bar near the sports complex, Chickie's & Pete's, two days before the NFC Championship Game between the Eagles and San Francisco 49ers. It was the first time in a decade and a half that I was re-engaging with the booze-infused festivities that were so much a part of my pregame tent duties.

During the height of the Friday-night event—chainsaws were not allowed, by the way—with a crowd of 1,000 or so crammed into the bar, my co-host at WIP, Ava Graham, introduced me. I still can't believe what I experienced.

A roar of approval shook the bar for seconds that passed like minutes. Pete Ciarrocchi, the owner, said it was the loudest ovation he had ever heard at one of his establishments—and he has 17 all over the country now. I met with hundreds of fans that night, and I felt like a superstar myself—like Dr. J at his height, like Bobby Clarke and Mike Schmidt and Brian Dawkins, all wrapped into one shy, nerdy old man from Rhode Island.

That's the night I decided I needed to write this book. As my journalism professors at Columbia taught me many years ago, presenting the truth is always the ultimate goal.

At the risk of turning lots of those cheers back into boos, this is my story.

Chapter 2

Life as a Journalist (For a While)

The idea that I would someday leave the comfortable confines of Providence, Rhode Island, and head to big, bad Philadelphia was inconceivable until well past the dawning of adulthood for me. I was the quintessential dork, the son of a toolmaker and housewife, Angelo Sr. and Ida, who excelled in school from the outset. Back then, before psychologists and lawyers got involved, kids would skip grades if they exhibited unusual aptitude.

My sister, Phyllis, never went to second grade. She was the true brain of the family, and I was deemed worthy of the slightly less respectable level of achievement—attending classes with the grade ahead of me without actually skipping. This made for a horrible sixth grade because I had already done the work when I was a grade below, and seventh grade was two miles and year away at junior high.

By the time I got to high school, I qualified for what amounted to the biggest honor available to a young Rhode Island student, admittance to Classical, a place reserved for the smartest (and nerdiest) kids. I continued to excel in class, but nowhere else. I was already approaching six feet tall, and as thin as a string bean back then. (In fact, for a few years, my nickname was actually Bean.)

My dad's love for baseball, and specifically the New York Yankees, was my introduction to sports, and I embraced the highs and lows mostly in solitude. I had a few good friends, but my constant companion was television. When I wasn't studying, usually I was watching *Leave It to Beaver*, *The Twilight Zone*, and sometimes even the movie matinee with my grandfather, Nicola, who lived with us and with whom I shared a room. (I can still hear his snoring 50 years after his passing.)

In a sports city ruled by the nearby Boston teams, I quickly became a contrarian, first with the Yankees in a Red Sox town, and then with the 76ers in a city ruled by the Celtics (and, even more so, the Providence College Friars.) My favorite athlete then was Wilt Chamberlain, the greatest NBA player of all time. (You can look it up. He still has most of the major records.)

The sports highlight of those early years was a rare visit to a dilapidated, smoky old building called "The Arena" (or "The Auditorium"—Rhode Island fans never could make up their minds) when Wilt and the Sixers faced the Celtics. Back then, the Celts would occasionally play a regular-season game in Providence, 40 miles from Boston Garden.

I managed to sneak down near the court during the warmups, and it was love at first sight. Chamberlain was (and still is) the most magnificent human being I had ever seen—over seven feet tall with massive shoulders and legs that went on forever. Before the game, Wilt stood to the side of the free-throw line, about 17 feet from the basket, and pumped shot after shot off the backboard and into the net. He must have put up 30 shots and never missed. It was mesmerizing.

This love for sports most definitely did not translate into any athletic success of my own, however. I did play in Little League, often in right field. I was usually the center in basketball because of my height, but my hands were stone and my feet were clay.

I sucked.

In an apparent effort to win status as King Nerd, I did manage to ascend through the hierarchy of the Classical Chess Club until I reached vice president. Hey, at least my parents were proud.

Even less impressive than my athletic exploits were my efforts with the opposite sex. I didn't go on a date until my senior year, and I missed the Senior Prom because my cousin declined my invitation. When I did start a relationship, right near the end of my senior year, I ended up marrying the girl. (I assumed she was the only female who would ever agree to it.)

As my attention turned to my many weaknesses back then, my commitment to education wavered. In fact, I ended up applying to only one school, then rated among the top party colleges in America, the University of Rhode Island. My girlfriend, Linda, and I moved into the first coed dorm in Rhode Island, Heathman Hall, and became a couple. We even boycotted classes in our freshman year, 1969–70, during a period of student unrest over the Vietnam War. (I actually did it only because I didn't want to take final exams.)

URI was a much better school for drinking than thinking, so I maxed out my credits every semester after that freshman year and graduated with the class ahead of me in 1972. During my final semester, I interned at the local weekly newspaper, the *Narragansett Times,* and was offered a permanent position by the editor, Gerry Goldstein, when I graduated.

Soon after I turned 21, I was named the assistant editor at the newspaper and got married. Making the situation even more improbable, my wife and I were hired to be house parents at Sigma Del Tau, a sorority of around 60 mostly Jewish women who were only a year or two younger than us. In the end, we got free boarding in a small apartment and $1,250 a month to protect the girls.

And protect them, I did not. One night the jock fraternity, Sigma Nu, broke into the sorority in the wee hours and proceeded to scare the bejesus out of the girls, and me. The extent of the damage was a few broken windows and walls drenched in pungent, beery urine. I called the campus police and stood in the doorway during the break-in. When the fake cops arrived, unarmed, they did likewise until the jocks got tired and left.

Meanwhile, I started planning my future beyond campus life and a small weekly newspaper, and I decided to aim high. I can remember telling my URI adviser, Wilbur Doctor, that I planned to apply to the Columbia journalism school and eliciting a snort from the professor. Though I had a 3.5 grade-point average and made it through URI in less than three years, he was aware of how I did it. My transcript was clogged with cookie courses. I took three on horticulture, including advanced bush arrangement. I was the only male in two different home-economic classes. I had gamed the system, and surely an esteemed institution like Columbia would see right through my con.

When I got my letter of acceptance, no one was more shocked than Mr. Doctor. He said I was the first URI journalism student ever to get into the Columbia journalism program—though, he pointed out, I was far from the worthiest. (I'm sure many have followed me since that unlikely occasion in 1976.)

Then a very strange thing happened. Right after I was accepted, I went for a visit to the massive old journalism building in New York, met with a few of the top people there, and was on my way out when I stopped at the bulletin board. It was still months before I would start there, but I saw a job notice for editor of the very newspaper I would be leaving in six months. Huh?

I hadn't shown any indication yet that I would be giving notice at the *Narragansett Times*, so how was the job above mine being advertised at Columbia? I told my boss, and he was equally mystified. Gerry Goldstein was so much better than that small newspaper, but the same could not be said of the owners. They were planning to fire him, for reasons never explained by anyone. He quit before they could execute their plan, leaving me, at 24, as the interim editor.

Since the newspaper didn't fold in the months when I ran it, the owners asked me to stay permanently. No, thanks. Gerry was 10 times better at the job. How long before the position, my position, would be back up on the Columbia bulletin board? I departed for New York as planned, leaving behind a great lesson on business mismanagement, and a pregnant wife.

The moment I arrived by train at Columbia, I learned that this was most definitely not Providence. I was assigned a dilapidated old dorm named Ruggles Hall, which greeted me with a sign informing all visitors and occupants that the building was condemned.

Once I crossed the threshold, I could see why. It looked and smelled dangerous. I used the elevator one time in my nine months there, on that first day. When the doors finally grinded open, I knew I would be climbing the four flights every time I came and went.

The morning after my first restless night, I walked through the front door and almost stepped in a puddle of blood. Someone had been knifed—and killed—on the doorstep of the mangy dorm. Welcome to New York. Our first instruction during orientation at Columbia was not to leave the subway stop if we went past 116th Street on the 1 train because we would be entering Harlem, a dangerous place back then for anyone who looked like many of us. I never missed my stop.

Within a few weeks, I developed a fungus infection in my fingers that took a decade to overcome. Not long after that, I also started getting severe nosebleeds, becoming a regular visitor to the hospital near campus. The doctors there were not shocked by my condition. Apparently, I had Ruggles Syndrome, a health risk inevitable when you live among the cockroaches and rats that had squatter's rights in our infamous dormitory. Hey, I survived. That's the best thing I can say about that dump.

On the other hand, the classes themselves were exhilarating, filled with brilliant students and extraordinary professors. On the very first day, right after the introductory speeches, we picked slips of paper out of a fishbowl with our first assignments. I was told to travel to Co-Op City (a long subway-plus-bus trip north of Manhattan), and to do a man-on-the-street article about an imminent primary election.

I knew I was at Columbia when I compared assignments with an attractive young woman later identified as Katherine Field—daughter of Chicago department-store magnate Marshall Field. I was definitely playing in the big leagues now.

A meeting in the first week of my time at Columbia changed my life. I was assigned as an adviser to a serious-minded man named Norman Isaacs, who most recently had run the *Louisville Courier-Journal* and was regarded as a journalism visionary. I will never forget plopping down in the seat across from this impressive man and announcing that my goal in life was to write about sports.

Sports? Columbia had produced the best foreign correspondents, the most accomplished editors of major newspapers and magazines, countless best-selling authors, and not one—as far as anyone could recall—sportswriter.

I convinced him that this was the right track for me when I proposed as a master's project an in-depth study of Yankee Stadium, including promises not kept when the city funded a massive and costly renovation of the ballpark and its neighborhoods. The park reconstruction went as planned; the neighborhood work did not. In fact, there was virtually no neighborhood work.

Isaacs liked the seriousness of my proposal and, in the moment, saw the potential of a well-trained journalist taking on the frivolous world of sports. Ultimately, he approved my educational track, but I had to make two pledges: First, I had to cover sports the way the media covered the White House—ask the toughest questions and hold the people in power accountable. No hero worshipping allowed. Make no friends of the people you cover. Bring journalism to sports. And second, I had to breathe to no one at Columbia my intention to cover sports. When someone would ask, I would say I wasn't sure yet.

During my year at Columbia, I did take one diversion from sports to pursue my other major interest—Hollywood. I love TV and movies, and always have since those afternoon matinees with my grandfather. When I looked at the catalogue and saw a film-criticism course with the revered writer Judith Crist, I jumped. She was, without question, the best teacher I ever had. She hated most of what she reviewed, using some of the same colorfully derogatory terms I would later apply to sports.

She also made even more unclear how I ever got accepted into Columbia in the first place. I had always assumed, with a few years of practical experience under my belt, I had dazzled the acceptance committee with the essays that I had presented as part of the application process. I was wrong. One day, Ms. Crist read passages from those essays during a class, and the one that received her biggest verbal demolition was mine.

"Mr. Cataldi," she said as she looked up from her reading glasses. "Did you write that?"

"Uh, er, I guess," I stammered.

"Well, we've got a lot of work to do, don't we?"

"Uh, er, yes, Ms. Crist."

Forty-five years after I graduated from Columbia, I can still provide no clear answer as to why that amazing school approved my weak application. Bad essays and a course load filled with landscaping and cooking classes are not the usual route to a master's degree at the best journalism school in the world.

The fungus infections and nosebleeds aside, though, the nine months at Columbia rivaled any period in my life. It was everything as advertised, if not more. I was still the nerd from Providence, but I accepted my diploma with a newfound confidence that served me well for my entire media career.

In the 46 years that followed my graduation in 1977, I often reminded myself that I must be right. I went to Columbia.

Just before I left the campus for good, I had one last meeting with Mr. Isaacs. He made a final attempt to talk me out of sports by offering me the job as the labor reporter at the *Courier-Journal*. It wasn't sports, but it was much better than the entry-level position I would get anywhere else. I had a baby daughter by then, and the extra money in a less expensive city was tempting. But no. Sorry. I wanted sports.

Using my Columbia connection, I got a job back home at *The Providence Journal-Bulletin*, starting—ironically—as a bureau reporter right back in southern Rhode Island, just a few miles from the URI campus. And my new boss was my old boss. That's right, Gerry Goldstein was the bureau chief. (Rhode Island is a very small state.) He is still one of the best journalists I have ever met. He was a brilliant mentor.

Once I had been promoted to the big city after a few months, I bartered a deal that would pave the way for the next four-plus decades of my career. I met with the executive editor, Chuck Hauser, and told him I wanted to jump to the sports department, and I would do anything to get there. Anything? He then proposed that I work for one calendar year on his pet project, Action Line, a daily column that took consumer complaints from readers and resolved them by using a socially acceptable form of extortion.

We would take a complaint from someone not happy with, say, the now-defunct Outlet Department Store, and we would talk to an executive there about the two options the powers-that-be had. They could either fix the problem—refund the money and apologize—or we could write in the column that they didn't care about their customers. Almost without exception, they relented. We then wrote in gushy language how responsive they were to their customers, and they ended up with a free ad. Win-win.

It was a horrible job. Companies would dodge us for weeks, and then they would often react with profanities when they could avoid us no longer. (Great training for a sports talk-show host in Philadelphia.) The last few months for me were a slow trudge through the muck of corporate America. I hated every minute of it. But Chuck Hauser was a man of his word. He added a position to the sports department and, finally, he gave me the only job I had sought from the time I was a teenager.

After a year or so of high school games and copy editing, I slowly gained favor with my bosses by taking on the sports heroes of Providence—especially beloved Providence College and Big East king Dave Gavitt, who despised me for pointing out his many foibles. By early 1979, I started getting better assignments, including the Boston Celtics. It was in my early days of covering them that I received my first exposure to national attention.

Right after Larry Bird had signed his first contract with the Celtics that year, he was making a public appearance at a school in Providence, and I was assigned to talk to him. The only one not aware of my challenge that day was Bird himself, who was habitually tongue-tied even in the carefully controlled environment of Indiana State. It's safe to say he was no more ready for me than I was for him.

Before his introduction to the students, Bird was standing alone and looking down at his feet in a tunnel outside the gym when I approached. I started by congratulating him on his five-year, $3.25 million contract, eliciting little more than a grunt. I tried a few other questions, with similar results. My first thought was, how could I write this story? I didn't even know how to spell the noises coming out of his mouth.

Then I made a connection. I asked him how the money would change his humble life in French Lick, Indiana. He actually looked up and said it was all the money he would ever need, so he planned to retire after the five years and realize his dream, to become a gym teacher in French Lick. It never occurred to me as I drove back to the office that a young man with Bird's unique skills would dream only of teaching dodgeball and rope climbing, but who was I to question him? He said it, and I wrote it.

When my editor saw the story I had typed on my electric typewriter—this was a few years before we got our first computers—he called me over and asked if I was sure this is what Bird had said. Yes, I was sure. Still, *The Providence Journal* had so little faith in my reporting at that point that they didn't even run the story on the front sports page. Within hours, however, many other publications did.

The next day, Bird denied saying anything of the sort. He called the story ridiculous and pledged his love for the Celtics until the end of time. Immediately, I was summoned a second time by the top sports editor, Gene Buonaccorsi, who started the conversation by saying we had a problem.

Actually, we didn't. From my first day at Columbia, I was taught to record all conversations, and the Bird interview was no exception. I played the tape, which I had transcribed while writing the story. It was word-perfect. Gotcha.

The report faded away quickly once the *Journal* backed my story, and I was left with four years of awkwardly encountering Bird in the locker room, never again exchanging a single word with him. I quoted him rarely as he made his ascent to the top of the NBA, and only when I got the comment in a group setting.

Once a liar, always a liar.

Shortly after I began covering the Celtics on a regular basis, I quickly learned that my main nemesis would be the coach, Bill Fitch, and not

Bird. My troubles with Fitch, a belligerent bully, began when I wrote a column about how different he actually was from his image as a quick-witted basketball curmudgeon. In other words, to know him was to loathe him. The column came out just before the playoffs in 1982, and it did not resonate with the coach of the reigning NBA champions.

When I arrived at the game the next night in Boston Garden, I was disappointed to find that my regular courtside seat near the scorer's table was assigned to someone else. Even though my newspaper was one of the top circulation outlets covering the game, I had been banished to the auxiliary press box near the nosebleed seats.

When I asked the PR director, Jeff Twiss, what had happened, he simply said "See the coach." I had a much more effective plan than that. I went back down to the court, told the most powerful basketball writer in America, Bob Ryan of the *Boston Globe*, what Fitch had done. Soon I was holding my own press briefing just a few minutes before the game.

The next morning, I was amused to see that I had become the top sidebar after the game. Fitch, never beloved because of his woe-is-me demeanor even after winning the NBA championship in 1981, got drowned in bad ink. There had been rumors that Fitch was not a favorite of the front office—which included the legendary (and extremely likeable) GM Red Auerbach and the team owner Harry Mangurian—but I didn't know how thin the ice was under Fitch until my phone rang.

"Please hold for Mr. Mangurian," I heard right after I picked up the phone.

The furniture and cement magnate was not calling to defend his coach. Quite the contrary. He apologized on behalf of the Celtics organization and promised that he would deal with the matter privately after the playoffs.

He sure did. Despite a 56–26 season and the championship a year earlier, Fitch was fired. Now, I'm not here to tell you the coach lost his job because of the way he bullied me, but I will theorize confidently that my incident exposed a deeper breach between Fitch and his bosses.

In future dealings I would have with Jim Fregosi, Buddy Ryan, and Gabe Kapler, among many others—the template of my life with coaches was set back there in Boston. Most of them would despise me, for valid reasons. What none of them understood in the chummy world of professional sports was that I didn't care what they thought. They were never the target audience. The readers were—and later, the listeners.

By far the best assignment I got in my six years at the *Journal* was interviewing, one on one, the most famous man in the world at the time, Muhammad Ali. He was in one of the many lulls during his historic career, and he chose Providence for an exhibition against his good friend and sparring partner Jimmy Ellis. Even in a boxing town like Providence, the idea of getting 10,000 fans to pay for an exhibition was daunting, but not for Ali. He could sell a cheesesteak to a vegetarian.

One of the advantages I had in my media career was that I was rarely starstruck. I never aspired to be an athlete, so I was not overwhelmed when meeting a superstar. Ali was a rare exception. He arrived at the Biltmore Hotel a few minutes late and—after greeting a horde of well-wishers—sat at a table for two alone with me for our interview.

All of these years later, I have little recall of what he said to promote the match—which was a sellout, of course—but I remember vividly the moment when he reached for my slim reporter's pad and borrowed my pen. The biggest celebrity in the world then drew a chart entitled *World Power*, trying to illustrate how best to make the world a better place.

He was gracious, funny, and, above all, charismatic, and I treasured that chart for years. Unfortunately, it got lost in one of my many moves, but the memory of it will stay with me for as long as I live. In my eyes, he was, is and will always be, the greatest sports figure I ever met.

My biggest claim to fame in my six years at the *Journal* was attending the longest baseball game in history, a cold, miserable eight-hour and 25-minute exercise in endurance between Triple A teams Rochester and Pawtucket that was not decided for two months and remains a charming benchmark in the sport, at least by those who didn't have to endure it.

The truth is, it was one of the worst nights of my life. A power outage in disgusting Pawtucket, a suburb just north of Providence, delayed the game for a half hour, during which time the temperature was approaching the freezing mark and wind was howling in from center field on April 18–19, 1981. The star on Rochester was future Hall of Famer Cal Ripken, while Pawtucket countered with the best self-promoter I ever met in sports, Wade Boggs.

By my first deadline at 11:00 PM, the players had grinded through 11 innings, and most of the crowd of hundreds had shivered back to their cars and wisely returned to the warmth of their homes. I had no choice but to stay until my final deadline at 2:00 AM. It was after that first benchmark at 11:00 that I began to develop my skill at complaining, something I used to far better advantage years later in Philadelphia. The handful of people who were there till the bitter end can attest to my non-stop patter of despair. I ripped the umps for calling the game fairly, I ripped the players for not blowing the game on purpose, and—above all—I ripped the International League for not calling a halt to the insanity.

To no avail. Once my final deadline passed around the 25th inning with no sign of an end to the misery, I was free to leave. But I didn't, having been reminded by the heartier crew braving it in the tiny, unheated press box that the contest was nearing the record for the longest game, 29 innings.

"You don't want to leave before the record, do you?"

I grumbled through frozen lips and pressed on. The game finally was halted after 32 innings when an executive for the Pawtucket team was able, at 4:00 AM, to reach the league president, who—according to legend—had been out partying and was unreachable, as it was more than 15 years before the advent of cell phones.

The game did not resume until June 23, at which time I crossed paths for the first time with my future radio co-host, Al Morganti, who was covering the resumption for the *Boston Globe.* I didn't actually exchange words with Al that night, but he haunted me for many years after that by saying he, too, had been to the longest game in baseball history. (The game was decided on a balmy June evening in the 33rd inning, 18 minutes after it resumed.)

Since then, millions of words have been written about the magic of that night. Every one of these words is bogus. Those who were there, without exception, hated the experience while they were enduring it. Only in retrospect, with violins playing the background, has the game become lyrical.

As for me, I am called every time a writer or broadcaster is looking back on that night as the lone voice of reason amid an ocean of hogwash.

My commitment to get to the truth was not a good fit for Providence, where hero worship was a prevailing theme throughout my life there. With Larry Bird, Carl Yastrzemski, Bobby Orr, Bill Russell, and so many more, there was no appetite for my warts-and-all approach to journalism. New England likes its heroes pure.

I found this out for sure when I wrote an article that challenged the legacy of the only undefeated heavyweight champion, Rocky Marciano. Although he was actually a native of nearby Brockton, Massachusetts, Marciano was a god in Providence, especially among Italian sports fans like my father. That an Italian journalist (me) would set out to question that record was a great way to wear out your welcome fast.

During my two-year stint covering boxing for the *Journal,* I got closer to athletes than at any other time in my half-century in the media. I ran (very briefly) with Marvin Hagler during one of his early-morning workouts before a big fight, I was spattered with the blood of Wilford Scypion while seated courtside at the Providence Civic Center and I got to schmooze with the colorful characters in America's most accessible sport.

Unfortunately, I was in it for more than the passing friendships. I was looking for stories. So when someone told me about the strange boxing match between Marciano and "Tiger" Ted Lowry that took place at the Rhode Island Auditorium on October 10, 1949, I was intrigued. Rocky was 20–0 with 19 knockouts at that point, but he was not ready for the ring savvy of Lowry, who was 64–49–9.

In the second, third and fourth rounds, Marciano was near collapse after flurries by his cagey opponent, and Rocky lost the first four rounds on all of the judges' cards. Then an amazing thing happened. Lowry stopped fighting. Marciano won the last six rounds and kept his perfect record by a unanimous decision.

Why did Lowry stop? Why did he go into a shell when he was so close to victory, and maybe a knockout?

The great thing about boxing is, everyone talks. Or at least they did back then. And I got a source inside the boxing commissioner's office willing to describe what was said to Lowry before the fight, and during it when he was leading. Basically, Lowry was threatened with banishment if he followed through on his victory. Instead, he laid down for six rounds and lost the decision.

As far as I could tell, my story was unassailable. I had witnesses saying Lowry should have won the decision anyway. I had insiders saying the Mob got to Lowry before and during the fight. And Lowry himself went silent, eyes down, when asked what happened in the last six rounds of the bout.

I was convinced the fight was fixed, and that's what I wrote. No one else was convinced at all. And that included my own father, whose love for another Italian superstar, Joe DiMaggio, is what inspired his love of sports—and ultimately, mine.

"Why do you have to be writing stuff like that?" he said. "Leave well enough alone."

The letters that poured into the newspaper after that story were, let's say, a bit aggressive. For a few weeks, I laid low. Norman Isaacs never warned me that my promise to him might be life-threatening.

I stand by my Marciano–Lowry story all these years later. I really do believe the fight was fixed. I also believe that the negative reaction to the story was a clear sign that I was not welcome in my hometown anymore.

Shattering sports myths did have its benefits, too. In fact, it got me a free ticket out of town not long after my Lowry expose. I wrote a column one day, years after Yankee catcher Thurman Munson was killed in a plane crash, lambasting the gushing adulation he was receiving. I argued that Munson himself would have recoiled at all the hyperbole. I started the article by using a quote he had provided to broadcaster Frank Messer not long before the accident.

"All I want to be remembered for," he said, "is a player who went from first to third on a single."

Why do we always have to make sports heroes into superior beings? Why can't we just accept them for being good at one thing, not everything? Those were the questions I asked. I doubt the readers were impressed, but the *Journal* nominated the column for an Associated Press award, and it won first prize in our circulation category.

Shortly thereafter, I got a call from Jay Searcy, the executive sports editor of the *Philadelphia Inquirer*. He invited me to come to the big city and talk to him about a job. This overture was beyond my biggest dreams at the time. More than any other city in America, Philly fit the challenge I had accepted from Norman Isaacs seven years earlier. Philly wanted me to ask the tough questions, and to get to the truth.

At the time, Philadelphia had the toughest and most talented sports writers anywhere, with columnists Stan Hochman, Ray Didinger, Bill Lyon, and Mark Whicker and beat writers Bill Livingston, Bill Conlin, and Jayson Stark, among many others. It felt like a perfect fit for me, but apparently not to Searcy. He didn't call me back for 19 months after my visit. It wasn't until I sent out a résumé and package of my clippings to a half-dozen of the best newspapers on the East Coast that he got back to me, this time with an offer.

He wanted me to join the *Inquirer* and cover the one sport I had never written about, and about which I had zero interest or knowledge. Al Morganti—remember him?—had recovered from that grueling one inning at baseball's longest game and was leaving the *Inquirer* hockey beat for a year to cover the Olympic Games in L.A. My first big assignment in the big city would be the Philadelphia Flyers.

Hockey?

Gulp.

Chapter 3

Did You Just Say I Have a Chance to Win a Pulitzer?

When I took the job at the *Inquirer*, I had no inkling that I was about to meet the person most responsible for my second career in the media as a radio broadcaster five years later. His name was Al Morganti, and for the next 40 years he would be there, offering a unique form of guidance that started my very first day in Philadelphia.

Since I would be replacing Al on the Flyers beat for one year, my bosses entrusted him with teaching me the intricacies of hockey, and also how to cover a sport I knew nothing about in one of the most sophisticated hockey cities in America. Al had been there in Philly for a few years and had already established himself as a future Hall of Fame hockey writer, so who better than him to school me?

Let's just say Al's plan was, much like him, unorthodox. He taught me nothing about the game, dismissing the idea by saying I would never pick it up in a year anyway. Instead, he told me how to survive. Lesson one: Don't worry about the game stories. Just stick a lot of quotes in there.

Most readers just scan for the quotes anyway. Lesson two: Spend more time on the notes columns. People love notes columns. And lesson three: Never—absolutely never—write for Saturday's edition. No one reads the paper on Saturday.

Meanwhile, when Al heard that I was living in a seedy motel just over the bridge in Cherry Hill, New Jersey, he offered me a deal to sublet his apartment until I found something more permanent. Al would just move in with his future wife, Carole, in the interim.

"Don't you have to check with Carole first?" I asked.

"No, she's fine with it," he said.

For the next six weeks, I lived in Al's world—at the rink during the day, in his apartment at night. He was there for both phases, providing answers on how to deal with the players and where to buy bread. In return, I paid a lower-than-market rent for his place. He always rebelled when I tried to thank him. Silence suited him much better. In fact, four decades later, he cringed when I did a testimonial to him during our final show. Al was never comfortable with any display of emotion.

In retrospect, Al did skip one lesson when he was preparing me for my first big assignment. I did need to know *something* about hockey. That's when I made my first mistake. I told everyone—the coach, players, and my fellow media members—that I was clueless. A New Jersey writer, Jeff Jacobs, took me under his wing, even though I was working at a much bigger paper than he was. And a Flyer, Tim Kerr, was always there after practice to tell me what I needed to know.

Still, there were problems. The legendary play-by-play broadcaster Gene Hart was relentless in needling me whenever I was trapped on the team bus with him, and some of the officials around the team were shocked that I was chosen, on a major American newspaper, to cover I sport I didn't understand.

It was inevitable that the situation would lead to my first physical confrontation early in the season. The coach and GM that year was a hockey nomad, Bob McCammon, who had two sides—a jovial quipster when the team was doing well and a snide jerk when they weren't. I definitely caught him on the wrong day after a bad loss to the Boston Bruins.

Ironically, Al was the cause of the problem, though it was no more his fault than mine. He was at the game helping me the night before, and he fed me a quote by Boston GM Harry Sinden that inflamed McCammon. When I arrived in his office at the practice rink the next day, the coach had been popping sugar-coated mini donuts into his mouth, but his mood was far from sweet.

"That quote was bullshit!" he bellowed.

"He said it, Bob. I just wrote what he said," I replied, trying to hide my discomfort.

"Well, it's still bullshit!"

The conversation deteriorated from there, so I made a hasty exit as he rose from behind his desk. I never saw him coming. By then I was walking near the bench, where Kerr spotted what was going on and stepped between the coach and me. Kerr was a solid 230 pounds. No way the pudgy McCammon, with sugar from the doughnuts still rimming the outside of his mouth, was getting past Kerr.

When I heard the commotion and turned around, I realized two things simultaneously. One was that Kerr had just saved me from my first media assault, and the other was that I wasn't in Providence anymore.

I saw Al later that day and told him about the outburst his quote had caused; his reaction was one I would encounter many times in the years ahead. He laughed. Nothing tickled Al as much as causing trouble. He taught me how to do that, too—a talent that would serve both of us well in radio.

One recurring theme of my journalism career was the trouble star players had with how I covered them and their team. Larry Bird was my introduction to this problem, but hardly the last. Even more dramatic was my feud with Flyers great Bobby Clarke in that one year I covered the Flyers.

Al had warned me that Clarke and McCammon were at odds on a strange plan by the coach to give his star player—then 34—a week's vacation before the playoffs. McCammon had toyed with the idea the previous season, and he was determined to get Clarke some rest before the biggest games in 1984. This was a generation before load management became a thing, and Clarke was as blue-collar as any athlete I ever covered. The idea of sunning himself in Jupiter, Florida, while his teammates played was unthinkable to him.

As the spring approached, McCammon brought up the idea during a press session, and I took it right to Clarke, who responded with the toothless scowl that had become his trademark. Clarke neither sought nor would accept a vacation. He was clear about that. So I wrote what he said, assuming that would be the end of the discussion. It was only the beginning.

McCammon, stupidly, then decided to engage in a power struggle with a legend. The coach said it was his decision, not Clarke's. After all, he was the both the coach and GM. The fact that I was the bearer of these bad tidings added to McCammon's irritation, I'm sure, since he still hadn't forgotten the Sinden controversy.

I was not ready for what happened next. Clarke denied pretty much everything he had said to me, and—while still not happy with the vacation concept—he said had no interest in challenging the coach. My rival beat reporter, a far more accomplished hockey writer, Jay Greenberg of the *Daily News*, peppered his coverage with snide shots at me over the next few days. Jay didn't like when he was beaten on a story.

Finally, I had had enough. One day in the locker room, while waiting for the players to come in after a practice, the topic came up again among the media, and I this time I was ready. I produced my tape recorder—just as I did with Larry Bird—and played the quotes I had supposedly made up. Clarke was lying. Thank you again, Columbia.

I learned two very important lessons that day. One was to be doubly vigilant when reporting about superstar players. They often got their way with the media, most of whom were not about to challenge the most important player on the team and lose access to him. And two, when a media person is right and the star is wrong, the story disappears quickly. It did with both Bird and Clarke. But hey, at least Greenberg stopped taking shots at me.

The Clarke vacation story has an ironic final twist. After the season, Clarke shocked the world by retiring. He was leaving the ice for a new role. He would become the new GM of the Flyers, replacing, yup, Bob McCammon.

You don't mess with Bobby Clarke.

After my year in hockey purgatory, my editor used me as a utility player, but it was hardly a secondary role. I was part of the coverage of one of the biggest stories in Philadelphia sports history, the imminent move of the Eagles to Arizona. (Like the longest baseball game, I often lucked into huge stories.)

My job for a few days was to stake out a posh hotel in Phoenix and look for Eagles president Susan Fletcher, who was also the daughter of the bon vivant owner of the team, Leonard Tose. There had been rumors that Tose was about to take a sweetheart offer from a consortium of rich Arizona businessmen. The deal would allow Tose to retain some control of the team and to get out of serious debt caused by his love for wagering—and usually losing—at blackjack.

Sure enough, I found Susan, as did a horde of other media detectives, and the story exploded in Philadelphia. At the height of the fan outrage, a crowd gathered outside a barber shop where Tose was getting a $100 haircut and booed till the foundation shook.

This was my introduction to the passion of Eagles fans, and it was spellbinding. No trucking magnate with a bad gambling habit was going to steal their football team. I got to know Tose later in his life, and that display of passion was the turning point. He told me he just couldn't do it to these crazy fans. He wasn't a villain. So he gave up football and sold the team to a car dealer—in every sense of the word.

Norman Braman was a pompous ass. Like many in his business, he had no more than a nodding acquaintance with the truth. He is best known for charging his players for their socks, creating a culture of penny-pinching and player dissent. And now Braman was my problem because I was assigned as the main beat reporter covering the Eagles for the *Inquirer* in 1985.

I definitely felt better covering football than hockey, but there was still a steep learning curve. Helping me in a role similar to Kerr with the Flyers were two Eagle players later described as "joined at the hip," Ron Jaworski and John Spagnola. Both of them tested my vow to keep a distance from the people I was covering, but I found a comfortable middle ground as they gave me insights into what was happening in the locker room.

During those first days on the beat, I realized the biggest problem with applying Mr. Isaac's no-friend policy. When you distance yourself from sports figures—while other media people are exchanging family photos with them—you are at a disadvantage trying to get the personal stories. Also, you build up no good will, which is handy in times of stress.

All of these years later, I have no recollection of what outraged a strong, powerful defensive back named Ray Ellis the day I slinked into the clubhouse—I'm not sure I knew then—but there was no question he was not a fan of my recent work. He started screaming at me, waving his fists, and approaching with evil intent as I backpedaled.

Just before he reached me, I was rescued for the second time in three years by a player. This time it was wide receiver Gregg Garrity who jumped between me and an onrushing Ellis. Soon, a few other Eagles helped to quell the one-sided dispute, but I noticed how many were sitting there doing nothing. I had very few admirers in that room, for good reason. I curried no favor, and I sought no friends.

The only beat reporter who reached out was a character right out of a 1950s gangster movie named Barry Levine, who worked for the *Delaware County Daily Times*. Barry admired my negative style, and he, too, sought out every dark twist involving those 1985 Eagles. Whenever there was a contract dispute or an off-field issue, Barry would pound the keys of his first-generation computer with relish.

"Classic tabloid-style," he would announce while he was writing. "This is great!"

It should come as no surprise that Levine enjoyed a lucrative career as a top reporter—and later, executive editor—of the *National Enquirer.* Back then he shared a foxhole with me, the two biggest outcasts in the Eagles media corps.

I knew I needed something to combat the advantage that my fellow reporters had when it came to breaking stories, and it was early in my first year when I was presented with it. I was covering the team during a week on the road in joint training-camp practices with the Detroit Lions at Oakland University in Rochester, Michigan. My biggest thrill back then was driving back and forth from practice every morning with the big-voiced, big-hearted play-by-play broadcaster, Merrill Reese.

On that trip, totally by accident, I would find the best source I ever had in my journalism career. Mr. Isaacs would be proud to know even now that I will not give up the name of my fount of great inside information. I'm pretty sure the source chose me only because I represented the biggest media outlet covering the team. Surely, it was not because of any brilliant maneuvering by me.

From that day until I left the beat three years later, I knew a lot more about the inner workings of the front office, but it came with a stiff price.

Every night, usually after 10, I had to take the malcontent's calls and listen to an hour or more of complaints about the people working behind the scenes. In the course of these ramblings, I would learn who the Eagles were thinking of trading, who they were keeping but no longer liked, and how enamored Braman was, or wasn't, with his coach.

My reward for these months of listening was a huge story. On the night before the last game of the 1985 season, I got a call telling me that Braman—who had just fired head coach Marion Campbell—had interviewed David Shula, the son of legendary NFL Hall of Famer Don Shula, for the head-coaching job.

What? Not possible! Shula was 26 years old, six years younger than the youngest coach in NFL history. My source said the magic words that night: "Write it." So I did.

Before the *Inquirer* published this implausible story, the editors checked with longtime columnist Frank Dolson, who most certainly did not subscribe to Isaacs' no-friends philosophy. In fact, one of Dolson's best buddies was team president Harry Gamble. To Dolson's shock, the story was true. Braman was a huge fan of the Shulas because he had his car dealerships in the city of Don's greatest success, Miami.

The story ran across the top of the front page of the *Inquirer* that Sunday, thereby pretty much ending any chance it would have of ever actually happening. The reaction in the city was second only to Tose's plan the previous year to move the team. Braman was depicted by the powerful Philadelphia sports media as a boob, a miser, and—worse yet—a car dealer. A couple of weeks later, Buddy Ryan was hired as head coach, after the Bears had obliterated the Patriots in the Super Bowl.

I didn't know it at the time, but my unlikely pursuit of a Pulitzer Prize was about to begin.

Philadelphia was always a passionate sport city, but it never reached its exalted status of today until the arrival of a pugnacious football lifer named Buddy Ryan. He was the architect of the 46 defense, which led the Bears to a dominant 1985 championship with a take-no-prisoners approach toward the enemy offense, and especially the quarterback.

Ryan's personality fit his defense. He was bold and blustery, totally lacking in concern about the accuracy of what he was saying. His only goal in those first weeks as Eagles coach was to connect with a hungry, frustrated fan base desperate to win a Super Bowl for the first time. Before his ascension to the head job, Ryan had been a career assistant in the NFL, too braggadocious for the tastes of most NFL owners.

Norman Braman was not intimidated. He knew business, and Ryan was great business for his Eagles. Big headlines every day added up to better ticket sales—Eagles games did not always sell out back then—and a bonanza in advertising, fan apparel, and pretty much anything else carrying the Eagles logo.

It would be a reach to say Ryan figured out the fans in those first eventful weeks at training camp at West Chester University. More likely, his attitude and that of the long-suffering fans was a perfect match. Ryan was heavy, loud, brash, and uninterested in how other people (beyond the customers) saw him. Years later, when the Eagles finally won a Super Bowl, the entire city sang: "No one likes us. We don't care." It could have been Buddy Ryan's anthem that first year.

From the very beginning, Ryan set a new standard for outrageousness. At his first two-a-day practice session in the blistering heat of West Chester University, 13 Eagles had to be treated for dehydration and other maladies because of the ferociousness of his drills. The coach merely snorted the next day when asked if he was already being too hard on the players.

Ryan also didn't like the two leaders of the offense, quarterback Ron Jaworski and tight end John Spagnola, because they were, well, too smart for their own good. Ryan hated players who thought for themselves. And he had no real use for people on the offensive side of the ball anyway. He liked defensive guys—big, strong, violent men willing to sacrifice their bodies in the ongoing effort to intimidate the opposition.

After grooming young defenders like Seth Joyner, Clyde Simmons, Andre Waters, and the best of them all, Reggie White, for a week or so, Ryan knew he had something to sell to the fans—hope. And sell it he did, before a capacity crowd of about 7,500 at tiny John A. Farrell Stadium.

With no warning, Ryan announced to the crowd that his Eagles—coming off a disappointing 7–9 season—would sweep all eight games against NFC East opponents, at a time when the NFC East had powerhouse teams in Dallas, Washington, and New York. Predictably, the crowd went nuts. It was love at first boast.

Year later, Ryan would say he knew his team would be lucky to win half the division games, but he did it to take pressure off the players. I still have my doubts about that. Coming off a championship with the Bears, Ryan was an egomaniac. He had convinced himself that he was the brains behind the dominance of the Bears, not head coach Mike Ditka. I think Ryan really believed his Eagles would dominate for no reason other than his presence on the sidelines.

In fact, pretty much everything Ryan said in the first half of that season—in which they went 3–5 and lost all three division games—was a lie. Whether or not he believed what he was saying doesn't really matter. My job was to dig for the truth, so I asked for a week off the Eagles beat to put together a long analysis of Ryan's work so far in Philadelphia.

What I produced was a searing indictment of his coaching and, even more, his contempt for the truth. Remember, I was only eight years removed from Columbia, and I was still totally committed to my promise to Mr. Isaacs. The article pleased my editors, and pretty much no one else. It's safe to say now that I was the only one who took seriously everything Ryan said those first few months. The fans didn't care that he was wrong; they loved the attitude anyway.

Of course, the person who liked the article the least was Ryan himself, who greeted me on my first day back on the beat with a stony glare. I tried to break the ice by asking a mundane question. Crickets. The silence was broken only when a reporter asked a different question. Even my pal Barry Levine sat this battle out. I was on my own that day, and for the rest of the season. To Ryan, I was the Invisible Man.

At first, I was uncomfortable not communicating with the coach of the team I covered, but I adjusted. It's not as if Ryan was going to shut his mouth during news conferences. He was just going to ignore me. I could live with that.

The team ended that season 5–10–1 and Ryan was the toast of Philadelphia anyway. Ironically, the closest that team had to winning anything that season was, well, me. My sports editor at the *Inquirer* was Glenn Guzzo and the executive editor of the paper was Gene Roberts. Both were geniuses at putting together a Pulitzer Prize entry, and they did so with a package of my beat work from that season.

I was on assignment in Miami, doing an off-season piece on Florida's efforts to attract an NBA franchise, when I got a call in my hotel room from Guzzo telling me to sit by the phone. I was a finalist for the ultimate award in journalism, and we would know soon if I had won. Until then, I had no idea my work had even been submitted, but I did have a home-field advantage. The Pulitzer awards were administered by Columbia University.

For an hour or so, I sat there with visions of grandeur dancing in my head. What if I won the award? That would be the ultimate revenge for my many early nemeses like Larry Bird, Bill Fitch, and yes, Buddy Ryan. Then the phone rang again. I lost to the *New York Times*, not exactly an upset at the time—or ever, really.

Losing that prize was the best thing that happened to the rest of my media career. First of all, I didn't deserve it. In retrospect, I never really grasped the genius of Ryan's plan to win over Philadelphia. I took everything he said way too seriously. To this day, interest in the Eagles is greater and deeper because of Ryan's five years as head coach. Second, if I somehow did win the Pulitzer, I could never could have made the decision I did to go into radio full-time four years later. And third, I would have to maintain a standard of serious journalism that really didn't match my personality.

Thank you, Pulitzer committee.

Chapter 4

Goodbye, Journalism

Being on call every minute of every day was taking its toll on me after three years covering the Eagles, and now, with the Pulitzer nomination, I had the gravitas at the *Inquirer* to tackle investigative pieces that were sure to bring more awards and maybe that ultimate prize.

I left the Eagles beat for two reasons. First, the pressure of having the most important sports beat at the most important newspaper in Philadelphia was not conducive to raising a young family. And second, deserved or not, where do you go on a beat after getting a nomination for a Pulitzer? It was time to try something else.

In my years after the Eagles, I investigated (with future WIP co-host Glen Macnow) the chummy relationship between the NFL and its team doctors, I reported on a fixed harness race by spending a month in Vegas tracking the crime, and I did the best journalism of my career on corruption within the sports-memorabilia business—long before it became a national story.

Unfortunately, Guzzo had left to run the *Denver Post* shortly after my near-miss on the Pulitzer, and he was replaced by the man most responsible for the creation of WIP, new sports editor David Tucker.

I was never good with authority figures, and Tucker was a challenge like no one I had ever faced before. He was insufferable, an editor who thought he was a wordsmith. In my eyes, he was not. Tucker had no reluctance taking a story that was months in the making, and changing it at his own whim. The fact that he had no discernible people skills did not improve the situation.

When he butchered our team-doctor piece, I bitterly resigned, until he had restored the article the way Glen and I had written it. Ultimately, Tucker's heavy hand led me into radio, with Al Morganti, Macnow, and Mike Missanelli not far behind. If Tucker were not there, would we all have left? I can only speak for myself. Probably not.

Two years before the mass exodus began, Al came to me one day with a bizarre proposition. He had set up a meeting with legendary broadcaster Tom Brookshier, who had just joined the brand-new all-sports radio station, WIP, as program director and on-air performer. Brookie was a great Eagle player—his No. 40 was retired—and an even more successful national broadcaster, with 25 years at CBS, many of them as the top NFL game analyst with Pat Summerall.

Al and I had served as guests on the local sports shows—dominated back then by Howard Eskin and Steve Fredericks—but we had zero experience in radio beyond that. I assumed that Al was trying to get us a show that would include a professional host and a bunch of *Inquirer* contributors. Actually, Al had no idea what Brookshier had in mind, if anything.

We met Brookie on a Friday afternoon in the confined quarters of the WIP studios on Rittenhouse Square, with Al doing all of the talking. Like most things involving Al, there was no real plan. He pitched Brookie on the idea that we would do a one-hour daily show talking about our specialties. On days after Eagles games, I would appear. When there was a Flyers game, Al would be there the next morning. And so on.

I can still hear Brookie's always-jovial voice booming: "I love it! Let's do it!"

Wow. Getting a job in radio was a lot easier than it was in newspapers. But now a couple of issues presented themselves.

"How much do you want?" Brookie asked.

"How's $75 per show for each of us?"

"Perfect," Brookie said. He had been making hundreds of thousands at CBS. I'm pretty sure he couldn't believe how low our proposal was. "Can you start on Monday?"

Monday was three days away, but who were we to say no to our new careers in radio? So we shook hands, and that was it. In a space of maybe 10 minutes, we had crossed the threshold into a new medium.

We reported a few minutes before 9:00 AM on the following Monday, and only then did we learn that there would be no professional host working with us. No, it just us, with a producer behind the glass as the only person with any idea how to do a radio program.

There is no recording of that first show, and for that I am eternally grateful. All I remember is that Al was the lead host—it was his idea, after all—and that we bumbled our way through the hour, not knowing how or when to go to breaks, or how to bring callers on, or what topics to cover. We just babbled for 60 gruesome minutes and then handed the mics over to the midday host, Joe Pellegrino.

I was convinced as I packed my pad and pen and left the studio that day that there was zero chance we would ever get invited back. Instead, we were greeted by a smiling Brookie gushing over our maiden effort, laughing heartily at all the things we had screwed up. The sports-talk format had been christened just a month or two earlier at WFAN in New York, and there were no rules back then in 1987. We were all an awkward work in progress.

Did we get better as went along? Well, I can say for sure only that we couldn't possibly have gotten worse. I do recall that I took myself way too seriously, pontificating ad nauseum about the Eagles. Our lead-in for most of my two-year apprenticeship was Brookie himself, and his homespun manner was an immediate hit.

The *Inquirer* writer with the most potential on our show was a football authority named Ron Reid, whose booming voice and razor wit made him a radio superstar in the making. There was just one problem: Ron was terrified of the microphone. He would be covered with flop sweat from the moment the On Air sign flashed on, and he would face-plant even worse on those rare occasions when he took on the main hosting role. Go figure.

The rest of us comprising *The Morning Sports Page*, as our show became known, were there because we needed something to distract us from the poor morale gripping the *Inquirer* sports department. Matters only grew worse when Tucker and the upper management of the *Inquirer* began pushing back on our budding radio careers. More than once, we were warned that if we showed any sign of the shock-jock mentality taking root in radio back then, we would have to make a choice.

Surprisingly, the squeakiest wheel in our radio operation was actually the assistant sports editor, Jim Cohen, a talented leader who had a tendency to wear lunch on his shirt and a propensity for outrageous on-air comments. His skewering of Joe Paterno years before the Penn State coach fell into disfavor during the Sandusky scandal is still considered (at least by me) as one of the earliest hot takes in sports-radio history. Cohen was removed from our show by the *Inquirer* bosses after one of his classic rants, leaving the rest of us wedged between a rock-head (Tucker) and a hard place.

At the height of my discontent at the *Inquirer*, I got an unsolicited job offer from the *Los Angeles Times* that answered my every journalistic prayer. I would cover the San Diego Chargers for the entire football season, and then I would work on investigative projects the rest of the year. It was a combination of my two most recent jobs at the *Inquirer*, only at an even more esteemed newspaper with a significant bump in salary from $55,000 to $62,500.

The only reason I hadn't accepted the job when I visited L.A. was the unfortunate fact that the two executives wooing me that day got so drunk, I doubted they would remember our agreement. Instead, I waited—just long enough for WIP to come calling with a better offer.

As I was pondering a whole new life 3,000 miles away, the program director who had replaced Brookshier, Tom Bigby, asked me to lunch with him and WIP GM Jack Williams. This was my first look at the bad cop/good cop style of the new WIP bosses. Bigby was a heavy man with an even heavier style. He knew a lot about radio, and nothing about people. He was the biggest bully I ever met in 50 years in the media. On the other hand, Williams was a folksy leader with a booming laugh and a diplomatic style. How he coped with Bigby for more than a decade is a mystery.

But Bigby was at his charming best that day, telling me I had more potential than anyone he had ever worked with and declaring that I was ready to carry a morning-drive radio show as the lead host. Then he and Williams said the magic words: I would be making $75,000 a year—$20,000 more than at the *Inquirer* and $17,500 more than the offer at the *L.A. Times.*

Was I really going to give up a career I had trained my entire life for over $20,000?

Absolutely.

As I look back on that life-changing decision 33 years later, it seems even more ridiculous than when I made it. People working in newspapers had careers of 30, 40, even 50 years back then. With a powerful union behind us, working at the *Inquirer* was pretty much like having tenure as a college professor. As long as you avoided scandals, you could stay until you were ready to retire.

But the idea of working one more day for Tucker was unfathomable to me, and moving across the country to work for bosses who had impressed me only by their alcohol consumption was not much more appealing. So I took the money and ran to radio.

First, though, I had to sit through one more lunch, this time with a top editor at the *Inquirer*, Jim Naughton. A journalist at the absolute pinnacle of his profession, Jim had accomplished everything Columbia wanted me to set as my goals. He was a White House reporter and foreign editor for the *New York Times*, oversaw several Pulitzer wins at the *Inquirer*, and was the right-hand man to one of the most powerful executive editors in America, Gene Roberts. Oh, did I mention Jim was also a decorated Marine?

In other words, he was everything in charm and smarts that Bigby was not. Then Naughton turned on the pressure. He pointed out that I didn't go to Columbia to become a "shock jock"—his words. He said I was a serious journalist, not some shill voicing lame pitches for dubious products. I promised him that would never happen to me, that I just needed a break from newspapers and Tucker. (The second week I was at the WIP, I voiced a pitch for a non-alcoholic beverage called Buckler Beer, and then hundreds more over the following 33 years. Jim was absolutely right.)

Before our lunch was over, I did make one final offer that would keep me at the *Inquirer*, but Jim was almost as appalled by that possibility as he was by my prostituting myself on radio. I said I loved television and would stay if he gave me a job as a TV critic. At the time, the *Inquirer* had the best television writer in America, David Bianculli, whom I knew personally and admired. Working as an apprentice to him—and watching TV all day—was my dream job. Or so I thought.

Jim dismissed my suggestion, wished me well, and left the restaurant that day shaking his head at my insanity. I always wondered if Jim—who died in 2012 after a brilliant career in journalism—re-thought my decision after newspapers went into a steep decline and radio emerged as a stronger and more lucrative medium in the years that followed.

Probably not.

He thought I was selling out.

And he was right.

To say I was intimidated by Tom Brookshier would be a laughable understatement. He was everything I would never be—handsome, athletic, likeable and experienced—but what I never knew until I worked with him was how diligent he was about his career. Brookie didn't need the money. He had worked for a quarter-century at CBS after a lucrative (for that era) career in the NFL. Why he chose to get up at 4:00 AM every day, schlep into the dark, cold studio, and prepare a show is hard for me to understand, even today.

What I didn't know until years later was that Brookshier had no intention of staying in radio for long. He started WIP, and his plan was to aim it in the right direction and get out of the way. I guess at one point early on he thought I was the right direction.

But there I was on Day One, sitting across from a legend, still knowing next to nothing about how to function in front of a microphone—but earning a record high (for me) of $75,000 a year. Those first few months, I did little more than watch and listen as Brookie carried both of us through the three hours until the *Inquirer* reporters showed up at 9:00 AM to relieve us.

As I listen to tapes of those early shows—I sincerely hope you won't—I hear a tremor in my higher-pitched voice on those rare occasions when I said something. Even though I gave my bosses very little to promote, they launched an advertising campaign on TV and billboards that was a jarring reminder that I was in show biz, not journalism. (In fact, after my very first show, Bigby called me in, said I was awful and told me to forget everything I had ever learned at Columbia.)

When I saw the TV commercial, I grimaced. It had Brookie reveling in his jovial style while discussing something, and me responding with a dumb line about lasagna. Every time the ad played after that first time, I switched the channel the second I saw it.

The billboard campaign was even more embarrassing. It had two garish athletic supporters hanging on hooks below huge print. *Brookshier & Cataldi. Mornings. The Two Most Colorful Jocks in Town.* (I was the polka-dot one.) I am not embarrassed to say I altered my routes to avoid those billboards, which stayed up for months. I really wasn't ready for radio at that point.

Ten months into my two years with Brookie, it became clear to everyone that I was not blossoming into the new star who could replace a legend, and he was getting increasingly edgy about it. He snapped only one time, the week of Thanksgiving in 1990. We had just finished a show that clearly hadn't met the high standards of a former network superstar, and he let me know it.

"I'm getting tired of carrying your sorry ass," he grunted as he gathered his gear and left the studio.

Those words were a turning point for me, a wake-up call that it was time to make the same commitment to radio that I had to journalism. I became more of a true co-host after that, contributing more and even involving myself in interviews. This was usually a good idea, but not always.

Brookie had the best guests in the history of sports radio because he was, well, Tom Brookshier. One day he booked the hardest get in sports, Bobby Knight, the snarky and highly successful coach from Indiana. Even though he knew my tough questions would not always be appreciated by his guests (who were often also his friends), Brookie never tried to silence me. Occasionally, he would yelp, "Why are you asking that?!" after an uncomfortable question, but then he would always allow the guest to answer it.

Bobby Knight was a different story. Brookie did the introduction, of course, and asked the first few questions. Then it was my turn. I have no recollection of what I asked Knight that morning, but I'm sure it was not as friendly as Brookie's queries.

There was silence for a second or two, and then Knight said: "Brookie...who the hell is that?" Tom burst into that infectious guffaw of his and said: "Oh, he's my co-host! Angelo, say hi to Bobby Knight."

I asked no further questions in that interview, but I learned an important lesson. Don't change the tone of a show to serve your own needs. Brookie was doing a fun interview, until I opened my mouth. Sometimes the best option in radio is to shut up.

Of all the shows we did together in those two years, the one I remember best came the day after Magic Johnson announced that he had the HIV virus and would be stepping away from sports. It was November 7, 1991, and I wonder if it had any impact on Brookie's decision to leave our show at the end of that year.

When something big happened in sports, it was always a little bigger for Tom because he knew everybody personally. That day he told stories about his adventures with Magic and how shocking the announcement had been for him personally. Tom was old-school, rarely showing emotion. But that day was a special challenge for him.

When we went to breaks, Brookie was not his jovial self. I can remember long pauses, and deep sighs, as he came to grips with the fact that his friend Magic had just been handed a death sentence. Back then, everyone knew how deadly AIDS was, but it didn't really resonate with the sports community until Magic made his announcement.

"Because of the...the HIV virus that I have attained, I will have to retire from the Lakers."

What I will always remember most is the verb *attained*. It was such a strange word to use. Brookie even mentioned it when he was lamenting what had happened to his friend. Mostly, though, Tom wanted to know how many other great players would soon fall victim to the same deadly disease.

The great irony of this story, of course, is that Magic is still alive 32 years after that announcement, thanks to the miracles of medical science. He outlived his friend Tom Brookshier by 13 years, and counting.

No one would be happier about that fact than Brookie himself.

Maybe it's just a crazy coincidence, but just a few weeks after Magic's announcement, Brookie had one of his own—and it was shocking in its own right.

Almost exactly a year after he gave me that wake-up call, he suddenly announced that he would be leaving WIP at the end of the year. Not only had Brookshier never told me of his intentions, he had never breathed a whisper to our bosses, either. Afterwards, he simply explained that he wanted no one to try to change his mind. He was done getting up early every weekday.

And, I was thinking, two years of working with me was more than enough.

During Brookie's last month, we had lots of meetings after our show, at which nothing was decided. How do you replace a legend? Also, was I actually ready to lead a show? Brookie had done all he could do. Now it was sink or swim—and you should know I always had a morbid fear of water. I was pretty sure I would sink.

Before I was left to fend for myself, however, there was one last curtain call for Tom Brookshier. After my own goodbye show, I have an even greater appreciation for Brookie's last hurrah, one of the most star-studded in any city in radio history. Here's a list of just some of the sports heroes who among the 34 who appeared that one day:

Pat Summerall, John Madden, Dick Vitale, Ron Jaworski, Harold Carmichael, Rich Kotite (ugh), Dallas Green, John Chaney, Tommy McDonald, Buddy Ryan, Frank Gifford, Gene Shue, Billy Cunningham,

Bill Giles, Keith Jackson (the Eagles tight end), Mike Golic, Allie Sherman, and 18 other big sports names, all of whom reinforced my fear that it would be impossible to replace Tom Brookshier.

When it was over, Brookie smiled, gathered his stuff for a last time and looked at me.

"It's all yours now, kid," he said. "Good luck."

Chapter 5

You'll Never Make It without Brookie

On my very first week after Tom Brookshier, I remember attending a big dinner honoring the FBI in Center City, Philadelphia. I was milling around during the cocktail hour looking lost—no one is more awkward at cocktail hours than me—when a listener approached. I can still hear his voice and see his smug face today. His words inspired me for the next 31 years.

"What are you going to do now?" he asked.

"What do you mean?" I replied.

"Without Brookie, what are you going to do?"

"We're going to keep the show going. What else?"

"Ha, ha. Good luck with that."

The troll did have a point. So many people listened to our show because Tom Brookshier was there. The ratings were okay—middle of the pack, really, among the top 10 in our target demographic, men aged 25 to 54. Take away all of the Brookie fans, and we were bottom feeders, no? Who would listen every day to a geek with a New England accent and no experience leading a show? I needed help. Fast.

Tom Bigby made it clear from the outset that I would require a radio pro with me, especially for a year or two while I got comfortable introducing the topics of the day, leading the interviews, and going to breaks on time. I needed a good partner (or two.)

Thus began the worst week of my long radio career. Because he was sadistic, Bigby decided to hold on-air auditions, to parade my discomfort right out there on the WIP airwaves. What could possibly go wrong? The listeners would love it, he predicted. And who knows? Maybe so would I. After all, I've always been good with change. I roll with the punches so well. I blend.

Yeah, right.

I began this awkward experiment with a heavyset partner who ended up suing the station when he didn't get the job. (He claimed it was weight discrimination. I just remember we had zero chemistry, mostly because he had the sense of humor of a turnip.)

Next up was the real heir apparent to Brookie, New York shock jock Joey Reynolds. It is not much of a reach to say Joey had hit a bit of a lull in his terrific radio career, since he was trying out for a job not in New York, with a partner who was a complete nobody. Joey absolutely bombed the radio audition that day. He came in—on a sports station, no less—with a page of George Bush jokes and a screaming void of sports knowledge. Compared to Reynolds, me and the heavy guy were Laurel and Hardy.

After the show, Bigby informed me that he was holding Reynolds over for a second day. Then I informed Bigby that Joey would be working alone. I quit that day (and countless others over the years, to be honest). Jack Williams stepped in to mediate the dispute. Bigby's argument was that it would take time for me and Reynolds to build chemistry. Mine was that being on a sports station required at least a rudimentary knowledge of sports. I won.

Begrudgingly, Bigby then took my advice and had Al Morganti—my original partner on the 9:00 AM show and the brains behind my move to radio—substitute for the rest of that week. Shortly after, the perfect radio pro became available, Tony Bruno. The new *WIP Morning Show* was born.

Bigby didn't do his on-air auditions for this reason, but after those hideous experiments with two miscast partners, I was determined to make it work with Al and Tony. And they were perfectly suited for the roles that they quickly developed.

Al, who has a surprisingly small ego for someone honored by the Hockey Hall of Fame, blended from the beginning, even though his role was less than it had been when we worked together on the 9:00 AM show. Tony had a knack for knowing what worked in radio. We learned a lot from Tony over the next three years.

It's hard for people to believe now, but back then Al was loud and even flamboyant at times. On one occasion, a naysayer who called all of the WIP shows, Baseball George, showed up during a remote broadcast marking the beginning of the baseball season at the Vogt Recreation Center in Northeast Philadelphia. Al had barely tolerated his negative calls over a period of months, and when George started in again, face to face, Al snapped.

Suddenly, Al jumped up from our broadcast table and took flight after a terrified Baseball George, chasing him across the baseball diamonds and onto a side street. I have often wondered what would have happened if Al had caught George that day. It's probably best for all of us that he didn't.

Even more memorable was a one-sided debate Al had with a reporter from the *Allentown Morning Call* named Terry Larimer. That morning, Larimer had written something that Al didn't like, and the columnist had the misfortune of being booked on our show. Right after I introduced Larimer, Al launched a verbal attack like none before or since at WIP.

If Larimer had ripped Al over his radio work, I doubt Morganti would have objected. More than once, Al admitted he "left [his] conscience at the door" before our shows. But the columnist said Al's weekly hockey column in the *Inquirer* was "a juvenile embarrassment." Al took great pride in those columns, and they helped make him a legendary hockey writer. But back then we were all fair game for criticism. After all, we doled out more than our share.

"Tell me to my face that I'm a fraud, Terry!" Al screamed.

"What do you mean?"

"Tell it to my face. I dare you. Tell it to my face!"

This went on for several uncomfortable—and compelling—minutes, until I dismissed Larimer, who in the column had also ripped our show as too loud and too dumb. Looking back, Al and I proved Larimer's point with venom instead of humor. We both would have handled it much better years later. (Maybe.)

Moments like that, while embarrassing on one level, are exactly what our show needed to gain some traction in the years after Brookie. A confrontation like that never would have happened in the presence of Tom Brookshier. This was a much different show now—a show more in step with the belligerent nature of the fan base. We connected. The ratings began a steady climb into the top 3 in our demographic—behind only Howard Stern and KYW's all-news station.

No one was more responsible for our climb than Tony Bruno, whose quirky persona slid snugly between my incessant bombast and Al's witty counterpunches. Tony was a showman, and his act was not reserved for his time on the air. He was naturally funny, entertainingly opinionated, and—beyond the bluster—a terrific person. Unlike me, Tony had no enemies. He knew how to rip sports figures with a twinkle in his eye. It took me years to pick up that skill, if indeed I ever really learned it.

During football season, Tony took over a segment every Monday morning that was among the best elements any show has had on WIP since the format change to sports in 1988. He called it "Mr. Monday Night," and he brought with him an adoring chant recorded for shows he did long before he got to WIP. At a time when *Monday Night Football* was at its peak in popularity, Tony would predict the games that night, in a manner unlike anyone else.

With the words "Mr. Monday Night, Mr. Monday Night!" echoing in the background, Tony would break down the game with searing criticism of players he didn't like and glowing praise for those he did. His top target was the Dallas Cowboys—of course—and Tony was not above getting personal in those unhinged early days of sports talk.

For example, Michael Irvin, the controversial—and spectacular—wide receiver on the Cowboys, had been implicated in scandals involving prostitutes and cocaine back then, and Tony would deftly include those juicy nuggets in his breakdown. Doing it with a gravity only his rich baritone voice could deliver, Tony was a revelation not just to our audience, but also to me.

It took years for me to refine the technique, but Tony showed me there was a way to rip into sports figures using a stiletto instead of a hammer. I never got as good at it as Tony, but I added it to a repertoire that definitely needed some changeups to mix in with all the fastballs.

The only real problem with Tony in the three years on our show was his availability. Tony was a morning-radio host who was not at all a morning person. In the first months of our show, Tony drove me and (occasionally) Al nuts with his tardiness. Then, unwittingly, Tony handed us another valuable lesson in how to make lemonade out of our own bitterness.

Many mornings in those early years, we would monitor Tony's tardiness—I can remember a few days when he wasn't in much before 8:00 AM—and his arrival was something radio shows treasure. A big moment. He would plop down in his seat, the few hairs on his bald head askew, and tell a story about what had happened. What he said wasn't important; how he said it was. He used that amazing voice to adopt the tone of an innocent victim, howling about dumb drivers or bad weather or anything else that would lower the volume on his inevitable meeting with Bigby after the show.

Tony also had another problem with being there on time, or at all. Shortly after he joined our team, he got a job offer he couldn't refuse—a spot on the new ESPN Radio Network as a lead weekend host that included a shift from 8:00 to midnight on Sunday nights. He was working with someone who quickly became a powerful friend to him, Keith Olbermann. It was obvious right from the start that the ESPN job had far more potential than being a No. 2 (or 3) host on our show.

Because he is Tony, he accepted the new position without hesitation and subjected himself to seven-day workweeks that also required him to drive from Bristol, Connecticut, to Philadelphia early every Monday morning. He told some great stories about trying to keep his eyes open while flying down I-95 to make it on time for our 5:30 AM start. (Actually, Tony was more likely to make it on time from Connecticut than from his home 25 minutes away in Lower Gwynedd, Pennsylvania.)

By the end of his third year with us, he was tired and I was scared—of losing him. We were creeping up on KYW for second in the ratings books, and Tony was every bit as irreplaceable as Tom Brookshier. Negotiations went into overtime, as I got involved with pleas to Bigby to find a way to keep Tony. In the end, Tony left WIP for the same reason I left the *Inquirer*. He hated his boss.

Before Tony's departure, however, we all became embroiled in arguably the ugliest controversy between a sports-radio station and a big-league organization ever, and it centered around a miserable bully named Jim Fregosi and a WIP still trying to find its way in the new take-no-prisoners world of sports talk.

The 1993 season was magical for the Phillies, with the notable exception of the four hours on WIP every morning. Led by the snarling demeanor of the manager, Fregosi, that team made a connection with the fans like none in Philadelphia sports history, right down to the blue-collar ethic and the screw-you attitude.

Darren Daulton, Lenny Dykstra, John Kruk, Pete Incaviglia, Mitch Williams, and Dave Hollins comprised a group of belligerent star Phillies that became known as Macho Row. They were the ultimate prototype for the us-against-the-world mentality of overachieving teams, and they did so with a distaste toward the media that paralleled mine toward them.

I was relentless in my criticism of that group of smartasses despite their growing popularity in the city. Daulton was the titular leader of Macho Row, and when I would engage with him, it was not a fair fight. He was handsome, tough, and an inspirational leader. I was none of those things. When it became clear I couldn't win this battle, I began offering to female listeners "Dutch treats," sound bites of him speaking words that I imagined tickled the women in our audience. (Yes, I was sexist, too.)

Meanwhile, Dykstra was a perfect player for Philadelphia, but all I saw was a crass jerk (which he was). Kruk was funny, but with far more of an edge than he had later in his broadcasting career. Williams and Hollins were great competitors, but subtlety was not their specialty. They suffered no fools. Incaviglia was a big, blustery hairball. I hated them all, never understanding that I was merely channeling my own high school days, when star athletes like "Man Mountain" Steve Hickey ridiculed me and the other members of my Dork Patrol.

My silly emotional commitment to belittle that beloved team led to the ugliest moment in my radio career. Constantly looking for attention in those hungry early years, I consented to having a reporter, Larry Platt of *Philadelphia Magazine*, shadow me for a day. This was a chance to show what a cool and clever fellow I was behind the scenes, a fun guy around the clock. (I was never any of those things.)

During a break, the topic of Jim Eisenreich came up, and I thought it would be hilarious imagining what Eisenreich might say about Fregosi during a bout with Tourette's Syndrome, an affliction that Eisenreich battled nobly every day of his baseball career and beyond. Then I put into Eisenreich's mouths words he would never use—the most profane imaginable (beginning with CS and MF)—and had him aiming them right at Fregosi.

I knew what I had done was stupid and wrong—I would be fired immediately, and with good cause, in today's world for mocking someone with a disability—but the unforgivable lapse landed only a temporary blow to my career, though an indelible one to my psyche.

In early 1994, when the article appeared, that quote turned our feud with the Phillies from ground combat into a nuclear war, and my apology did nothing to quell the trouble. Fregosi said in a private moment something that made its way to WIP afternoon host Howard Eskin—who had stayed above the fray throughout that season. When Eskin reported what the manager said, Fregosi didn't deny it.

"People who listen to WIP are a bunch of guys in South Philly that [fornicate with] their sisters, and the people that work at WIP [fornicate with] their mothers," he said.

The quote made the front page of the *Daily News*, inspiring days and days of debate over what to do with Fregosi—and, even more so, what to do about WIP. As I recall it today, my quote in *Philly Mag* was never directly blamed for what Fregosi said, but I believed it to be true then, and I still do now. I was wrong—more wrong than I've ever been about anything—and even today, writing these words, I am humiliated all over again.

When I look back on those stressful early days, I cringe at how far we were willing to go to get attention, and I was far more guilty than Al or Tony. The microphone, which had intimidated me for the first four years of my radio career, had become a battering ram I used for the entertainment of our growing audience.

No one was safe from my vitriol in the 1990s. My favorite targets were anyone playing quarterback for the Eagles (Randall Cunningham, Rodney Peete, Ty Detmer, Bobby Hoying, Doug Pederson, and, of course, Donovan McNabb). Free-agent busts like Danny Tartabull, Chris Gratton, and Matt Geiger faced my wrath every day. Good players like Curt Schilling and Ron Hextall were ripped relentlessly. Bad players like Juan Bell and Charles Shackleford got it even worse.

And then there were the coaches and managers, my favorite targets. What we did to Eagles coach Rich Kotite in those early years would probably be grounds for a slander lawsuit today. Same for Eagles president Joe Banner, whose lack of sympathy for the fans was made worse by his insufferable snugness. Even Hall of Famers like Larry Brown didn't escape unscathed. Phillies managers John Felske and Nick Leyva had no chance with us (for good reason). Every Flyers coach named Terry—there were several, all lousy—was fresh meat for me.

After I was done having my way with these constant disappointments, Al and I set loose our secret weapon, Joe Conklin, on them. Joe is an extraordinary impressionist, and he was the best I have ever encountered at taking a dumb comment, turning it into a catch phrase and then hammering the victim into submission with it. Kotite was a terrible NFL coach, but the way Conklin depicted him—stammering and shouting out nonsense, losing track on the sideline because the ink on his play sheet ran in the rain—made the coach's life a living hell at the end of his final season in 1995.

With the advantage of hindsight, I guess it was inevitable that I would go too far someday, though never as far as I did in *Philly Mag*. Of all the howling and protesting I did over 33 high-volume years, I feel no actual regret for skewering all of the players and coaches, big and small—except, of course, for Eisenreich. I would like to believe I learned from the Jim Eisenreich experience.

Although it didn't occur to me at the time, Tom Brookshier had warned me years earlier about the steep price of media empowerment.

"See that microphone?" he said early in our time together. "It's a loaded weapon—and it's pointed right at you."

Chapter 6

Dealing with Depression

The daily combat on WIP was bringing us sustained success by the end of 1995, but at a heavy cost. Sleep never came easily for me because of our terrible hours. I tried napping so I could stay up to see the games live, but that didn't work. I was too high-strung to nap. Then I tried cheating the number of hours I would sleep, but I would struggle the next morning after only five or six hours. Finally, I developed a way to watch the games quickly the next morning—DVRs were just coming into vogue then—and I would sleep from 7:30 PM to 3:30 AM.

There was just one problem with that plan. I felt pressure every night to fall asleep quickly, which led to me sleeping very poorly, and occasionally not at all. When I finally gave up and sought the help of my doctor, she said I should try Ambien. Later in my career I would turn to sleeping pills with far better results, but it became clear that Ambien and I were not meant for each other.

I never reached the most ominous side effect of the drug, suicidal thoughts, but I was sinking into a deeper and deeper emotional hole as we pressed for even bigger numbers—all the time knowing that Tony was in the final year of his contract and could be leaving for ESPN full-time in a matter of months.

Trying to do a show in 1995 was like hiking through beach sand with heavy boots. I would wake every morning with a sense of dread, knowing I would be performing for four-plus hours with a brain that craved rest. Always obsessed with order, I found myself rashly improvising rather than following my basic plan. The show would often escape my grasp, drifting into chaos. Tony jumped to my aid in those challenging times, though we never—not once—discussed my lapses.

The lowest point in my descent into what was later diagnosed as clinical depression came one day while I was sitting in the back of a limousine, on one of the countless extra assignments designed to raise our profile. When the car pulled up to the destination, I couldn't get out. I sat there and ignored the repeated announcements from the chauffeur that it was time to disembark. The Radio Guy persona that I had adopted was being swept away in a wave of sleeplessness and stress. I never got out of the car.

Right after the limo episode, my voice was not heard on WIP for the longest period in my 33-year tenure—three full weeks. During that time, I was juggling my career crisis with equally puzzling troubles at home. My daughter, Meredith, had reached her teen years without the daily involvement of her father. Before radio, I was often an absentee dad while I was covering teams on the road, and then I often checked out mentally when I was home. She had developed a rebelliousness I was not equipped to handle.

I can remember one time during the crisis when we were all at the dinner table, and I sat there in a stupor. My fork remained on the plate as I stared into space. Meredith turned to my wife, Linda, and said: "What's wrong with Daddy?" Linda said not to worry about it, that I would be okay soon. Maybe she believed it. I wasn't so sure.

During my three-week hiatus, at a family counseling session, the psychologist detected my problem. There was no actual joy in my life. I was overwhelmed at work by the pressure of higher and higher expectations, and I was clueless on how to handle a teenage daughter and a son two years younger who, in order to survive, was trying to block out the chaos all around him.

When the psychologist asked me what I did for fun, I had no answer. As she probed deeper, she uncovered issues that I had never acknowledged about my marriage. Linda and I met at the end of our senior year at Classical, and we were married when she was 20 and I was 21. Time and stress had worn away the foundation of our relationship. Then the psychologist said something that I can still hear today.

"You have a decision to make," she said.

"About what?" I asked, thinking she wanted me to quit radio.

"About your marriage," she said.

That comment sat there, with no response from either of us, but it planted a seed that grew into a whole new direction in life, for all of us.

I managed to survive my bout with depression thanks to the aid of an antidepressant, Effexor, which has remained part of my daily pill regimen for the past 28 years. After the Ambien had dug me deeper into my emotional hole, Effexor lifted me back up into a lighter world. It was not a dramatic change at the time, but it was enough to restart my life.

That first show after my hiatus was like no other I ever did, including that very first one with Al back in 1988. I didn't feel just nervousness that day; I felt genuine fear. As he always did, Al jumped to my aid and carried me when I took those baby steps post-depression. He was uncanny in his ability to know when to jump in and when to sit back. This is what I mean when I say Al was every bit as responsible for our success as me. He was always there in times of crisis.

(By the way, I never said any of this to Al because he is uncomfortable with any self-analysis. And I'm positive he will never read this book. Let's keep this a secret just among us, okay?)

My radio career reached a new high within months. Effexor was giving me the peace of mind I needed, and well, you know the old saying:

"What doesn't kill you makes you stronger." I was effectively juggling my radio work with a TV show called *The Great Sports Debate* and even a teaching gig at La Salle University.

This was by far the most active period of my life. When I wasn't doing one of the three jobs, I was speaking at dinners and making public appearances for anyone who would have me. I turned nothing down—sometimes to my own detriment.

By then I had perfected my 20-minute dinner spiel and then finished out the half-hour or so by answering questions. It was like stealing money, until one night it wasn't. I appeared before a young group called the Pro Painters of America—an organization primarily composed of college kids who made a few extra bucks by painting houses, inside and out.

A sign that my mental health was solid again came when I stood before this group of 100 or so young people—I was in my early forties then—and bombed worse than Joey Reynolds had on our show a few years earlier. A rock band was standing behind me, tuning up before a rollicking set, and I was the only obstacle to the young crowd's good time. I still got my $500 for the 10 minutes that seemed like three hours (even my Charles Barkley joke failed), before the organizer of the event put me and the crowd out of our misery.

Comics will tell you there is no worse feeling than the awkward silence of a crowd waiting to be entertained, but I weathered the storm with barely a shrug. Thank you, Effexor.

I was definitely much stronger now—except for my marriage. I kept hearing the psychologist's voice saying that I had a decision to make. Did I really? Linda didn't think so. She kept reminding me that marriage was a lifetime commitment. Was it? Or was the promise of a life together contingent on both partners enjoying that life?

By the spring of 1996, I made the decision the psychologist had warned me about half a year earlier. There is no easy way to ask for a divorce, especially after 24 years, and I concocted a dubious plan to deliver the news. Linda's sister, Cynthia, was getting married in a beautiful mansion in Newport, Rhode Island, and I decided I wouldn't say anything until after that happy event.

Those familiar with my radio work know I am totally inept at keeping secrets, and I was no more skilled at this critical juncture in my life. Less than an hour after the vows were exchanged that night, Linda and I ended up walking along the grounds at The Breakers, and looking out over the water on the back end of that picturesque estate.

She asked me if I was leaving.

I said yes.

We both cried.

The next day we went to visit my parents, who were in a nearby hotel room and had attended the ceremony the night before, and we delivered the news. Ida and Angelo Sr. were married for 40 years at that point (and remained so until my dad died after 59 happy years with my mom), and this was the first divorce in our immediate family.

"That's bad news," my dad said, shaking his head in shock. "I can't believe it. That's very bad news."

Throughout my radio career, I have mastered one emotion above all others, awkwardness, and I can say without fear of contradiction that those six hours in the car with my soon-to-be ex-wife driving from Rhode Island to our home in New Jersey were the most uncomfortable of my life. What do you say when there's nothing left to say? I still shudder at the memory.

My co-workers found out about the end of my marriage one week later at a party hosted by my producer, Joe Weachter. Joe had been with me from our days with Brookie, and it's safe to say he was never a devotee of social conventions. I arrived at the party alone that night, carrying fresh-baked pies in each hand. Where was Linda?

"She's not coming," I said, and the look on my face told the entire story.

"Holy shit!"

By the time I reported to work on Monday, everyone at WIP knew. That wasn't the problem. How would I tell the audience, whom I had conditioned to hear every twist and turn in my boring little life? I was never any good at secrets—so much so that I actually took a call from my daughter's boyfriend one day and had to fend off, on the air, his declaration that "You're a terrible father!" I always said I hated secrets, but mostly because I was no good at keeping them.

Unfortunately, before I could inform the listeners, the story broke on the front page of the *Daily News*. There were photos strung across the top of ex-DA Ron Castille, sports anchor Don Tollefson, and me—all three going through a divorce at the same time. The day that story came out, I vowed to divulge pretty much everything going on in my private life. Listeners counted on me to be honest, win or lose. For the only time, I got scooped on my own story.

With a high-profile figure suddenly available in the dating market, there was a frenzy of activity among our female listeners.

Not really.

In fact, not at all.

I had a face for radio, and most of the potential dates had already gotten a good look at me on TV. In all, during that period when I was "back in circulation," as I liked to say, I got one offer and it was strictly for charity. Embracing my new-found freedom, I agreed to be auctioned off. This was a terrible idea, since all of the other men on stage that night were hunks. I was a different kind of hunk, if you know what I mean.

When I strode out in my finest suit and twirled so the hungry women in the crowd could get a full view, I was greeted with silence. The auctioneer started the bidding at $100. Crickets. (In my defense, that $100 would be more like $200 today). Eventually I got a few sympathy bids before a woman named Lorraine phoned in a $500 offer, which was accepted.

The highest bid came from a woman who wasn't there to see me up-close. What does that say about my appeal? I ended up paying the $500 myself. I was pretty sure Lorraine would have been disappointed when we did meet, so I bought myself out of the inevitable dating disaster. It was the best $500 I have ever spent.

Meanwhile, my divorce was turning bitter. After a failed attempt at mediation, we went to court in Haddonfield, New Jersey, where my on-air reputation as a radio jerk had proceeded me. It was clear from the outset that the judge was not a fan, and even my own lawyer seemed less than sympathetic to my cause.

When we reached the late stages of hammering out an agreement, the opposing counsel—also not a fan—invoked an obscure clause in New Jersey marital law called "the Joe Piscopo amendment." During the *Saturday Night Live* star's contentious divorce a few years earlier, his ex-wife received a bigger settlement because being married to a celebrity carried with it certain privileges. What was my name worth?

Apparently, quite a bit. I ended up with a divorce deal that required me to pay more than I am allowed to disclose here, and I would be required to pay it for—get this—the rest of my life. Wow. For the next 27 years I paid those bills twice a month—we came to an amiable agreement when I retired—always quietly resenting Piscopo, even after he had made a series of highly entertaining appearances on our show.

Finally, one day I took Joe aside during a break and told him how much money his divorce had cost me.

He laughed right in my face.

"I won that case on appeal," he said. "You got screwed."

Once you are a victim of depression, you never react the same way to adversity—and then were plenty of down moments over my long career, even with the aid of Effexor.

What I never could master, right to the end, was my obsession with making every show the best it could be, at all costs. Even after a terrific four hours, I tended to focus on the one awkward moment, the one question I should have asked a guest but didn't, the perfect line that I failed to deliver in the moment.

I had many sessions on the air with a brilliant sports psychologist, Dr. Joel Fish, who tried to get to the source of my perfectionism. In school, I was never satisfied with anything less than 100 on a test, A in a course, or summa cum laude at graduation.

Why? My parents were forgiving. The rest of my family was supportive. My life was better than most. Why was I always looking for a reason not to be happy?

Then I met someone who knows me very well, with a theory that haunts me to this day.

"I think you're on the spectrum," she said. "I think you have a mild form of Asperger's."

What?

I realize I will need another whole book to consider this possibility, but I did take a moment to consider the symptoms:

Inappropriate or minimal social interactions.

Conversations that mostly revolve around yourself.

An intense obsession with one or two specific, narrow subjects.

Becoming upset at any small changes of your routine.

Speech that sounds...high-pitched or loud.

Check, check, check, check, and check.

Is it better to know what the root cause of your psychological struggle is, or is it best to block out the noise and just live your life the most comfortable way you can?

Oh, I guess you should know who offered this armchair diagnosis.

It is my wife of the past 23 years, Gail Cataldi.

Chapter 7

A Tutorial from Tony

Hanging over our heads for most of the three years Tony Bruno was on our show was the realization that he was worth more than he was getting, and he clearly deserved a bigger role than we could offer. Those three years, he, Al Morganti, and I were together are often referenced as the heyday of our show. I don't know about that. All I can say with confidence is that the 28 years that followed Tony's departure would never have happened without him.

Those years were known for our tireless desire to get attention with the kind of stunts that were so common in the early and mid-1990s. Our first venture into this approach was one of my favorite moments in our long history—Honk for Herschel.

Herschel Walker was an extremely talented running back at a time when running backs were more valued than they are today. He had played out his contract in Minnesota—after a brilliant four years in Dallas—and we decided to recruit him to our city early in 1992, shortly after Al, Tony, and I became a team.

Back then, Al was our street reporter—a really good one, by the way—and he agreed to travel to the sports complex early one morning to gather together all of the people heading into work and to demonstrate to

Walker how much the Eagles fans wanted him to sign with their favorite team.

The plan was to corral hundreds of motorists and start an impromptu parade—we had no permits—culminated with a honk, in unison, at precisely 8:00 AM. When Al arrived outside Veterans Stadium, he called us off the air to report that the hundreds of cars we anticipated were barely a dozen or two. (This was only a couple of months after Tom Brookshier had left, and our audience was not that familiar with stunts like this, nor as committed to our show.)

It was too late to shift gears, so we went down to Al, who did a convincing job selling the idea that Honk for Herschel was going great. Fortunately, no one from the sparse gathering called in to dispute Al's exaggerations. Time was drawing near for the big horn-honk, and it exceeded our highest expectations. At first, the noise was tepid, but then it kept building to a ground-shaking crescendo. I was overwhelmed with the fan support, congratulating everyone for a job well done—at least until we went to break.

Then Joe Weachter broke the news to us. The tepid first part of the Honk for Herschel was the only actual honk. The rest he had enhanced with a seamless blending of many, many horn-honking effects that sweetened the sound many-fold. The campaign was bogus.

My biggest test in this blatant fraud came when Walker indeed did sign with the Eagles, a transaction for which we took full credit, of course. Walker was a guest on our show shortly after he did his deal as a free agent, and I proudly played for him our doctored honk. He was awestruck.

"Wow," he said. "I really appreciate that. Thank you so much."

Walker ended up playing three seasons in Philadelphia, with declining results. After his playing career—and before his brief flirtation with politics in 2022—he became a restauranteur, a business venture that led to lawsuits contending he had exaggerated the number of people employed by his companies.

I wonder where he got that idea.

Encouraged by the success of the Honk for Herschel campaign, we sprinkled throughout Tony's tenure stunts that often got us headlines, and occasionally caused us problems.

The most notable was a bet I suckered Tony into taking. Back then I had adopted a false narrative that I was a bad athlete with a golden arm. (The bad athlete part was not false.) I referred to my right appendage as my "soup-bone," and I wanted to prove to Al and Tony—especially Tony—that I could throw a ball harder and farther than he would ever believe.

For example, I suggested, I could throw a baseball from the 700 Level in left field at Veterans Stadium beyond second base—a distance of well over 300 feet. Tony scoffed at the notion, and we made a bet. During our show before opening day in 1993, I stationed myself in the walkway between the 600 and 700 Levels and, at the appointed time, let loose with a scream as I over-emoted the stress I was putting on my gifted soup-bone. The ball landed somewhere in straightaway left field, where it did what a couple of experts told me it would do.

It bounced a couple of times and then rolled...and rolled...and rolled past second base and all the way into the first-base dugout.

"He made it!" Tony screamed. "It's still going....Wow."

Much like Honk for Herschel, this was a bogus stunt, as was proven by what happened next. A young woman—maybe 18—was seated in a 600 Level seat just below us, and—unannounced and unplanned—she took one of our practice balls and flipped it just beyond the overhang in left field, and it bounced a couple of times and then kept rolling all the way in the dugout, exactly like mine.

Tony never paid off the bet, but we got such a big reaction to an obvious scam that we kept looking for more ways to toy with the audience.

The next year, as a season-opening stunt, I said I could catch a pop fly dropped from the helicopter where our new traffic person, Kris Gamble, gave her daily reports. Kris agreed to take a ball with her one day and drop it upon my command. I would then deftly track it and snag it before it hit the ground.

Nothing about this plan made sense. First, it was unlikely I would be able to catch sight of a ball dropped from an hovering aircraft, especially once the ball got swept up in the wind caused by the spinning rotors; second I would almost definitely not catch it even if it miraculously hit my glove; and third, if it smacked me on the head from that distance, I would probably die.

Nevertheless, down came the ball, as I scooted across the parking lot, my trusty Bob Gibson glove thrust out in wildly optimistic anticipation. Fortunately, the ball eluded my grasp, but it landed close enough for me to hear the impact when it landed on the asphalt. When I picked up the ball, it was flat on one side.

Hey, better the ball than my head.

As our final opening-day stunt, I went back to the soup-bone, predicting that I could throw a fastball 85 miles per hour. In fact, to make sure there was no funny business this time, I would do it as an esteemed place of advanced science, the Franklin Institute, which just so happened to have a baseball exhibit opening that week.

As usual, Tony expressed grave doubts, but he said it was worth seeing, if for no other reason than to make me look stupid. Back then, before a newer, more generous radar gun replaced the old ones, there were members of the Phillies pitching staff who didn't throw 85 mph. The one thing worth noting at this point is that I had recorded my fastball at an amusement park not long before the stunt, and I was unable to break 60.

But hey, the Franklin Institute had a sense of humor, no? The scientists there would help me fake the reading in return for a free advertisement of their baseball exhibit, no?

No. Not a chance. We exchanged letters for a couple of weeks—the museum wanted everything in writing—and the only hang-up was that I would actually have to throw the ball 85 mph.

Undaunted, I began a search for someone who was as crooked as me. Our audience came immediately to our rescue. A man with his own radar gun could create exactly a reading of 85 mph simply by striking a tuning fork at the moment when I released the ball. The only thing the guy wanted in return was the satisfaction of conning the fans. Perfect.

The morning of the season opener, in a tent across the street from the Vet, I went through all of the motions. As Tony scoffed, I warmed up, wind-milling my soup-bone between warmup pitches for added effect, and then uncoiled the hardest pitch I have ever thrown in my life. It was high, and (for me at least) pretty hard. The man with the radar gun barked out: "85 miles per hour!"

Tony ran over to the gun, saw the number, and was buying none of it. "No way that was 85!" he informed the listeners. "This was rigged."

Here's the crazy twist to the story. I actually thought I had uncoiled a pitch that reached 85. Honest. For one delusional moment, I believed that the adrenaline, the rigorous warmup, the pressure of the moment turned me into a stud pitcher.

Later, I sidled up to the guy with the radar gun and asked him if he had actually rigged it.

"You told me to," he said. "I just did what you wanted."

"So I didn't throw it 85?"

"Are you serious?"

In the midst of our uncertainty over Tony's future at WIP, Al and I were presented with an unexpected opportunity of our own. WEEI in Boston called and asked if we would be willing to come back home to New England to take over its floundering morning sports show. The only difference between these negotiations and the discussions that led to our radio careers was that I was the one doing the talking this time, at least for a while.

We got far enough in our talks to hear a magic salary number, and that was enough for me. Even though I had no affection for Rhode Island, or Boston, or anywhere in New England, I loved the money, which was almost double what we were making at WIP. There were two main hurdles to clear: Our contracts ran for more than one more year, and Al was reluctant to head back home.

Al's thinking made no sense to me then, or now. He loves Boston so much, he still actively roots for all of their sports teams, and especially the Red Sox. He visits his hometown several times a year. He has family and friends there. On the other hand, I rarely missed the opportunity to rip my former hometown of Providence as minor league and corrupt. I hate Boston's teams, and the city where they played.

In the end, the one year left on our WIP contracts became a moot point. Tom Bigby had violated the basic rules of radio negotiations by denying us the use of agents. Against his edict, I had finally hired someone to manage me, and he was prepared to take WIP to court. WIP acknowledged the problem by matching the Boston offer, and agreeing to tear up our contracts.

Still, I had my bags packed. My father was getting older, and—15 years before our radio signal was available anywhere through the internet—I wanted him to hear our show every day. Al wanted nobody in his family ever to hear our show. He said it was far too loud and aggressive for Boston and would flop spectacularly. I told him we would adjust.

He told me to adjust this.

We stayed.

WEEI went through many phases in the following years, dominating Boston for a while and then plunging to depths we had never experienced in Philadelphia. How would we had done in Boston?

The best thing that ever happened is, we never got to find out.

Can you believe this fetching young man couldn't get a date for the Senior Prom? *(Photo by Loring Studios)*

My first day in the WIP studio with the legendary Tom Brookshier. I was terrified. *(Photo by WIP)*

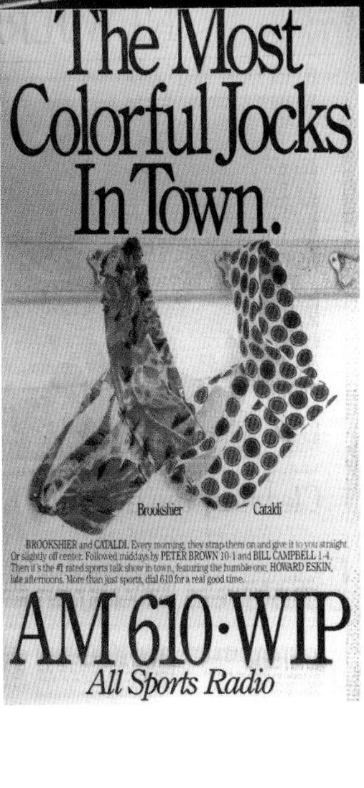
The Most Colorful Jocks In Town.
Brookshier
Cataldi
BROOKSHIER and CATALDI. Every morning, they strap them on and give it to you straight. Or slightly off center. Followed middays by PETER BROWN 10-1 and BILL CAMPBELL 1-4. Then it's the #1 rated sports talk show in town, featuring the humble one, HOWARD ESKIN, late afternoons. More than just sports, dial 610 for a real good time.
AM 610·WIP
All Sports Radio

The ad campaign included this print ad and big billboards all over town. I had no say on the style of my jock. *(Photo by WIP)*

In my first year with Brookie, I represented a weight-loss program and dropped to skeletal proportions. The company dropped me. *(Photo by WIP)*

For over a decade, we did Eagles pregame shows in this claustrophobic, drunken tent. It didn't smell great in there, either. *(Photo by Kenny Justice)*

I spent one day in the 700 Level at Veterans Stadium with Torchman and the other lunatics. The only thing my son talked about on the ride home was the bloody fistfight he witnessed. *(Photo by Neil Cataldi)*

No person outside of our show had a bigger influence than former mayor and governor Ed Rendell. Here he married Gail and me on December 31, 1999, in the famous heart exhibit at the Franklin Institute. If you listen closely, you can actually hear the thumping. *(Photo by Caitlyn D'Amico)*

Give Donovan McNabb credit for something. He sure could fake a smile. *(Photo by Cindy Webster)*

Even though we hated each other, Andy Reid sent his good wishes when I retired. That greeting was no more sincere than these smiles. *(Photo by Cindy Webster)*

The early years were filled with attention-getting stunts. We spent four hours up on this billboard. I have no good explanation why. *(Photo by Gail Cataldi)*

It is six o'clock in the morning and 20,000 fans are crammed into the Wells Fargo Center to watch fat guys eat chicken wings. It was the biggest annual promotion in radio history. (I think.) *(Photo by Cindy Webster)*

Chip Kelly's introduction to Philadelphia was at the Wing Bowl. He was so overwhelmed by the ovation, all he could say was, "Yo, Philly!" *(Photo by Cindy Webster)*

At the behest of Ed Rendell, I hosted an event for Barack Obama on Ben Franklin Parkway. These people did not turn out to see me. Bruce Springsteen performed in support of Obama that day, after I finally got Rendell to give up the mic. *(Photo by Angelo Cataldi)*

Bruce Springsteen was obviously awestruck when he finally got to meet me after the Obama rally. *(Photo by Gail Cataldi)*

I lost some bets along the way. There was no public outcry for me to keep this look. *(Photo by Gail Cataldi)*

Tony Bruno worked with us for only three years, but his impact was profound. Here, near the end of our long run, Tony came back to recreate an early photo. Al Morganti (left) seemed even less thrilled the second time. *(Photo by Cindy Webster)*

THE GREAT
SPORTS DEBATE
PRISM
IS THE ONE
(Clockwise, Fenway, Al Morganti, Jayson Stark, Glen Macnow, Angelo Cataldi)

In the early 1990s, we tried our hand at TV. The breakout star was the furry one on the lower left. *(Photo by CCI Communications)*

Two broadcast legends, Harry Kalas and Merrill Reese, honored me with joint appearances on both my radio and TV shows. They were the most popular Philadelphia sports figures in my 33 years at WIP. *(Photo by Cindy Webster)*

I promised my *Inquirer* editor when I left for radio that I wouldn't become a commercial shill. I lied. *(Photo by Gail Cataldi)*

One of our biggest thrills was meeting movie star Ray Liotta in 2002. Al was not in the photo because he was feuding with Ray over *Field of Dreams*. Rhea Hughes loved the movie. *(Photo by WIP)*

Hanging over our heads throughout Tony Bruno's tenure was the fact that we valued his contribution to our show much more than Bigby, who often said to me that Tony was a dime-a-dozen radio voice, likening his work to that of a carnival barker—all volume, no substance. This began a period of diminishing returns with Bigby; we had learned most of his inside-radio lessons, and now we were dealing with his many quirks and shortcomings.

Bigby's formula for success in Philadelphia radio was very simple: Talk about the Eagles most of the time, and stir up a commotion whenever possible. For example, Al and I were mortified one time when the *Daily News* reported on its front page that we had written letters of support for an executive we knew at a BMW dealership that we represented at the time. The service manager had gotten caught with a huge amount of marijuana in his garage, and he was facing serious jail time.

Letters like ours are common before someone is sentenced, and we merely said in those documents that our dealings with him were positive. Quickly, the story got twisted. Al and I were soft on drugs, the articles repeatedly implied. (Actually, we had no valid opinion on drugs, or anything else outside of sports.) Still fairly new to our celebrity status, Al and I were both upset by the negative publicity. Bigby was delighted.

"Do you think fewer people are going to listen to you now, or more people?" he asked. "You didn't do anything wrong. This will help us."

He was right, I guess. But he was wrong about Tony, who knew a lot more about radio than Al and I did, and often locked horns with Bigby over our boss's many uninformed takes on sports. Tony's three years at WIP made me see Bigby in a less favorable light, and the boss thought the best way to get me back in line was to let Tony's contract run out.

Indeed, Tony's contract did expire at the end of 1995, much to the chagrin of Al, me, and our audience. I have heard two stories about why Tony left. One is that WIP never made him an offer to stay. The other is that he wanted to be paid like the national voice he had become—probably more than I was getting—and Bigby didn't think he was worth it.

Either way, we lost the one true radio professional employed by our show. Now, ready or not, it was time for me and Al to embrace that role ourselves.

Tony was a pro right up until his last day. In those final weeks, he was game to do anything to add some fun to the proceedings. For example, a tree had grown in front of the window in our broadcast studio on 5th Street, so Tony said he would take care of the problem. (He always liked to brag about his prowess with a tool kit.)

Sure enough, one day he climbed up the tree, balancing himself precariously on a shaky limb, and cranked up his chainsaw.

I am happy to report Tony was much more adept with that device than the idiot who nearly severed his cousin's arm a couple of years earlier. At the perfect moment, Tony sliced away the end of the offending branch, and then took a bow that lasted till the end of his days with us.

On another occasion, Tony couldn't make it to work on time because his home in Lower Gwynedd often got the brunt of snowstorms, and he was buried in the white stuff. He offered to create some radio fun on his way in by shoveling out people who were snowed in like he was. No charge. Tony Bruno to the rescue.

Shortly after 8:00—halfway through our show—he showed up at the home of a "little old lady," as he described her, and proceeded to huff and puff until her driveway was clear. She showered him with praise, which he accepted with typical aplomb. (We think one of his neighbors played the part of the elderly women. And we doubt he cleared anyone's driveway, including his own.)

Tony never made it into work that day.

We were not surprised.

I have always embraced my sedentary lifestyle, proudly declaring many times on the air that I will never need any replacement body parts because the ones I have are almost like new. I will acknowledge a bit of an overstatement there. I was an avid runner in my early days at WIP, even finishing the 10-mile Broad Street Run one year. (I was the runner with the blood covering the front of his shirt, the result of nipple burn. Ouch.) Nowadays, I pedal 90 miles a week on my recumbent exercise bike, largely because I can do so while in my preferred sitting position.

My last major physical stunt came 20 years ago when the Borgata Hotel Casino and Bar opened in Atlantic City. Actually, this was a month or so before the official opening. Larry Mullin, the original CEO at Borgata, was a big fan of our show, and he booked us for weekly remote broadcasts every Friday at his sparkling new facility. Before there were lawyers who prevented stuff like this, he even invited us to start while the building was still a construction site.

It just so happened that the PR director at the time was a world-class athlete who also happened to be a woman. I was a bit past my prime at 51, but hey, I was a man. I was in the midst of my typical sexist schtick back then when a challenge evolved. Could I beat the PR woman in a 40-yard dash?

Hey, let's find out.

What could possibly go wrong?

One Friday, we measured off the 40 yards, even before the floor had been fully installed, and we lined up for the race. Al had told me to stretch, but I assured him I wouldn't need to do that to "beat a girl."

Ready. Set. Go.

Rhea Hughes assures me that I never actually had a chance to beat the woman, though I briefly harbored dreams of an upset when I saw she was only a stride ahead as we neared the finish line. (She was barely jogging, Rhea claims.)

I lengthened my stride to get to the tape first—but I never made it there. My right hamstring popped first; I felt a distinct tear and then a jolt of pain. What happened next is, in many ways, virtually impossible. With the next stride of my left leg, I snapped that hamstring, too. Two hamstrings in one race, ripped to shreds.

"Oh my God, Al!" Rhea screamed. "Angelo is really hurt!"

"Ha," Al laughed. "He pulled a hammy...I told him to stretch."

That Rhea had sympathy and Al only sneering contempt says a lot about both of my co-hosts. I didn't finish the show that day because I was in the back of an ambulance, en route to Shore Memorial Hospital.

The back of both my legs were turning purple by then, a memento for my absurd male ego. I spent the next month in a wheelchair, though I did return to work the next Monday, feeling only shame.

In those weeks after the mishap, I underwent the most arduous rehab I could ever have imagined, under the direction of one of our sponsors (of course), NovaCare Rehabilitation. I even eventually consented to deep-tissue massage by a male rehab specialist, though it became a running joke that I would always ask for a woman first. (I told you I was a sexist.)

Every step of the way during that rehab—and many other medical issues in the years ahead—was Ray Pennacchia, the senior vice-president who stood with us at WIP unwaveringly for over a generation. The fact that I was made whole again is a tribute to Ray and his extremely patient staff.

The NovaCare people were also very helpful with their medical advice. They suggested, gently, that I stopped doing physical stunts. For once, I followed my doctor's advice. I never attempted another stunt in the 20 years that followed.

Chapter 8

Spreading My Wings

Timing truly is everything, and it was especially so for me in the 1990s. Not only was I doing a radio show I had no clue how to do, but soon another opportunity, on a medium I was even less equipped to handle, presented itself. ESPN had a new show called *The Sports Reporters*, populated by a bunch of writer types just like us.

If they could do it, my old partner at the *Inquirer*, Glen Macnow, figured, why couldn't we?

Well, there were a lot of good reasons, starting with a host who didn't look the part. The ESPN show had Dick Schaap, a veteran TV guy who also wrote best-selling sports books. Our show would have me as host, a year or so into a radio career not projected to go much further than that. But Glen is nothing if not persistent, and he didn't stop until he convinced the regional sports-and-movie station, PRISM, to hand us a spot on the lineup.

It would be called *The Great Sports Debate*—a television show by four people who knew nothing about TV. The original cast would be Al Morganti (wearing a stylish mullet), me (absurdly skinny because of a weight-loss product endorsement I took too seriously), Jayson Stark (who would soon become a breakout TV star), and Glen Macnow (the real brains of our operation).

Ironically, the main attraction was none of us. For the first time in TV talk-show history—another claim we never bothered to check—a regular part of the panel was a dog, Al's beloved pet, Fenway. The lovable but lethargic canine would sit on the edge of the set, rarely moving, but his presence provided most of the drama. Would he stand? Would he walk? Would he do anything, ever?

In an opening that was high camp even for that cheesy era of sports TV, I was shown in front of the set, reeling off the big topics we would be tackling during the program, with the rest of the panel in silhouette behind me.

We had no cue cards—this was truly bargain-basement TV—so I had to memorize the open. Unfortunately, we always recorded the show right after our radio program, and my brain was too tired to remember all of my lines. We scrapped the open for that reason alone. Each of us would deliver one headline after that. It was almost as bad.

At the time when we started *The Great Sports Debate*, the only one of us with any TV experience was Al, who was a contributor to the hockey coverage on ESPN. Stark would become a star at ESPN, and later at the MLB Network, but back then his preoccupation was baseball writing, which earned him honors from the Baseball Hall of Fame in Cooperstown, New York, a generation later.

Early on, we all agreed that the TV show had to be different from our radio work because, hey, we had the benefit of the audience actually seeing us when we were talking. At the same time, we did not have access to highlights, which cost money we didn't have in our budget. So, primarily to entertain myself, I began to incorporate visuals into my commentary.

One time, to emphasize how easy Georgetown's schedule was, I smashed a line of cream puffs with a cinder block, leading to a mess on the stage. (Fenway didn't even bother to get up and lick the smushed pastry.) All of that first year, I was trying to come up with big visual moments that went beyond our trademark yelling and screaming about sports.

For the finale of our first season, I thought it would be a great cliff-hanger if I was shot with a fake gun in the final scene, leaving viewers to wonder if I would be back for season two. (Of course, if they turned on the radio the next morning, they would know I was okay.) The plan was to have me launch into a tirade against a sports figure, and then a gun would appear right in front of the main camera, a shot would erupt from the firearm, and I would fall back in my seat.

The money shot would be blood soaking through my white shirt right near the heart. (I was able to get a blood pack used in movies, which I squished at the appropriate time.) The credits would then roll as I lay on the set, motionless.

How we executed all of this is a matter of opinion. (My humiliation, and the lack of a VCR, prohibited me from studying the tape all over again, though it is included in a special video package of the greatest moments in *The Great Sports Debate* history.) I think it's safe to say it fit the so-bad-its-good vibe of the show.

Much later in the 10-year run of that silly show, I had joined the original cast of the new regional sports network, Comcast SportsNet, with my own TV show, and the boss then was Sam Schroeder, who oversaw the early seasons of *Debate*.

Since they had come to me with an offer I couldn't refuse, I assumed Sam was a big fan of my goofy antics—until he talked to me before my debut.

"All I ask," he said, "is that you don't do any of the stupid stuff you did on that show."

Okay. Got it.

By the mid-1990s and post-depression, I reached the period of my career that was the most productive, and also the most turbulent. Soon, I would have more jobs than I could handle, and new partners both on and off the air.

Looking back, I never forgave Tom Bigby for letting Tony Bruno go. The inside phone line would still ring during shows—often right near the beginning—but I would either dismiss what he ordered me to do, or not even take the call. When I would retire many years later, I referred to this period as my "jerk" years, but I was never going to show deference to Bigby. I have no regrets about how I dealt with him.

For several years, in fact, I didn't deal with him at all. After the flirtation with Boston, I hired an agent who would have a major impact on the rest of my career. Guess who recommended him and set up my first meeting. Who else? Al Morganti. Al had met Steve Mountain while covering hockey. Steve has been one of the top representatives of hockey stars for a generation, and he dabbled with lesser talents like me and Al in his spare time.

Whenever my hatred of Bigby nudged into desperation, I would call Steve and unload. My therapist had told me not to hold in the negative feelings, and I had no shortage of those when it came to my immediate boss. The GM of our station, Cecil R. "Butch" Forster, was also a good outlet, and his hatred of Bigby may have surpassed even mine.

More than once, Butch made it clear he was ready to display his Marine background during altercations with Bigby. In a conversation for this book, Butch told me things got so heated that he threatened, at least once, to punch Bigby's lights out. Tom was a typical bully—tough right up until he was actually confronted physically.

Finally, my frustration with my immediate boss had reached a point of no return. I said I doubted I could keep working under the oppressive atmosphere created by Bigby, and then Steve got an idea so implausible, all these years later I still can't believe he executed it. Steve said he would try to eliminate Bigby from my life.

Huh? How?

Well, what if Steve wrote into my contract a clause that prohibited my boss from criticizing me? This was 1995, before I had the contract leverage that I would get in later decades as I proved my longevity. Steve acknowledged at the time that it was a long shot that our parent company, Infinity Broadcasting, would allow such a dangerous precedent, but there's no harm in trying. Right?

At no point during those talks did the following clause become a point of contention. It is right there, on page five, of my contract, signed on January 1, 1995:

> *Infinity and Employee agree that employee shall not be subject to criticism or sanctions by Thomas Bigby, the present Program Director. All criticisms, advice and sanctions shall be imposed by the General Manager only to Employee. In the event Thomas Bigby would become General Manager during the term of this agreement or any extensions hereto, then another officer of Infinity, who would be mutually agreed upon between Infinity and Employee, would replace the General Manager's role for purposes of this agreement.*

I was free for the rest of my time with Bigby, at my own discretion. It was almost too good to be true, and I assumed Bigby was aware of the clause because the next two years were surprisingly amiable. Always a man whose mood was governed directly by ratings, maybe Bigby was so happy with our rising numbers that he decided to back off. At least that's what I thought at the time.

But then, in 1997, Bigby was back to throwing his substantial weight around, and I finally snapped. Late in June 1997, I started a show talking about what the world was obsessing over: Mike Tyson biting off a piece of the ear of his opponent, Evander Holyfield, in a heavyweight championship match televised worldwide. It was an extraordinary event, in every way fulfilling Bigby's own litmus test—to parrot the conversations that day in the corner taverns of Philadelphia.

The boss was having none of it that morning, however. He was on the hotline even before I had gone to the first break. When I picked up the phone, I didn't even get a hello.

"No one gives a damn about boxing!" he barked. "Get off this—now!"

"Boxing?" I snapped back. "What the hell is wrong with you? The world is talking about this!... No. Fire me! I don't give a bleep!"

The argument continued right up to the end of the commercial break, at which time I purposely defied Bigby by inviting comment on the incident. If I took a call that morning about anything but the ear bite, I have no recollection of it. The war of wills was at hand.

The Tyson ear-bite dispute exposed me to another round of abuse by Bigby, but this time I put an end to it quickly. I invoked the clause in the contract. I told Bigby we were done. If he had any problems, he could tell Butch Forster, who was more likely tell him to go to hell than to pass on the complaint.

Bigby had no idea that the clause existed until that moment. I know this because he told me so—a violation of the agreement that I let pass. For years after that, the program director who had taught me radio had no influence on me or our show. I'm not sure he ever recovered. All I know is that, thanks to that clause, I was able to work at WIP for 28 more years of relative peace.

Thank you, Steve Mountain. Thank you, Butch Forster.

This sudden burst of energy, post-depression, also led me back to the halls of academia in 1995, 18 years after I had left Columbia. Following a meeting at La Salle with the head of the communications department, Brother Gerry Molyneaux, I joined the faculty as an adjunct professor. I would teach a two-hour journalism class on Tuesdays and one more hour on Thursdays every week.

The job itself was not exactly lucrative—$2,000 per semester—but it became more important to me than any other in my career when I was assigned a grad student named Gail Cox to help me with my computer. The first thing I noticed was the red hair. The second was the patience. I am not just inept with technology; I often lose my mind very quickly. She smiled through our lessons until I had a fundamental grasp of what I was doing.

This was literally weeks after my separation with Linda, and Gail was nine years younger than me, but, as the saying goes, the heart knows what it wants. What boggles my mind all these years later is why I thought I had a chance with someone so out of my league. Still, at our last computer lesson, I asked if she would like to go to lunch someday. She said yes.

At that lunch I learned the news that she, too, was in the midst of a breakup after a 13-year marriage. She made it clear that she was not ready for another relationship, especially with a 45-year-old dork on the rebound. She used a fatal word at that lunch. Friends. She wanted to be friends. Ugh.

Was there a moment when I knew Gail was really The One? I'm glad you asked. Yes. It happened one day in 1997 when we decided to do a show just before a big Eagles game against Dallas from a billboard hanging precariously over I-95 just north of the city. Since this was an all-too-common radio stunt in that era, I decided to act as if we had come up with it for the first time. We even billed it The First Billboard Sit-in in Radio History! The irony eluded most of our listeners.

This was one of our very early shows with Rhea Hughes, and none of us (especially Al, who we later learned had a morbid fear of heights) was in a good place, literally or figuratively. The wooden board that had been placed on the base of the billboard was shaking with every gust of wind, and if we looked down, well...we were instructed never to look down.

We were cold and starving when, rising like a phoenix through the trees in a bucket truck was my new girlfriend, Gail. She has always looked beautiful to me, but never more so than on that day, on that billboard. She got close to us without leaving the bucket, handed over some soft pretzels, and waved as she went back down to the safety of terra firma.

I was a goner. All it took was that bucket, those pretzels, and that smile.

While I was placing my romantic intentions on the back burner, I adapted to teaching quickly by using some of the theatrics I was still working on in my radio and TV jobs. One of the benefits I had was that few, if any, of the students knew who I was at the start. Early in the semester, I grabbed a theater major and concocted an experiment in observation.

The lesson was about how to report what you observe first-hand, and I had a trick to demonstrate a special technique. At my designated cue, the actor burst into the classroom wearing a mask and stole my briefcase. (Yes, I had a briefcase. Stop laughing.) Just as quickly as he entered, the burglar then ran out of class and headed for the exit.

I will never know how many of the kids caught on to what I was doing, but I can say the ensuing discussion was one of the liveliest of the semester. Who could describe the thief? What did he steal? Where did he run? Of course, the accounts varied, with some students arguing vociferously with others about what they had seen. The point of the exercise is that eyewitness accounts are not reliable, and that a reporter has to train him or herself to take a visual snapshot of what he or she sees in the moment.

The great reveal at the end of the class was always the best part. The theater student would reappear exactly as he had 30 minutes earlier and the students could then either take a bow or hide their heads. I did the same stunt eight times over my four years at La Salle, and it worked every time. (It also helped me get among the best student-feedback scores at the end of every course.)

In my final year at La Salle, I designed my own course for the curriculum called Sports Reporting 101, and it was truly a labor of love. It brought me back to my journalism days with a joy that I never had when I was actually reporting. I also got to work with young people like Mike Sielski and John Gonzalez, both of whom have gone on to great careers in sports media.

Mike even went into sports after attending the Columbia Graduate School of Journalism. He tells me no one swore him to secrecy about his intentions. In fact, his advisor had previously written for *Sports Illustrated*, and there was actually a course on sports journalism in the catalogue.

Go figure.

Back at WIP, we were doing well, but how long could we do without the wit and wisdom of Tony Bruno? If there was a long-term plan on what to do with our show, I was never made aware of it. The consensus was, no one person would be able to replace Tony, so initially we kibitzed with our traffic people, Max Vierra and then Kris Gamble—until Kris took on more of a regular role as our foil. Kris was a sexy, fun person who appealed to our male demographic, but she was the first to say her knowledge about sports was not exactly extensive. We needed someone to fill that void.

Our prayers were answered when Kris, a bit of a radio vagabond back then, departed in 1997 for a rock station in D.C., and was replaced by a wild-haired young woman who had left WIP as a producer years earlier and made her mark on a local country station. Rhea Hughes was everything Kris was, and more, plus she had a knowledge of sports that rivaled ours at the beginning and far exceeded mine at the end.

Rhea came to us with previous experience at WIP as a producer for several shows, including the legendary and headstrong Howard Eskin. In other words, Rhea was battle-scarred. She also came with some hurdles to clear because she wasn't doing traffic. She was doing sports—a young woman in a man's world at a time when those who crossed the line did so at their own peril.

The howls of protest against a woman talking sports, especially in Philadelphia, the manliest of manly sports cities, never stopped over the 26 years she worked with us, but she was more powerful than the loudest voices. Rhea handled all of the news updates—brilliantly—and interrupted our show repeatedly with breaking stories that added an element of impending drama to every show.

And that was just the start of her emergence as a voice that broke through the cacophony created by Al, me, and our many guests and callers. Though she was new, Rhea never hesitated to launch counterattacks against Al and me (especially me) that deftly toed a very thin line between fun debate and personal attack. Above all, she knew what she was talking about. She was a perfect replacement for Tony, before we got more reinforcements a few years later.

Radio was becoming a real career for me by the late 1990s, when I was approaching a bigger salary than I ever imagined having, but money ultimately ended my ventures into TV and teaching.

At *Debate*, we went weeks with no pay because the producers simply didn't know how to sell the show. We were surprised anyone was watching, but over time we became a cult hit, or so it seemed. To generate some cash, we were sent out on remote locations—mostly auto dealerships, but any business that would write a check—and the turnouts were astonishing.

We did one at the Exton Mall—40 minutes outside of Philadelphia—and at least 500 people showed up right outside the Strawbridge's department store, hooting and hollering at four middle-aged journalists who suddenly felt like rock stars. Then Fenway, Al's dog, sauntered out, to the biggest ovation of all. All these years later, it amazes me that no other panel show has ever featured a dog.

I was reminded many years later that one of our early producers, Rob Kuestner—a young man who became very successful in TV—had to wait outside a business for three hours the day before one of our last broadcasts because I said I wouldn't show up the next day if I wasn't paid. The other panelists were also frustrated—we added another ex-writer, the telegenic Mike Missanelli, shortly after we started—but off the air no one knew how to play the role of obnoxious jerk as well as me.

We ended an improbable 10-year run with a final *Debate* in the Roosevelt Hotel, with a sellout crowd of hundreds and a guest appearance by our longtime leader, Mayor Ed Rendell. People pleaded with us to bring back the show, and we did try a time or two, but it was never the same.

Now that I think about it, I'm not sure we ever got paid for that last show, either.

Walking away from teaching was even more painful for me because it was the job that I enjoyed the most, and probably the job I did the best. I fed off the energy of the students, who responded well to many of my off-the-wall theatrical efforts to keep their attention. It was a way to perform with less pressure. I flourished in the classroom setting.

By then my daughter, Meredith, had outlived her rebelliousness and was doing well in school. When she said she wanted to apply to La Salle, I encouraged her—until I saw what the school was charging. In the end, I was making $4,000 a year to teach at a university where my daughter was being charged $14,000. (There were no special tuition dispensations for adjunct faculty.)

Still, I was willing to accept the $10,000 shortfall until one day when the acting dean of the communications school—the brilliant head of the department, Brother Gerry, was on sabbatical—informed me that I was losing my parking space near the communications hall and would have to pay for parking up the street.

Hello? I had just developed a new course for the curriculum, pretty much gratis. And that wasn't good enough to win me a parking space?

The woman in charge back then said, yes, that's right, take it or leave it.

I left it.

I should have figured something like that would happen. That woman was from Syracuse, the biggest journalism rival to Columbia back then.

She must have been jealous.

As I look back on those days today, I realize the four years at La Salle were worth every penny I never got for my work. Some amazing students have tracked me down over the years to thank me for aiming them in the right direction. Nothing I did in any realm gave me the sense of accomplishment I got teaching at La Salle.

And even more beneficial was my introduction to Gail, who eventually moved me out of the friend zone and into the best relationship of my life. To this day, I get people she befriended—which is pretty much everybody she meets—wondering, right in my presence, how the heck a beautiful woman like her ended up with a doofus like me.

When I helpfully suggest it must be my winning personality, they inevitably shake their heads.

No, they reply every time, it's definitely not that.

Chapter 9

Wing Bowl

The biggest disconnect in my career is that my résumé includes both Columbia University and Wing Bowl. It's hard to imagine a wider abyss between quality and sloth than that.

Wing Bowl is the most successful promotion in radio history. (Again, we never researched it for verification, but often recited it as fact. This one was probably true.) It was an annual bacchanal in which WIP would gather a bunch of the fattest, grossest sports fans for a 30-minute chicken wing eating contest at major venues throughout the city. It lasted for 26 years, and it received international media coverage for most of its tenure.

The original concept came from—of course—Al Morganti. We were grumbling before a Super Bowl in the early 1990s that the Eagles were never going to make it to the biggest game on the sports calendar, and so we needed something to replace it.

Hey, why not try a big event of our own?

The Super Bowl was not the epic extravaganza it is now, 30-plus years later, but it is absurd to compare that game with the pitiful contest we planned for the first year. The Bills were annual also-rans in the Super Bowl back then, and Al's extensive exposure to the NHL made him an expert on Buffalo cuisine. The Anchor Bar in that frost-bitten city made the best chicken wings in the world, so why don't we have our own contest?

I know, I know. The logic eludes me, too. How a bar in Buffalo would inspire a Philadelphia tradition is a pretty big stretch, but I was never one to question Al's quirky genius. We couldn't get wings from the Anchor Bar, so Al did the next best thing. He asked his neighbor to make a batch. We had no trouble recruiting six fat slobs to eat wings in the lobby of the Wyndham Franklin Plaza Hotel that first year, and the hotel saw nothing wrong with a few extra people turning out for our show.

To our shock and delight, at least 200 loyal listeners attended that first Wing Bowl, which featured the gluttonous stylings of Carmen Cordero, who won so easily that he lit up a cigarette with a couple of minutes left, clearly the best of our blubbery crew. For this herculean effort, Carmen won a dusty old hibachi from the back of our contest closet. A great time was had by all.

Well, maybe not by all. The hotel management was not happy with the disruption caused by the Wing Bowl and made us promise never to do anything like that again in their quality facility. (The Wyndham thus became the first in an endless line of Wing Bowl critics.)

What would happen if we found a place more suitable for the event—like, say, the Mike Schmidt's bar on Market Street? After having to delay Wing Bowl 2 because of an ice storm, we held it the following week there, with around 700 people turning out at 6:00 AM to watch fat guys eat chicken wings.

Huh? Were these people all nuts? Or were we?

That second Wing Bowl ended with a new everyman hero, Heavy Kevvy (Kevin O'Donnell), a man even larger than Carmen. The winner of the first Wing Bowl quietly walked away after the loss and never returned. Little did Carmen and Kevvy realize back then that they had a part in what would soon be a radio promotion like no other.

Wing Bowl 3 featured our first overtime battle, and when Kevvy won again, a star was born. Over 1,000 listeners turned out at the Schmidt bar that morning, with hundreds shivering outside before we opened the doors at 6:00 AM. The whole city was talking about us, or rather, our stupid event—and this led us to find new ways to make it even crazier.

Now that we had outgrown the bar, we took Wing Bowl 4 to Club Egypt, a night club on Delaware Avenue that was not prepared for the 3,000 fans who turned out on a snowy morning. I remember that event well because it featured a contestant angrily pelting Al and me with undercooked wings as the final seconds ticked off the clock. We finished that Wing Bowl while hiding under the broadcast table, with greasy wings flying over our heads. No one cared. We had a monster on our hands, for reasons we don't understand any better now than we did then.

It was at Wing Bowl 5 that we headed in a direction that would make the event a true phenomenon, and ultimately would bring about its end 21 years later. The field of contestants was growing, and we needed volunteers to help us count the wings. Who better than beautiful women? Thus, the term Wingette was born. Would any women be willing to demean herself and join the tomfoolery every Friday before the Super Bowl?

Yes. Lots of women. Lots and lots of women.

In fact, there were so many people on the stage at our first concert venue, the Electric Factory—15 contestants and 30 Wingettes—that we were not prepared when a contestant invited a group of Mummers to accompany him as he marched to his place at the table. As the decorative musicians poured onto the stage, we heard a crack, then another. The stage was collapsing.

The Mummers were urgently invited to leave at that point, and we held our breath for the rest of the show. We resumed the festivities, but only long enough for Heavy Kevvy, our breakout star, to stop eating in the first minute of the contest, drop to his knee, and propose to his lead Wingette. (We hadn't noticed that he had snuck his girlfriend onto the stage.) She said yes.

A stage collapse and an impromptu wedding proposal? All for free? And none of it actually planned by us, of course. Wing Bowl, from the fifth year on, would be like a wild bronco we could never fully contain. It had a mind of its own. All we could do was hold on for dear life as it got wilder and crazier. And yes, dirtier, too.

By Wing Bowl 9, we had outgrown every minor venue in Philadelphia, leaving only the Spectrum as an indoor option. It had a capacity of 20,000—far more than the 5,000 we were drawing at Electric Factory. Maybe we could use just one side of the huge building. But how could we get it for a chicken-wing eating contest? At 6:00 AM?

To the rescue came Mayor Rendell, yet again. He called our show one day and said he would offer for Wing Bowl 9 one of the dates the city had available as part of its Spectrum contract. The mayor had no idea what he was offering back then, but I can report that Wing Bowl 9 was the last one he ever attended. It was the first one when the Wingettes took center stage, dressed in the minimum allowed by law. (In retrospect, we probably should have renamed it "Thong Bowl" after that.)

By then, we had a new superstar, a protégé of Heavy Kevvy named El Wingador (Bill Simmons), and he alone was worth the price of admission (free). In many ways, El Wingador's career in wing-eating paralleled Wing Bowl's—successful beyond comprehension for a long time, and then a sharp decline before a very sad ending.

He was a local hero, often featured with wing juice smeared over his bearded face on the front page of the *Daily News* the morning after every conquest. By the time we moved to the Spectrum, the prizes had improved dramatically. Instead of a used hibachi, the winner got a new car—though I must humbly admit the first couple of cars were too small to accommodate the heft of the winners.

Moving to a new site provided a new dimension to Wing Bowl, which added elaborate processions into the arena for most of the contestants and their growing entourages. Now Mummers were infiltrating every event, playing, and dancing. We began giving our prizes for the best entrances, which led to floats commemorating Philadelphia's hatred of the Dallas Cowboys, which led to a constant barrage of debris, which led to beefed-up security, which led to the hurling of even more debris.

Since we had no idea how to actually pull off an event that was attracting 12,000, then 15,000, and finally 20,000 every year, we had no choice but to ride the wave for as long and as far as it took us. There were signs all along the way that we needed to downsize it at some point, but we took no heed.

One time, Rhea Hughes got trapped between two almost identical processions of makeshift tanks. She was reporting from the walkway that led into the arena when the first tank turned around and aimed itself at the second tank. She dove up against the boards, right near the Flyers' bench, but still got sandwiched just before the collision of the floats. She did the rest of the show that day with blood dripping down her arm, a profile in courage.

In that first decade of Wing Bowl, I look back in disbelief at what we did, and how the station's lawyers were not yet aware of the dangerous stunts that literally threatened lives in the interest of promoting the event. For example, prospective competitors had to call during the show and propose an eating adventure that would impress the judges (us). These ideas would span the spectrum from mundane to insane.

The closest anyone ever came to dying was during a stunt in the early 2000s—before lawyers began scrutinizing our every move—when a competitor proposed eating two gallons of ice cream in 10 minutes. Simple enough. We said yes, and the poor fool showed up that morning at our studios in Bala Cynwyd with the ice cream in a cooler.

When we started the clock, the young man scarfed down the creamy delight with unbridled joy, polishing off the first container in less than three minutes. As he jabbed his soup spoon into the second gallon, his teeth started to chatter. My first thought was, *This guy must be really nervous.* After all, his family and friends are listening to him live on WIP. These are most likely his 10 minutes of fame.

The chattering of teeth became more pronounced as the eater slowed his pace, a lethargy setting in. Al was the first to notice his face was turning gray, and his lips were changing from rosy red to frozen blue. We called off the stunt less than halfway through the second container as the effects of the ice cream sent the contestant spiraling deeper into distress.

Emergency personnel showed up quickly after that, at our insistence, and they rushed the man to the hospital, deep in the grips of hypothermia. He recovered quickly once his body temperature had stabilized, but not before he scared everyone associated with WIP and Wing Bowl. From that day on, the station lawyers had to approve all stunt proposals. For some reason, they no longer had faith in our judgment.

Before that, there were no rules about what we tried in the interest of spiking excitement before the event. People listening couldn't believe we allowed a nutcase named Slushy Shelly into Wing Bowl when he proposed, and successfully executed, a stunt that required him to eat a big chunk of the dirt-caked snow clinging to the bottom of his front bumper. And then there was Corn Boy, who guzzled down six large containers of creamed corn, only to spackle our walls at 5th Street just a minute or two later. Yuck.

We even offered for eight consecutive years a halftime show featuring a character named Mize, whose claim to fame was to smash full cans of beer on his head. He would shake the six-pack vigorously for maximum effect, and then crush the aluminum cans against his upper forehead, digging gouges into his swollen forehead and usually finishing with his face cloaked in blood. The crowd went crazy. Eventually, the WIP lawyers went nuts, too. Game over for Mize.

One stunt that was the brainchild of Al Morganti would probably have gotten us fired a decade later. He thought it would be fun if our national anthem singer, a provocatively dressed woman named Tina Marie, delivered the sacred song while bouncing up and down on a trampoline. The drunken crowd urged her on toward the end of the anthem when she struggled for breath.

By now, I'm pretty sure you think less of us. I know, looking back on it today, I do. But back then our goal was single-minded. We would do whatever made the Wing Bowl more ridiculous, and our plan worked spectacularly. I knew we were making a connection when my son, Neil (then in his early twenties), and stepson, Brendan (a teenager), clamored for tickets. They would take hordes of their young friends, promising to drink not a drop of beer at the event. (We used the honor system.)

And I cannot leave out the love that Gail's own family developed for Wing Bowl. Her brothers would come every year, as would her dad, who was pushing 80 and loving every minute. One year, Adolph Autenrieth tripped on a float when he was on his way into the arena, opening a huge gash on his head. (It actually looked a bit like Mize after his beer-smashing show.) Once the first-aid people had wrapped Ade's head in a huge tourniquet, he refused further medical attention and took his seat in the arena, with blood soaking through the bandage.

For the first 13 years of the event, believe it or not, there was no ticketing, and absolutely no crowd control. First come, first served. Beer sales for the two hours allowed by law—yes, we served alcohol starting at 7:00 AM—topped the list of all events at the Spectrum and

Wells Fargo Center for alcohol consumption every single year without exception.

Then the unthinkable happened. The Eagles finally made it to the Super Bowl. Suddenly, Wing Bowl wasn't a way to forget about another failed Eagles season; it was the biggest pep rally in Philadelphia's history.

We opened the doors that day early in 2005 and filled all 20,000 seats and had another few thousand standing on the floor of the arena well before 6:00 AM. Fire marshals shut out the rest of the crowd, which, according to conservative estimates, totaled at least another 10,000. You can probably guess what happened next. The drunks not allowed entry started throwing cans and bottles and other projectiles at the windows of the arena, shattering several. After that event, as we were driving away, the parking lots around the building looked like Beirut after a war siege.

The long decline of Wing Bowl was under way. Starting the next year, we agreed for the first time to ticketing—$10 each—and supplemented our WIP security force. To appease the Philadelphia police, who listed Wing Bowl as the event they most dreaded each year, we pledged donations every year to the Survivor's Fund. The cops were really too kind. They had every right to close us down for good, but they realized at that point that the backlash would be huge. I apologize to them for those last 12 Wing Bowls or so. We were all out of control by then.

How out of control? The best example of our zeal run amok was our partnership with gentlemen's clubs in that final decade. It started when our Miss Wing Bowl, a beautiful woman named Jennifer Burmeister, had an affiliation with Cheerleaders, one of the more prestigious strip clubs in Philadelphia. Soon, she invited some of her fellow performers, which led to other clubs wanting representation as well.

Then our sales department saw a chance to monetize the event more by selling sponsorships, primarily to gentlemen's clubs, which led to an army of strippers arriving every year, in various stages of sobriety and dress. I knew we were in serious trouble when my wife, Gail, who I had generously assigned the job of checking in all the Wingettes, quit after Wing Bowl 22. The event had officially gotten too "sleazy"—her word—for the wife of the host. (Her family kept coming until the bitter end. They still loved it.)

In the final years, we were willing to try pretty much anything to keep interest high. We actually used as a co-host one year a porn star, Katie Morgan, who was excellent on the air. Soon, the clubs were issuing announcements that they would feature the likes of top porn stars Jenna Jameson, Mary Carey, and Ron Jeremy. (Yup. Even him.)

Spurred on by this infusion of decadence, the atmosphere at Wing Bowls deteriorated to the point where the video screens started showing women sitting in the stands who were urged by the drunks surrounding them to flash the crowd. I am not proud to admit I encouraged this behavior myself. Many did flash. We were no longer just politically incorrect. We were now wrong by all basic standards of human behavior.

In a failed effort to redirect attention to the eaters, we then sought out the biggest names in the competitive ranks, securing the services—sometimes with an appearance fee attached—of Joey Chestnut, The Black Widow (Sonya Thomas), and the legendary Takeru Kobayashi, among many others. By then it didn't really matter who was eating, though. The show became, for want of a better word, obscene.

Even the all-time biggest winner, El Wingador, fell on hard times. He was sent to prison on a drug charge, just a year after we had named him the first inductee to our Wing Bowl Hall of Fame. (He would serve another stint in prison a few years later.)

Our final desperate attempt to turn attention away from all the shamelessness led us to booking entertainment names to generate some positive spin. One year, I invited the terrific character actor Chazz Palminteri to attend, and he immediately marveled at the depravity.

"This is unbelievable," he shouted to me above the din. "Wow."

He never came back.

Same for Snooki Polizzi, fresh off her initial spike in interest from the TV reality show *Jersey Shore*. She even agreed to ride our mechanical bull, to the cheers of the crowd. We invited her the next year. No.

In 2016, we used some connections to convince rap star Coolio to perform. Our program director then, Spike Eskin, got Coolio—who was well past his peak of popularity—to promise he would use none of the profanities in his most popular songs and would not try out new music.

At our signal, Coolio grabbed the mic and announced: "I'd like to start with a new one." Moments later, he segued into a big hit, swear words and all. Coolio was not a good listener. His performances never got on the air, though the drunks in the crowd happily sang along.

And then there was Dennis Rodman, who agreed to come for a $15,000 fee that included his subsequent appearance at a strip club. For years I have trashed Rodman because of his attitude that day. He would answer none of my questions and bid a hasty retreat even before the first wing was consumed. Then I found out he had gotten hit in the head with a projectile—most likely a beer can—as he entered the arena.

Needless to say, he never came back, either. (Nor was he invited.)

Ric Flair is the only celebrity who did return, for our final two Wing Bowls in 2017 and 2018. The fans greeted him with his signature "Woo hoo!" and he speaks to this day about what a wonderful thing Wing Bowl is—at least by pro wrestling standards.

By that time, let's face it, Wing Bowl may just as well have been produced and directed by World Wrestling Entertainment. We were done. I just didn't accept it right away.

When the Eagles won the Super Bowl in 2018, Al knew immediately that we had a perfect exit point. There was no reason to hold the Wing Bowl anymore. At least that would be the best way for us to put to rest the monster we had created.

For most of 2018, I argued in vain to hold one final Wing Bowl, and to bill it as our last hurrah. I envisioned Wing Bowl 27 as a return to our roots, a good-clean-fun finale with a bunch of fat guys eating wings, in a smaller venue. No Wingettes. No big floats. Definitely no porn stars. Maybe the top prize would be a hibachi again.

What do you say, guys? One more day to honor the spirit of the original Wing Bowl? Let's do this for the fans. Let's give our listeners closure.

Other than me, the vote was unanimous: No.

Wing Bowl was dead.

Chapter 10

Bonding with the Listeners

As our first decade wound down, the line between my radio persona and the real me began to blur. I was immersing my personality more and more into the job, pretty much at the expense of everything else.

By the year 2000, I had bleached my hair blond on the air (I lost a bet), I had my head sheared and shaved (another bet), I had one of the first live on-air colonoscopies, and—believe it or not—I had breast reduction surgery broadcast live on our show and later that day on Channel 10.

It's pretty safe to say I was unembarrassable by then. I can remember no pain in my life worse than the burning of my scalp when the colorist first applied the bleach. And that includes the time I got a vasectomy, which we didn't do on the air (the urologist nixed the idea), but which I talked about incessantly for months.

The breast problem was one of my best-kept secrets. I became more conscious of it when I met Gail, and a great Cherry Hill plastic surgeon, Dr. Steven Davis, stepped forward with an offer I could not refuse: smaller breasts for free. To pay him back, I let the TV people in to film his artistry.

When I saw the piece that night, I retched. I knew nothing about that rapid sawing motion that the doctor uses to break down the fat, nor that nasty tube that channeled the bad stuff out of me. Still, though, my chest was flat. I could finally take my shirt off at the beach. (I never did.)

An even better example of this blurring between my public and private lives is the day of my second marriage, which happened either on December 31, 1999, or January 3, 2000. I still have no idea which is our actual anniversary. Neither does Gail, who still laughs at the bizarre circumstances that surrounded our blessed event.

Toward the end of 1999, I got a call from Mayor Ed Rendell—notice a trend here?—and he needed my help again. Undaunted by the Ricky Williams debacle months earlier, I told him I was there to help. The mayor wanted to marry 2,000 people on the day before the millennium, and it would give a big boost to the promotion if I joined the mass ceremony at the Philadelphia Convention Center.

I said yes—a bit too soon.

Gail understood the unique demands of my job, but she said it would mean a great deal to her if we got married earlier that day and then did the whole thing again a few hours later. (You know how people renew their vows? We decided to do it the same day we exchanged them.)

We worked with Mayor Rendell's secretary to determine where and when he would be on that historically busy day, and we all agreed to meet in the heart display at the Franklin Institute at 11:00 AM, three hours before the big event across town. The museum has a walk-in exhibit of a human heart, with all of the ventricles and arteries accompanied by the sound of incessant thumping.

The next few details have been in dispute for the past 23 years. I have one version, and Gail has quite another. I remember checking out the heart a few days before December 31 and discovering that the sound of the heartbeat made me woozy. I said I would only be able to stay upright if the Institute unhooked the heart for a few minutes. (Apparently, I hadn't been convinced of the Institute's inflexibility during my 85-mph-pitch debacle.)

In my version, the nice people at the esteemed science museum acquiesced and the heart was silent during the ceremony. In Gail's account—more believable, I admit—she told me to suck it up and I braved the ceremony with the thumping engulfing us. Either way, we got married, leading to the best 23 years (and counting) of my life.

Three hours later, we were back doing it all over again with throngs of others—some of whom we had recruited for the mayor right there on WIP. It was a heartwarming display of everlasting love. Unfortunately, in the group surrounding us, Gail and I are the only ones who escaped unscathed. As best I can tell, the rest all got divorced within the next decade. Go figure.

It wasn't until after New Year's Day that Gail realized we didn't have the legal documents proving our marriage, so I called Mayor Rendell on January 2 while he was in his limo racing off to another event. Because we had gotten married a few hours before the other 1,999 couples, our papers were kept separate. They were missing. They were gone.

Were we married or not? I'm not sure even now. No papers, no marriage, I think. We may have been living in sin for a few days. Sorry. We didn't know.

In a final twist to this rom-com, someone from the mayor's office met us at a destination halfway between City Hall and our home in Mt. Laurel, New Jersey—the Forman Mills outlet in Pennsauken, New Jersey. It was right there, next to a bin of $5 T-shirts, that we sealed the bond with our signatures.

They don't write love stories like that anymore.

Instinctively, one of the things I definitely got right during my 33-tenure on WIP was making a priority of bonding with the fans. In the early years, I did this face-to-face in the tent before Eagles games and on special bus trips to experience sports up-close with the biggest supporters of our show. These trips gave me some of our biggest laughs, and the most revealing experience of my long career.

Our very first trip sent me and a bus of zealots to the Baseball Hall of Fame in Cooperstown, New York, followed by a visit to historic Fenway Park before wrapping up our excursion at the original Yankee Stadium. I learned a very interesting fact on the first day of that trip. Our listeners do not like to read. (So why am I writing a book? Good question.)

After a few words of introduction on the bus's PA system, I plopped down in a seat near the front of the bus and cracked open a biography of union activist Marvin Miller.

"What are you doing up there?" asked a traveler.

"Reading," I answered. "Why?"

"Reading? Ha, ha. Hey guys, Angelo is reading."

The inside of the bus rocked with derisive howls, which soon lapsed into relentless heckling whenever I tried to pick up the book.

"How's Marvin Miller doing now?"

"Did he call for another strike?"

"Ha. Look. Angelo's reading again."

Somehow, we made it through the Hall of Fame and to Fenway without any arrests—though the consumption of beer was prolific—and the listeners didn't even seem to mind when the game in Boston was rained out. (We managed to con an usher into giving us an unauthorized tour of the magical old place.)

But by the time we made it to Yankee Stadium, the joviality had been replaced with an edgier form of humor. An old fellow who was a regular caller back then, Phil from the Northeast—he developed a big following by saying, during every call, "Shut the Front Door!" as if he were swearing—was a troublemaker, plain and simple. He concocted a practical joke that nearly cost another elderly traveler his life.

Phil convinced his traveling buddy that there was a raffle for a trip to Florida at Yankee Stadium after the game, and he had the bus driver read out the winning numbers in everyone's programs. (Phil had stolen the old guy's program earlier in the day and wrote down the numbers.)

Sure enough, as the driver barked out the numbers, the codger got increasingly excited. After the last number crackled through the speaker system in the bus, we had just pulled onto a clogged Major Deegan Expressway and were about to ride into a stream of traffic.

"I won! I won! I won! Let me out of the bus! I've got to claim my prize!"

The driver said he couldn't do that. Phil said, "Damn, bad break. If you don't claim the trip right after the game, you lose it." The old guy started pounding on the door of the bus, demanding to be let out on the expressway. Then he suddenly fell back and appeared to suffer a seizure.

At this point—way too late—I tried to explain to the gasping victim that the whole thing was a bad prank pulled by Phil. The old guy ended up getting some medical tests after our return to Philadelphia that day. The doctors called it "an episode."

The last thing I remember telling Phil when order had slowly been restored was, "Shut the front door!"

Only I used the swear words instead.

Phil didn't make a peep the rest of the trip.

Most of the excursions I took with the fans ended up in disastrous situations like that, though I kept trying them anyway. Even worse was a bus trip to Memorial Stadium in 1991 for the last game ever at that old Baltimore ballpark.

To sell the trip, I suggested (stupidly) that this visit might provide an opportunity to take home a memento from a nice old ballpark. I even reminded our fans of the final game at Philadelphia's beloved old Connie Mack Stadium, where you can actually hear on the radio broadcast the clanging and banging of tools making contact with the seats as fans disassembled them at the last game ever played there.

Sure enough, a few of our travelers that day brought with them their trusty toolboxes and planned to take a page—and a seat—out of the old Connie Mack playbook. There was only one big problem with this thinking: The world had become less tolerant of fan misbehavior in the 21 years between the final games of the two old ballparks.

When I told the people on the bus that they couldn't bring toolboxes into Memorial Stadium, they completely understood—or so they said. Of course, they had no intention of listening to me, or anyone else, for that matter.

The atmosphere was filled with nostalgia that day in Baltimore as some of the biggest heroes in Orioles history said goodbye to the ballpark, which was almost as decrepit as the neighborhood surrounding it. Meanwhile, our crew of 50 or so Philadelphia fans were scoping the place out for anything that wasn't bolted or cemented.

Around the sixth inning—approximately the same time when the dismantling at Connie Mack had really kicked in—two of our miscreants slid their toolbox out from under their seats—I have no clue how they got the big box through security—and proceeded to begin working on the bolts behind a seat. The problem was, these nitwits took aim at an aisle seat, where they were easily observed by everyone, including the ushers.

Before long, security arrived and threw the morons, and their toolbox, out of Memorial Stadium. Not knowing what my responsibility was at that point—after all, I was the host of the trip—I reluctantly followed the WIP listeners out of the ballpark to argue against their arrest. We spent the last three innings of the game in the bus, stewing for different reasons.

Eventually, the rest of our traveling circus showed up, arms filled with mementos. They had dismantled the seats, had several of the wooden spokes with the number that served as the back of the seats, an exit sign and various other priceless souvenirs. Of course, the two guys with the toolbox wanted their money back for the trip.

I don't think they ever got it.

I didn't care.

I still don't.

In a strange and totally unplanned way, I got to see a side of the Philadelphia sports fan that is never part of the national narrative about our passionate city. We were on a trip in 1992 that included stops at Wrigley Field and Comiskey Park in Chicago, with a visit to Milwaukee County Stadium sandwiched in between.

The bus was loud and drunk on the way back from Milwaukee—they were called "the Brewers" for a good reason—when one of the older and more subdued passengers learned some shocking news on his radio. (This was a few years before cell phones.) The beloved defensive tackle on the Eagles, Jerome Brown, had died in a horrific traffic accident. His nephew also perished in the crash.

The laughter and howling ended instantly as word swept through the bus. The party was over. In a matter of seconds, people on the bus that afternoon openly cried. Others sat there quietly, shaking their heads in disbelief. Passion comes in many shapes and colors. This was a side of Philadelphia fans no one ever gets to witness. Oh, you can see all of the misdeeds on YouTube, but never this. Never the flip side of passion, the unequivocal love of the city for a player taken way too soon.

The rest of that trip is a blur to me. Even after word spread that the larger-than-life sports hero was driving recklessly and was solely responsible for smashing his sports car into a tree—and for taking the life of an innocent victim—the love of Jerome Brown never wavered.

Philadelphia, a sports city that hates with no reservations, loves just as hard. I was often reminded of that fact in the many years following that trip.

One thing I never ran short of was my distaste for disloyal players. At the top of that list was a man I called "The Human Hairball," Jayson Werth, a journeyman bench player until Phillies GM Pat Gillick rescued him from irrelevance and signed him as a free-agent outfielder in 2007.

From the day he arrived in Philadelphia, Werth went on a growth spurt—growing into a terrific player and emulating a Chia Pet with hair spouting out of every follicle on his head and face. Werth became a valuable piece on that championship 2008 Phillies team, and beyond. He finally got paid, too, earning $7.5 million in his final season at Citizens Bank Park in 2010.

When the Phils refused to bid against an absurd seven-year, $126 million offer by the Washington Nationals, Werth left as a free agent for D.C. Most players would express gratitude for getting the opportunity to flourish as an athlete, and to win a World Series in Philly. Jayson Werth was not most players.

Phillies fans—okay, maybe spurred on a little by my negative commentary—were pleased one day when they traveled to D.C. and watched their fallen hero break a wrist trying to make a sliding catch. Werth heard the Phillies fans that day scream, "You deserve it," and he wasn't happy about the reaction.

The ingrate just got $126 million, and he didn't expect some backlash from the city he snubbed? Werth then made it worse with this obnoxious comment: "I'm motivated to see to it personally those people never walk down Broad Street in celebration again."

Now, a rational person might say the $126 million would be motivation enough, but then again no one said the Human Hairball was rational. I mean, look at him. So I went on the attack, setting up a trip to D.C. to greet him as soon as his wrist mended. We got seats in right field, and I found 40 grungy fans this time to bus it to D.C. and boo Werth until he saw the error of his ways.

I don't want to say we assembled a motley crew for this adventure, but both my wife and our crack PR person, Cindy Webster, chose to drive to the ballpark on their own. (Cindy was emphatic about not being trapped in a bus with the dubious characters we had assembled.) By the time we arrived after two-plus hours, the air in the vehicle was, admittedly, a bit ripe.

Everything went according to plan—at least for a while. We booed ourselves hoarse at every opportunity, and Werth even looked back at us a couple of times, encouraging a new outpouring of howls and obscene gestures. Unfortunately, as often happens on these fan trips, the evening inevitably divebombs as the consumption of alcohol takes its grip.

One of the couples on the trip was standing right behind the right-field section when the inebriated woman fell back onto the concrete concourse and was soon lying unconscious in a pool of her own blood. My reaction in times like this never varied. I panicked. I screamed for Cindy, who got an emergency crew from the stadium to whisk the woman away to a nearby hospital, accompanied by her soused husband.

While we boarded the bus after the game (with Gail now onboard, against her wishes), the injured woman was admitted for observation. She had a concussion and a big gash on her head. Her husband needed a ride home, so guess who got to take him? Ha, ha. Cindy.

By all reports, it was not a fun two hours for Gail or Cindy late that night.

As for Werth, the Nationals finally got a parade of their own—but not until two seasons after he had left.

The Phillies haven't had a parade since Jayson made that comment.

So I guess the dispute ended in a draw.

I never organized another bus trip.

We only ventured out with a fan group in the air once, and it is an experience none of us will ever forget. What appeared to be a tragedy at the time became the answer to our prayers during over very last trip ever with the fans.

This time, we flew coast to coast for a visit to Los Angeles to see the upstart 2017 Eagles face the Rams at the ancient Coliseum. Our dream season was well under way, thanks to a young, talented quarterback named Carson Wentz. We took a plane full of fans to L.A. to watch the Eagles stretch their NFL-best record to 11–2 that day. Would this finally be the season—our 27th at WIP—when the fans would get to celebrate a Super Bowl?

The trip was a monumental success—for most of it, anyway. Our group of 50 did a bar crawl on Saturday, working our way through the city and encountering hundreds of green-garbed enthusiasts craving the Holy Grail of sports.

On the morning of the game, we held a rally near the stadium, and we were all shocked to see more than 1,000 Eagles fans there to chant E-A-G-L-E-S and to scarf our free buffet of In-N-Out burgers. Our WIP co-host Hollis Thomas was there to address the crowd, and lots of our most famous callers—Eagle Shirley, Butch from Manayunk, and a couple of resilient souls from the original Dirty 30, took the trip as well.

We overwhelmed a bar across the street from the Coliseum and watched the early NFL games there, and then we made the trek to the decaying eyesore. Three thousand miles from home, it felt like an Eagles home game that day, even though the Rams were a worthy opponent.

Never in my long life as a sports fan has a win felt more like a loss than that game. Backup quarterback Nick Foles ended up pulling it out for the Eagles, but the only story that mattered was that Wentz was hurt, and badly. Even before we went on the air the next morning at 3:00 AM Pacific time in a dark studio on the outskirts of L.A., we knew the young kid from North Dakota was done for the season, having torn the ACL in his right knee when he swerved to avoid contact near the end zone.

Callers were literally crying, lamenting our rotten luck. Wentz was the consensus MVP in the NFL that season. Why didn't this ever happen to Tom Brady or Aaron Rodgers? Why, oh why, did this have to happen now? Rhea Hughes rolled out her familiar refrain: "Philadelphia sports fans don't get to have nice things."

The six-hour flight back to Philadelphia later that day was every bit as bleak as that bus ride between Milwaukee and Chicago where we learned of Jerome Brown's death. Even at baggage claim, the quiet was funereal. Not a chant was heard that day. Our hopes were gone.

"Any chance I can get a refund?" one traveler asked.

"No," I replied. "The Eagles won, you know?"

"Yeah, right. I forgot."

What happened in the next two months was the highlight of all of our lives as sports fans. Nothing could ever challenge the glory of those days.

Thank you, Nick Foles.

Chapter 11

Enemies for Life

One of the secrets of longevity in the media is luck. I will always believe luck was the biggest reason for our success. Our show evolved over the 33 years not because of any grand plan by us. It just happened organically. Never was that fact clearer than in 2001, just as Al Morganti, Rhea Hughes, and I were finding a steady rhythm on the air.

Again, Al was in the middle of the big change, though none of us had an inkling that our show would be heading in yet another new direction. One day he simply showed up with a former Flyer, Keith Jones, whose reputation as an NHL player was built as much on his tongue as his stick. Jonesy could talk, and he was looking for something new to do.

Jonesy's feisty career in the NHL was cut short by a botched operation on his left knee, and then a series of worsening knee injuries that evolved out of the first one. In a sendoff we would never let him forget, Flyers GM Bob Clarke announced the end of Keith Jones' career by coldly saying, "Jonesy's done." Fortunately for Jonesy, he was not done collecting his salary. He had just signed a new, three-year, $4.3-million deal, fully guaranteed.

That first show Jonesy did—for free—will be remembered forever by those who were fortunate enough to be listening. A star was born. Not only could Jonesy analyze strategy in any sport, he could get inside the heads of players better than anyone I had ever met, and he did it all with a blistering, low-brow wit.

No one tells a joke better than Jonesy—he recycled at least 25 that he told over and over during his tenure—and we burst out laughing when he ended his debut appearance with a joke about what happened one time when his wife, Laura, eagerly greeted him after a long road trip. I cannot repeat here what he said that day—especially now that he is the president of hockey operations for the Flyers—so you can imagine how inappropriate it was then, on the public airwaves.

Of course, that wasn't the biggest problem. Laura was. She had been listening, and was justifiably mortified. Jonesy and Laura made a pact that day when he got home. He would stop talking about Laura on our show.

And she would stop listening.

Jonesy got there just in time to help me with the biggest feud in my long history at WIP, my festering hatred of new Eagles coach Andy Reid.

When Reid took the head-coaching job in 1999, I went to a private lunch with him and ESPN's Sal Paolantonio at Dante & Luigi's iconic restaurant in South Philadelphia. It was hate at first sight for me (and probably for Reid, too).

Even then, the new coach—who was the QBs coach at Green Bay before his shocking promotion with the Eagles—came across to me as a phony, a first impression that would only deepen as time went on. He was evasive about pretty much everything that day. The only genuine moment came near the end of the meal when he looked at me and said: "I'll bet you wonder whether I can coach, don't you?"

Well, yeah. Reid at that point had never even served as an offensive coordinator, and I wasn't the only one asking that question.

In time, I guess you could say he answered it by building the Eagles into a perennial winning team that made it to five NFC Championship Games and one Super Bowl (which he blew). If you accept that answer, congratulations. It was the only answer Reid actually provided during 14 years with no championships.

There are more reasons than I can spell out here, even in book form, for my deeply negative feelings toward Reid. I will present it here its simplest form. Andy Reid never gave a damn about the fans. Put aside all of his family issues, the accumulation of criminals on his roster after he left for Kansas City, his constant struggles with clock management, all of that. The real issue was that he disrespected the fans, and I held him accountable for that every day of his 14 years in Philadelphia, and well beyond that in KC.

Any sports figure who develops a patter reminiscent of a robot would never win favor with me, even if he did win a Super Bowl. I had the opportunity to interview every Eagles coach from Dick Vermeil on, many times each, and Reid was easily the least sharing, least honest, least understanding of the responsibilities of a coach in Philadelphia.

I made it through 33 years with Eagles fans by constantly looking for honest answers to fair questions. Honesty and Andy Reid were complete strangers.

"I'll start with the injuries.... I take full responsibility for that.... I've got to do a better job.... I'm not going to get into that.... Hey Les [Bowen], clean your ears out.... [Blah, blah, blah].... The time is yours."

A trained parrot could do an Andy Reid news conference, and yet he won over most of the national media who covered him with an occasional fat joke or some other ingratiating trick in his repertoire. Obviously, he is a successful NFL coach; I can't argue that point. But at what cost?

Jonesy became my one ally on the show when I launched into my endless tirades against Andy Reid, making my fights with Al and Rhea—both supporters, to varying degrees—fairer and more grounded in reality. This would be a pattern that would continue to repeat itself as I jumped from feud to feud. I tried to take an inventory of all of the sports figures I hated—or hated me—over more than three decades, and I realized quickly that I would never be able to name them all.

But I will name some of them now. I regret nothing I said about any of them. They deserved every word of dissent. They were working in Philadelphia, the city in America that has never suffered any fools. I received an outpouring of support at the end of my time early in 2023, but what I embraced most is what no one ever said about me. No one ever claimed I pulled a punch against a sports figure there.

No sports figure got away with it when he acted stupidly in Philadelphia from 1990 to 2023. Not one. I am proudest of that.

In a world filled with insufferable sports fools, there can be only one king. His name is Gabe Kapler. The short-lived Phillies manager had the audacity one day to lie to me and my audience, and I let him know it in a way that made national headlines.

It was his first year in Philadelphia, and he already came with some dubious credentials. He was truly a new-wave guy, whose weird philosophies included the banishment of alarm clocks and the undeniable benefits of coconut oil for self-pleasuring. In other words, he was not exactly a perfect fit from the start. Nor were the two boobs who hired him, president Andy MacPhail and novice GM Matt Klentak.

I can't deny that Kapler offered us some colorful insights to baseball and life along the way—he wasn't a boring drone like Andy Reid—but his first rule was to protect his players at all costs, including his own credibility.

He was booked as a regular weekly guest on our show, and—in a quirk of timing—the Phillies had just announced that they had lost outfielder Andrew McCutchen for the season when the veteran player tore his ACL in a rundown that should never have happened. With McCutchen on first, Jean Segura hit a pop up near first base, and Segura saw no reason to run. As a result, the ball dropped to the ground, where Ian Kinsler of the Padres fielded it, got the out at first, and trapped McCutchen. A second later, McCutchen was writhing in pain.

I was ready for Kapler that Wednesday morning, and he was ready for me. It all started innocently enough when I said Segura not running led directly to McCutchen's injury. (After all, the game was televised. We could all see what happened, and why.)

Immediately, Kapler tried to insult our intelligence.

"You're not even acknowledging that him not running led to the injury to McCutchen?" I said. "You honestly don't see one and one equaling two?"

"I absolutely do not see one and one equaling two."

"Wow, that's amazing."

"What I see happened, like I said, [Segura] stumbled out of the box. He didn't have his feet under him. Once he got his balance, he wasn't able to run as hard as he usually does. He acknowledged that and talking about acknowledgement, I'm acknowledging that. He can do a better job running out of the batter's box. Also acknowledging that our center fielder at the time, our leadoff hitter, got hurt in a major way. I'm saying that's not Segura's fault and to say that is absolutely irresponsible."

"Oh, it is? Well then you better tell the whole city, because everybody thinks that was the reason."

"Angelo, you don't speak for the whole city."

"I talk to a hell of a lot more fans than you do."

"I'll tell you this, what you are plugged into are the people that call in to your show. Not all of the fans in Philadelphia like you represent."

"We actually polled this question and 85 percent of the people said that Segura should be held accountable far more than you did. So that's over five, six thousand people. That's not enough either for you, Gabe? How many do you need before you realize that you're actually not in tandem with what's going on in your city?"

"Your sample, the sample that you are drawing from, is a very specific sample."

"Last thing, would you do anything different this week, Gabe?"

"I may have handled this show a little different. I am very frustrated with you. Right now, I'm pretty perturbed. I think you didn't handle this show in a fair and reasonable way, and that's probably the thing I am most disappointed in, is the way you handled this show."

"I'm disappointed in some of the answers, so I guess we're equal in that."

I was right, of course. Segura himself, far more honest than his manager, publicly apologized for not running hard. McCutchen, a team leader, said Segura would learn from the mistake. Kapler never acknowledged his blatant lie. He was fired a season later.

Gabe Kapler was given one last chance to make amends. He was approached to tape a final message the week I retired.

He was the only sports figure who declined.

He hated me. I hated him.

I respect his decision.

In all of my feuds over the years, only one figure went public and called me a "terrible human being," and that is a man widely considered to be an expert on the subject—Curt Schilling.

My first contact with Schilling took place not on WIP but in the early days of *The Great Sports Debate.* Someone booked him as a special guest on the TV show, and special he was indeed that year, his amazing first season on the Phillies. I will make no friends among my co-hosts on that show, but I recall them fawning over Schilling to the point of stomach distress for me. I was just never wired to be awestruck in the presence of a man who throws a baseball hard. Others were. Let's leave it at that.

Schilling was deferential to my TV partners and dismissive of me, and that was fine with me. I still believe he was showing up Mitch Williams by putting a towel over his head when Mitch was brought in to relieve him during that magical 1993 season. Beyond that, I think he was a blowhard then, and even worse now.

Despite our cold beginning, Schilling became a regular un-booked caller to our radio show, and as the games got bigger and his role expanded, his behavior became bizarre. When we would arrive in the studio in that fall of 1993, one line would already be lit. It was Schilling on the inside line, waiting to go on the air. It was 5:55 AM, and he was there already.

Can you spell M-E-D-I-A W-H-O-R-E?

What made Schilling's entry into our world even more bizarre was that it was happening at a time when the rest of his team was plotting ways to kill us. No team hated WIP as much as the 1993 Phillies, with one notable exception—the best young starting pitcher on that team.

It was clear to me during those early days, and in all the years that followed, Schilling was an incorrigible me-first player who would never win the love of Philadelphia, despite his undeniable greatness on the mound, and especially in big moments. I thoroughly endorse the best description ever offered about Schilling, by then-GM Ed Wade: "Curt is a horse every fifth day and a horse's ass the other four."

One thing I take pride in is my ability to remain consistent when I develop a grudge against a sports figure. When they would leave Philadelphia, I would monitor closely their bad acts, ready to pounce at the first opportunity. So when Schilling pitched a big game for Boston after he left our city, the game when he soldiered on despite blood soaking through one of his socks, I couldn't help but suggest that the big fella was probably eating a hot dog between innings and spilled some ketchup on his foot.

Thus began a years-long feud that landed me a few times on one of his very active—and relentlessly misinformed—social media accounts. On one occasion, Curt called me a "terrible human being." Wow. That crossed a line for me. I tried never to delve into the personal lives of the sports figures I hated, even when they provided ample fodder for that. (Of course, I did make a few exceptions.)

So, for once, I will take the high road here. Curt Schilling has become a national joke since he stopped playing baseball and exposed his many eccentricities, including his political views and other totally unsolicited opinions on matters about which he knows nothing.

Now that he's no longer pitching, Curt is a horse's ass all five days.

Not all of my enemies had dubious personalities. For example, Brett Brown, by all accounts, is a wonderful man. He just happened to be a terrible head coach when he was in Philadelphia overseeing the Sixers during their "Process" years, and beyond.

Brown was brought here by another one of my favorite targets—albeit too briefly—GM Sam Hinkie, the brightest executive (in his own mind) during my tenure in Philadelphia. Hinkie is the genius who made public his intention to lose as many games as he could until he accumulated enough top draft picks to build a champion. He carefully selected Brown as the loser to oversee his plan.

Sure enough, the Sixers were awful the first four years of Brown's tenure as Brown acted like the director of a swanky resort, fulfilling every request by his coddled young roster. Unfortunately, the plan bogged down as soon as the coach brought to the city to lose was suddenly expected to win. Hinkie had talked his way out of town by then, pretty much an enigma before, during and after his time in Philadelphia.

After Brown had ruined his fifth season by getting blatantly outcoached by Celtics coach Brad Stevens, I strongly suggested the Brett Brown experiment should end. It was nothing personal. He just had one tiny problem. He couldn't coach. Wasn't it obvious?

Not to Brown, it wasn't. One day my cell phone rang while I was lounging on the beach in Sea Isle. I thought it was spam, since I didn't have the Sixers' number in my phone. I picked it up anyway.

"Brett Brown wants to talk to you," a Sixer flak announced. "Are you available?"

"Sure. Tell him to call me."

Moments later, the phone rang again.

"Hi, Angelo. This is Brett Brown."

In my 33 years, I received two personal calls from coaches—Brown and Chip Kelly after he left the Eagles. These people were not my friends. There was no reason for a conversation unless we were on the air. But I never turned down a call, either. I knew what I said on the air, and I was ready to defend myself.

Brown was courteous, but unhappy, that day. He said I was wrong about the way he coached the Boston series. We spent at least 15 minutes on his description of an in-bounds play that cost the Sixers a key game. The message was consistent. Not his fault. Never his fault.

Somehow, Brown survived two more seasons after that loss, and that phone call. No one has ever given him another chance to be an NBA head coach.

But he is still available, for any team determined to lose.

Philadelphia's pro teams won only two championships in 132 tries while I was the host of the *WIP Morning Show*, so you'd have to believe I would feel a special bond to the manager (2008 Phillies) and the coach (2017 Eagles) who finished the job. You would be half-right. I will feel a debt to Doug Pederson forever. The boldness he employed in stealing Super Bowl LII will never be forgotten. As for Charlie Manuel, eh, no, thank you. He should have won three World Series with that roster.

It's a stretch to say I hated Manuel with the same passion as Reid and Kapler, but there was no love there, either way. Manuel is the only

Phillies manager in my 33 years who never appeared on our show—and we were the Phillies' flagship station for most of that time.

During the interview process before Manuel got the manager's job, I fixated on a far more qualified candidate, Jim Leyland, and I made no secret of my affection for the one-time champ and three-time Manager of the Year. When I heard that the Phillies eliminated him because he asked for a smoke break during the interview, I howled like a wolf in heat.

So when Manuel made his first appearance at his introductory news conference and sounded like a clueless hayseed, I went on attack. From that point in 2004 until my last show 19 years later, I missed no opportunity to twist the knife. Having Joe Conklin's brilliant impression at our disposal made the job much easier.

Manuel was a country bumpkin. That was my story, and I was sticking to it.

Unfortunately, the new skipper was also a new listener in his first weeks as Phillies manager, and he did not take kindly to our depiction of him (imagine that). So he boycotted our show, right up until the second-to-last day, when he sent a kind 30-second message that was about as sincere as my subsequent thank you to him.

So, even in these insincere times, let me say one more time what I said, ad nauseum, for the last 19 years of the show: Manuel was a terrible strategist. He simply could not think on his feet. He would have won the World Series in 2009 if he had managed with more urgency, and he would have won it all again in 2011 if he had just let Atlanta win the final series in the regular season and eliminate the hottest team, the St. Louis Cardinals.

I will defer here to a man who knows a lot more about baseball, who loves Charlie Manuel, and who happened to be the Phillies GM in 2009 and '11. His name is Rubén Amaro Jr., and he was a terrific co-host on our show for my final two years.

"True or false, Rubén," I asked, on the air. "The Phillies should have won two, or maybe even three, World Series in the time Charlie Manuel managed the team."

"True," he answered.

The defense rests.

The feud our listeners knew the least about during my long tenure was my total disconnect from the most powerful man in Philadelphia sports over the past quarter-century, Eagles owner Jeffrey Lurie. There was no final message of congratulations from the billionaire before I left; no one even tried to get one. He hated me, and I saw him for what he really was, a very good owner who was also pompous and insecure.

You would think the man owning Philadelphia's most important sports franchise for all those years would have developed a special bond with the fans. Not at all. His idea of connecting was his ritual of walking across the parking lots before home games and shaking hands with a handful of the zealots. The rest of the time? Forget it.

Lurie held no more than two news conferences a year, unless the team was going to the Super Bowl and he could pontificate about the brilliance of his leadership. I would clamor for months every year to hear more from Lurie, until he actually spoke. Then I would beg him to shut up.

Very few fans remember that our show's relationship with Lurie couldn't have started more promisingly. He appeared regularly on WIP, once even calling the fans his "compadres." One day, when we were raising money for the Eagles Fly for Leukemia, he even showed up at Suburban Station in Center City during a show and warmly greeted the many subway commuters.

Lurie spends money, he cares deeply about winning, and he is a charitable and environmentally savvy person. He checks a lot of boxes. What he lacks, more than anything, is a sense of humor. Our show was based on making people laugh. We were definitely not a good match.

As best I can trace the decline of our relationship, it all started—like many feuds—with the way Joe Conklin depicted Lurie and his dastardly pal, team president Joe Banner, in comedy bits that, shall we say, placed both top executives in uncomfortable situations. In those satirical pieces, Lurie did not come across as a manly man, and Banner was football's version of Ebenezer Scrooge.

Lurie was no longer a guest on our show long before the fatal blow in our relationship, the booing of Donovan McNabb. Lurie knew Ed Rendell was the catalyst of that unfortunate incident, but he needed the mayor's support—especially in getting some municipal funds for his soon-to-be-built new stadium—so he blamed only the people he could afford to dismiss. Us. WIP. As far as he was concerned, his flagship station had sunk.

What I didn't know until years later was just how much Lurie hated our show and our station. Near the end of his decade-long tenure as WIP's GM, Butch Forster called me into his office and produced a letter sent in 1999 from Jeff Lurie to the NFL commissioner, Paul Tagliabue, complaining bitterly about WIP's conduct. It was CC'd to lots of other interested (and a few uninterested) parties, including all of the executives of WIP and Infinity Broadcasting.

For this book, I tracked down Butch, a pioneer among Black radio executives from the 1970s through the 1990s, and asked if he thought Lurie was trying to get me fired. A lawyer till the end, Butch said he couldn't say that. All he knew for sure was that Lurie really, really hated us then, and he wanted everyone to know.

As someone who holds grudges for decades, I can appreciate Lurie's distaste for us—me, really—sustaining the final 24 years of our time occupying the same sports community, but I feel obligated to point out that, through all of those years, the Eagles owner kept re-signing with WIP to broadcast his team's games.

Let's just say, with Lurie, business always comes first.

What I realized only now, while writing this chapter, is that I could write an entire book just about all the enemies I made while at WIP. Instead, for a change, I will keep it brief and just touch on the others who crossed my path and felt my wrath. Here's my Dirty Dozen (other than the ones I have already mentioned):

Rich Kotite—Let's start with an oldie. Kotite was as big a jerk as I ever encountered in Philadelphia sports—and he was that way even before he got to be the Eagles head coach. Our show had a contract with him to appear after every game during Buddy Ryan's tenure. Kotite did so, offering us next to nothing as the team's offensive coordinator, until the day after Ryan got fired. Kotite was a top candidate for the job, and he was scheduled to be on our show that morning. He called just before his 8:00 AM appearance and told me, off the air, that he would honor the commitment but would not discuss Ryan or the job. I said there was no way we could avoid the topic. He hung up on me. His failure here, and his even more spectacular implosion with the Jets, brought me joy.

LeSean McCoy—Nothing upsets me more than when an athlete abuses the privilege of playing in front of Philadelphia fans, and this overrated Eagles running back did so, and more, at an after-hours club when his buddies pummeled two off-duty Philly cops and then escaped punishment because of his status. Smug, clueless, disconnected...McCoy was the quintessential ingrate. You may notice the often-vilified Chip Kelly is not on my enemies list. The reason is, he rid our city of this blight by trading McCoy to Buffalo. Bravo to that.

Howard Eskin—Never have I had more of a love-hate relationship than with the dean of Philadelphia sports talkers. He broke many stories on our show, including the unforgettable time he gave away his source

(Alshon Jeffery) during one of many crises involving Carson Wentz. I have no reason to start another feud now, so I will just say without Howard, none of us would have ever figured out the best way to do sports radio in Philadelphia. But we both had more crazy disputes over the years than anyone else. It was fun, really. We had something in common. We were both really good at hating people.

Joshua Harris and Scott O'Neil—I knew I would loathe these two carpetbaggers the minute they took over the Sixers in 2011 and immediately stopped using the arena's name unless the Wells Fargo Bank bought advertising for their then-horrible team. Harris was a billionaire who thought nothing of interrupting a kids' soccer game and landing his helicopter on their field. O'Neil was a Madison Avenue type who left an oil slick wherever he stood. O'Neil finally left. Harris will, too—as soon as it becomes a good business decision. Philly deserves so much better than these two.

Terry Francona—The fastest route to a feud with me was to disrespect the fans, and Francona did that when he rested his sullen star third baseman on a big Sunday game that the Phillies promoted as Scott Rolen Day. That's right, a big crowd turned out to honor Rolen—at a time when the Phillies were starving for fans—and Francona kept the honored player on the bench. After four fruitless seasons, Francona left, calling his time in Philly "a mulligan," and then won two championships in Boston. Here's where you can stick your mulligan, Terry.

Derrick Coleman—Somehow, this lazy underachiever got two tours of duty with the Sixers. At no point in either three-year stint in Philly did he show the least bit of interest in the fan base, and I crucified him for that. Then I got a rare chance one day to express my distaste in person. Not knowing what I planned, Sixers president Pat Croce got me courtside seats. All week, I had pointed out that Coleman was, shall we say, not in top shape. So I bought a dozen Dunkin Donuts, had them placed in a large bag, and waved them in Coleman's face every time he approached me. He never acknowledged me, but legendary referee Joey Crawford laughed and winked at me. That was a thrill.

Dick Stockton—I started this feud on behalf of my late father, who despised this sing-songy play-by-play broadcaster when Stockton did Red Sox games all the way back in the 1970s. Over the years, Stockton became an improbable network star, but he was atrocious doing NFL games by the time he was well into his seventies, and I said so. Word got back to him, and he called me "mean" in the *Philadelphia Inquirer*. I prefer the term honest. Stockton retired the year after my WIP attack. Of course, I took full credit for that decision.

Ben Simmons—It still amazes me how popular this No. 1 draft pick was in his early years as a Sixer. He refused to shoot, never improved at the free-throw line, was gutless at key moments, and never showed any concern about his many shortcomings. The Philly fans eventually turned against him, but by then it was too late. He ruined a couple of great seasons and then was dumped on Brooklyn in the trade for James Harden. Now he is hated in New York, too. Hey, don't say I didn't warn you.

Domonic Brown—He was often referred to as a five-tool player. To me, he was just one big tool. The first time he came on our show during a remote broadcast at spring training in Clearwater, Florida, he was a nobody who acted like he was already in the Hall of Fame. When he walked out of the broadcast booth that morning, Al Morganti proclaimed: "That guy will never make it." Except for one glorious month in May of 2013, Al was right. Rubén Amaro still says Brown was the best prospect he ever saw who didn't make it. For the past decade, I have referred to him as the man with the million-dollar body and ten-cent brain.

Jerry Jones—I know, I know. The Cowboys owner is the lowest of low-hanging fruit. But I can't leave him off the list because I have hated him longer than anyone else in my top 12. I disliked him when he bought the team, ridiculed him even when he won a couple of Super Bowls in the early days of our show, doubled down when his team failed year after year in the 2000s, and went into overdrive when he paired up with his dumbass buddy, New Jersey's then-governor Chris Christie. Stick with it, Jerry. I'm sure you will return the Cowboys to glory any day now.

Chris Christie—I offer this name with mixed emotions. I am not proud of something I did when he visited our show at the height of his popularity in 2015. With his usual bluster, he waddled into our studio one morning, turned to plant his ample derriere on our guest seat, and promptly fell with a splat right on his ass. (The video is still available on YouTube.) I covered for him. I stifled a laugh, bought a few seconds for him to recover, and continued on with the interview. Listeners might have picked up that something had happened, but I never let them in on the spectacular pratfall.

Fast forward a month, and the governor had gotten on our nerves with a series of appearances in Jerry Jones' luxury box at Cowboys games. By then I was filled with regret for the cover-up. What to do? Well, we had the video. And he had a perfect forum for it—Wing Bowl. Sure enough, at a perfect time in the festivities, we directed the attention of 20,000 drunks to the video screen, and we played the tape. The crowd went crazy. (But not as crazy as when women in the crowd flashed the camera with their boobs.)

In retrospect, the Wing Bowl that year featured one more boob than usual—the governor of New Jersey.

Chapter 12

Famous People

Despite her understandable early misgivings, Laura Jones generously shared her husband with our show for over 20 years, as Keith provided both the inside knowledge of life as an athlete and the humor of a stand-up comedian. He also gave me an ally in my constant disagreements with Al Morganti and Rhea Hughes.

(No, we never once compared notes on what position we would take during our show. Al and Rhea thought I was consistently illogical and overly emotional. I thought I was always right.)

Rhea and Jonesy gave us a sense of stability on the air that we lacked in our first decade, just as the upper management of WIP went into a state of flux. First, Butch Forster left, then Tom Bigby was ousted in a power struggle, then he was reinstated, and then he got booted again, as our bosses changed offices like a high-stakes game of musical chairs.

By the time of Bigby's first ouster—he was literally led out of the station he had built by security guards—our boss had very few friends left at our parent company based in New York. He lasted as long as he did because our ratings remained strong. We were making money. But it was no secret that Bigby's bullying manner was becoming less tolerable in the new corporate world of the early 2000s.

It was a day of celebration when we all learned of Bigby's dismissal. The new boss, Drew Hilles, arrived one day the week after our longtime program director was led out of our studios on 5th and Callowhill. It was the dawning of a new era. Hallelujah.

Except it wasn't—at least not yet. All these years later I can offer no logical explanation as to why, totally without notice, Bigby was back in his office three weeks later and back in charge of WIP. The best guess anyone had as to how Bigby got back in charge was his relationship with the president of Infinity Broadcasting, Mel Karmazin. No one else had the power to reinstate Bigby like that. No one else would have anyway.

Like most second acts, Bigby's final days at WIP were nothing like his first decade. I was no longer the only employee acting insubordinately. The blood was in the water by then. Bigby was fatally wounded. He became a source of constant ridicule, on and off the air. And no one was better at that than Joe Conklin.

Bigby had a contentious relationship with everyone at WIP, with Joe at the top of that long list. Joe's job was to go right up to the line of good taste, and if a joke was funny enough, Conklin wouldn't hesitate to step way past that line. It got to the point where Joe would include, right in his on-air bits when he was pushing the rules, Bigby's own Texas drawl saying, "Joe, see me in my office after the show."

One time, Joe had a film crew following him the whole day, and Conklin—never one to back down from a potentially funny situation—was summoned to Bigby's office to discuss his latest infraction. But this time something was different. Joe had a camera crew following close behind.

"Who are those people, Joe?" Bigby snarled.

"Oh, they're just doing a story on me," he replied, the picture of innocence. "Ignore them.... What did you want to see me about?"

Bigby raised his 300-plus pounds off his chair, his face flushed with anger, and yelled, "Out! Get out!"

Of course, Conklin began to retreat with the crew.

"Not you, Joe! Them!"

Another interesting twist in Bigby's background was his status as the owner of all Little Caesars pizza stores in Puerto Rico. If you ordered a pizza at Little Caesars in Puerto Rico, Bigby got a piece of the pie. (We have no idea how he got the franchise rights. No one ever had the guts to ask.) Then Joe either heard something or just concocted a fake narrative in which our boss was acquiring black-market cheese for his pizzas.

When he got the sign from someone that Bigby was otherwise occupied, Conklin would get on the station's PA system and announce, in Bigby's voice: "Tom Bigby, please come to the front desk. Your black-market cheese has arrived. Come get your cheese."

(Did I mention to you yet how much fun it was to work with Joe Conklin? He was exactly the same off the air as he was on it. He lived for the laugh. If it took some black-market cheese to set us off, all the better.)

The second time Bigby left, it was with a whimper, not a bang. For a decade after that, I stayed in touch with him despite my mixed feelings. Only now I can see, more clearly than I ever did then, that he is as responsible as anyone for my radio career. Yeah, he drove me crazy, but he also drove me to a level of success that I never would have reached without him. He often emailed me in his final years pleading with me to be invited to my retirement party.

In the end, I insisted on no retirement party, for reasons previously stated. (No one needed to see me flounder one more time in a social setting.) In Tom's case, it wouldn't have mattered. He died in 2021 at 77, two years before I hung up my microphone. I was lucky enough early in my career to meet up with someone who understood radio so well.

Thank you, Tom Bigby.

One of the messages that stayed with us during and long after Bigby's two tenures was the need to expand our audience beyond sports. For a time in those early 2000s, this meant bringing in movie stars. That's right. Movie stars.

Adding some star power was exciting to me—I always preferred talking to movie stars than athletes—but my co-hosts were ambivalent about the new direction. Even though it stretched our sports format, I reveled in interviewing Ray Liotta, Mark Wahlberg, Cliff Robertson, the Alfred Hitchcock blondes (Janet Leigh and Tippi Hedren), Kristin Chenoweth, Debbie Gibson (yes, even the teen idol), and song stylist Billy Paul than any of the athletes who got onto our show.

In the cases of Liotta and Wahlberg, they had a direct connection to sports. Liotta got on the A list in Hollywood by playing Shoeless Joe Jackson in the beloved baseball classic *Field of Dreams*. Beloved, that is, by everyone except Al Morganti. Al always hated that film, and he made no secret of his distaste.

Liotta was visiting in late 2002 to promote an okay crime movie, *Narc*, but it was inevitable the conversation would soon turn to *Field of Dreams*. After all—I kept reminding myself—WIP was a sports station. As I tended to do with all the movie people, I gushed about Ray's work in *Field of Dreams* (and *Goodfellas*, too, of course), but then it was time to acknowledge Al's dislike of the baseball film.

"Talking corn?" Al started. "Oh, please."

Liotta was not acting (I think) when his face dropped and he looked at Al with an equal mixture of disbelief and disdain. From that point to the end of Liotta's visit half an hour later, Ray became obsessed with changing Al's mind. (I could have told Liotta that that absolutely never happens.)

We went to a break with Ray still extolling the merits of *Field of Dreams*, but Al kept naming all the other baseball movies that were better than Ray's—starting with another movie that featured Ray's buddy Kevin Costner, *Bull Durham*. Al loved *Bull Durham*, which had everything in it that *Dreams* didn't—sex, philosophy, believable baseball action, Susan Sarandon, humor, and sex. Especially sex.

Then I saw something that I still don't believe a generation later. A major movie star, Ray Liotta, followed Al out of the studio and kept arguing the case for one of his favorite roles. I know how frustrating Al can be in moments like that, and I wouldn't have minded if Ray retreated into his gangster Henry Hill character from *Goodfellas* and pummeled some sense into Al. He didn't. Ray was a very likeable guy in real life, which is more than I can say for Al Morganti.

Not long before we bowed out at WIP in early 2023, Ray Liotta passed away suddenly in his sleep at 67. Ray went to his grave never convincing Al of the value of *Field of Dreams*, though I doubt it was ever much of a preoccupation once Liotta left our studios that day.

Still, I sought some closure for my favorite Hollywood visitor during the movie-star period of our show.

"One last time, Al, in honor of Ray Liotta, what do you say about *Field of Dreams*?" I asked. "I'm sure he's listening right now up in heaven."

"It still sucks," Al said.

Al was never much for sentiment—in movies or deaths.

The biggest highlight for WIP and our listeners in the first decade of the millennium was the time the Eagles finally made it to the Super Bowl at the finish of a brilliant 2004 season. The previous two years had ended in mounting frustration after a superior Eagles team lost to Tampa in the final game ever played at Veterans Stadium, and then the Birds squandered a nine-game winning streak and a miraculous 4th and 26th conversion in the playoffs with a brutal loss in the NFC Championship Game again.

Philadelphia had a love-hate affair with the cookie-cutter Vet—a round, all-purpose monstrosity with the hardest playing surface in sports made even more dangerous with crevices and craters underneath its fake grass. The fans loved it for football and hated it for baseball.

That old mausoleum brought out the beast in Eagles fans, especially in the upper reaches of the stadium, the notorious 700 Level. I went to only one game up there in my long tenure at WIP. One was enough. My son, Neil, watched his first fistfight up there between two drunks throwing haymakers until one slumped to the concrete, his face draped in blood. (Security never even bothered to intervene.)

There was a nutcase in the upper reaches of the Vet who rigged up a device in his right arm that sent sparks flying when he led Eagles cheers after big moments. He called himself "Torchman," and he was a hero up there for years. There were no pressure groups back then to stop a grown man from sending sparks right onto a section of fans. In the 700 Level, it wasn't even in the Top 5 of crazy rituals. The fights, the beer showers, the obscene chants, the projectiles, and the atmosphere of anything-goes were all part of the 700 Level experience.

It goes without saying that Eagles fans wanted to send the Vet out with one last thrill in the NFC Championship Game in early 2004, but then Blaine Bishop forgot to cover Joe Jurevicius and the Tampa wide receiver took a step into Eagles history with a season-killing 71-yard reception.

Shortly after the new stadium, Lincoln Financial Field, had opened, I got involved in a controversy that led to the only suspension in my long tenure at WIP. What the dispute was really about was my deep hatred for team president Joe Banner, whom I considered a blemish on the otherwise excellent reputation of the Eagles. Banner was a bully, a miser, and a jerk. I said so pretty much every day during his 17 years with the Eagles.

He finally went too far when he announced that, among the new rules in his pristine stadium, fans would not be permitted to bring in their own sandwiches, and the team would be adding security to make sure no one ate an unauthorized hoagie. His bogus explanation was that fans could smuggle "who knew what" into the sandwiches and cause trouble. My counter argument (the truth) was that he wanted fans to have to buy the obscenely overpriced food in the Linc.

Then I went too far. I said the new security force should wear swastikas like in Nazi Germany during World War II. Both Banner and owner Jeffrey Lurie are Jewish, so the comment was especially inappropriate. By no means was I alluding to their Jewish heritage, but I gave the Eagles a chance to punish me, and they did.

I was called into GM Marc Rayfield's office the day after the comment—Bigby was still not allowed to talk to me—and told to go home. I was suspended. I said I knew I didn't use the proper metaphor, but the bigger point was getting lost. The Eagles were screwing their fans. WIP needed to take a stand against that, regardless of how stupidly I had made my argument.

When I came back, I issued my only written statement in 33 years at WIP. Here's the key paragraph:

> *Do I wish I had used a different analogy? Yes, I do. The last thing I was trying to accomplish was to alienate anyone of the Jewish faith, or any faith for that matter. But the truth is, I didn't. There were no calls of complaint to this station—not one. I didn't even receive a single email complaining about the unfortunate characterization.... I don't believe my attack was against anything but the policies of the Philadelphia Eagles. It had nothing to do with any individual on the Eagles. I was angry at the rules. So were thousands of others.*

The suspension ended up being a two-day vacation because I appealed the ban and won the union case on appeal. I also won something bigger a few days later.

"The food policy at Lincoln Financial Field will be the same as the food policy that existed at [Veterans Stadium]," Eagles president Joe Banner announced. The good guys, the fans, had won.

If ever there was a day that marked the crossroad between my time as a reporter and my days as a fan advocate, that was it. From that day on, I spoke on behalf of the passionate, loyal Philadelphia sports fans with a fervor that matched their emotions.

Getting to do that was an even bigger honor than I ever imagined at the time.

After another devastating loss at the NFC Championship Game in the inaugural season at the Linc—a fancy new stadium that replaced the crackpots in the 700 Level with people financially able to spring for expensive seat licenses—the Eagles finally made it to the Super Bowl for the only time in the long runs of coach Andy Reid and quarterback Donovan McNabb.

By then, Reid and McNabb had become convenient targets for me, both because they choked in the biggest games and because they added to the distress by being absolutely horrible at explaining themselves. Reid had developed his robot persona by then, spouting non-answers like a trained parrot after butchering big games with dreadful time management. McNabb thought he was funny in interviews, often mugging for the cameras while also producing nothing of substance to explain the game he had just played. Neither one of them gave a damn about the fans.

Super Bowl XXXIX provided one of the most puzzling finishes in the history of the NFL's biggest annual game. The Eagles were so casual in the fourth quarter while running their offense that the opposing coach, Bill Belichick of the Patriots, famously asked his assistants if the 24–14 score on the scoreboard was correct. The Eagles ran out of time that day, and the fans ran out of patience with their phony coach and his maddening quarterback.

That I became enmeshed in a controversy involving McNabb—six years after the draft-booing incident—was a complete accident. I was simply preparing to do my live Monday night TV show on Comcast SportsNet when Joe Weachter—who also helped to produce my television work—told me he had found two Eagles players, Jon Runyan and Hank "Honeybuns" Fraley, at the airport and they were willing to be guests on the show.

What Joe didn't know yet was that the two big offensive linemen had been drowning their sorrows in beer since the loss, and they were in no condition to hide what everyone else on the team was concealing in the hours after that crushing loss. Namely, the failings of their quarterback.

Why didn't the Eagles rush to the line to save the clock in the four-minute drive that ended their chances to win that Super Bowl? Well, the two guests said, McNabb was sick to his stomach on that drive. At one point, in the biggest game of his career, McNabb was unable to perform the basic requirements of his position.

Time has altered the memory of that interview, but I remember it well. Neither player was trying to blame McNabb for the loss, and neither came right out and stated their quarterback had vomited. But the exact quote of what Fraley said was even worse. This is precisely what the center told me that night:

"He gave it his all. He was almost puking in the huddle. One play had to be called by Freddie Mitchell because Donovan was mumbling because he was almost puking."

Runyan confirmed Fraley's account, and then Mitchell joined in a day or two later and went further by saying that he had indeed seen McNabb vomit. To understand the insane nature of this moment, you need to know that Mitchell was the most improbable choice to take over play-calling (or play-relaying) duties. By all accounts, he was known a lot more for his hands than his brain.

There was a final chance to get the real story of what happened in one of the worst losses in Philadelphia sports history. The person who knew for sure because he was the one calling the plays was Andy Reid. He could have cleared up a mystery that still puzzles the greatest NFL coach of all time, Bill Belichick.

Good luck with that. Back then, and even now, the fans never got the true story from Andy Reid.

Do you understand now why I could never stomach that man?

If I was looking for a bad omen during that 2004 Eagles season, I didn't have to wait long. With the Eagles off to their best start at 7–0, I got a call to come home. My dad was in critical condition. Three years earlier, the doctors had told him he needed dialysis, and he balked at the suggestion. He even told me that once you get hooked to that machine, there's no turning back.

Before long, though, he had no choice. It was dialysis or die. His spirits remained surprisingly high in that period, especially when the Boston Red Sox were losing. My father loved the Yankees, but as he got older, he grew to hate the Red Sox more. Even with a Yankee game was on TV, I would find my dad watching the Red Sox, and actively rooting against Boston. (Can you see why I was so good at being a negative fan?)

I was at the hospital in Rhode Island on November 7 when the Eagles risked their perfect record against the Pittsburgh Steelers. Let's just say the worst loss I suffered that day was not the Eagles' 27–3 defeat. I was with my father in his final hours as his breathing became more labored and he drifted into and out of consciousness. He rallied one last time, near 11:00 PM.

"Ang, go home," he said. "I'll see you tomorrow."

One thing my father never showed, regardless of his age, was weakness. He never, ever called out sick—and his brother owned the toolmaking business. He was back at work in days after a serious hernia operation—before there was such a thing as an arthroscopic procedure. He was a product of his times. He was tough.

I left that night expecting a call, and it came around 7:00 the next morning. He had passed away in his sleep. The official cause of death was kidney failure, brought on by years of undiagnosed high-blood pressure. But I have developed a different theory over the years. Please hear me out.

My father was born on August 18, 1918, less than a month before the Boston Red Sox won the World Series. He died on November 7, 2004, less than two weeks after the Red Sox won the World Series. In the intervening 86 years, the Sox won nothing, much to the delight of my father.

"The Curse of the Bambino," they called it.

I think it was the *malocchio* my father gave that team. The Evil Eye.

I said it on the air many times—much to Al Morganti's disgust—and I will say it one more time here.

I think the Red Sox killed my father.

Now, I'm not saying that in a literal way. I'm just saying he loved so much when they lost, Boston's miracle comeback (against the Yankees, no less) in the 2004 American League Championship Series and the ensuing Red Sox win over St. Louis was a signal to him that it was time to go.

He would be proud of my theory, I'm sure. He would also be proud of what his obituary said the next day in the *Providence Journal*, right there in the seventh paragraph:

He was a member of many bowling leagues, and was a great fan of the New York Yankees.

This is one reason why it was so hard for me to switch allegiances from the Yankees to the Phillies.

In the first half of the 2000s, Rhea and Jonesy blended into our show in a better way than we ever could have planned. Rhea was a dynamic presence in the newsroom, and she was a perfect balance to my sexist leanings. No one was ever better at straightening me out when a gender issue came up—and protecting me in the process—than Rhea. I was painfully slow in gaining the gender sensitivity that we have today. Rhea got me there, eventually, by never allowing my dumb comments to go out on the air unchallenged.

For example, if I compared Martina Navratilova unfavorably to a man, Rhea would compare me unfavorably to a woman. She was joined by one of my favorite callers, Kim the Lesbian, who repeatedly saved me from myself in those awkward days. That they both did it in an entertaining way is a skill I am in awe of all these years later.

Meanwhile, Jonesy opened the door to a whole new direction for our show, the integration of player voices into our studio as co-hosts. Jonesy developed a style that was both unique and infectiously lowbrow. He had, by conservative count, around 20 funny responses to sports situations, and he was incredibly adept at knowing instantly when to roll one out.

My favorite made no sense, but still sent me into hysterics for 20 years. The moment a caller would accuse Jonesy of saying something stupid, I knew to back off until Keith delivered his line.

"My name is Dimple, not Simple," he would say.

Huh? His name is not Dimple. It made no sense. And yet, the more you heard it, the funnier it became.

Jonesy was always known for his flatulence, though I must now disclose that most of it was imaginary. He was not the gasbag he claimed to be. But whenever someone would say they had released a silent but deadly fart, Jonesy would quickly say: "Well, the first thing you need to check is your hearing."

And then there were these two classics whenever he was going for his annual physical.

"I asked the doctor where to put my clothes. He told me to just throw them in the corner on top of his."

Also: "The doctor said he needed a sample of my blood, urine, stool, and sperm. So I handed him my underpants."

Hey, I never said Jonesy was intellectual. Just funny. Really funny.

I have to admit I keep thinking of Jonesy as I write this book because there is almost no chance he will read it. He said many times that he read only one book in his entire life, a textbook for a class in Juvenile Delinquency while at Western Michigan University.

When I would remind him that he is actually listed as the author (with ESPN's John Buccigross) of his autobiography, *Jonesy: Put Your Head Down and Skate*, he would say he heard bad things about it, so he never bothered to read what John wrote. (Actually, it's very good.)

Hugh Douglas had the same potential as Jonesy, and we were thrilled to add him to our regular co-host lineup after he retired in 2005. He was a rarity among star athletes; he had the ability to laugh at himself. No athlete was ever better at going back-and-forth with the callers, asking questions that often trapped the fans into dumb comments.

Douglas was involved in two physical fights during his years with us in the mid-2000s, one I started and one I was unable to stop.

The first happened at Borgata in our early days there, where our broadcast table was stationed right in front of the Gypsy Bar. We were easy to reach by the patrons, some of whom were still up from the previous night—and lathered to the max—when they approached us during breaks.

One time an ignorant drunk came up to our table and said something that tested Hugh's restraint. (I didn't hear the comment.) He quickly rose from his seat, jumped off the low stage, and approached the beer-muscled intruder. Douglas then pressed his face right up, chin to chin, with the idiot, and bellowed, "Say that again. Come on. Say it again."

The moron then said something racially insensitive, extremely inflammatory, as he was backpedaling toward a railing in front of the

Metropolitan Restaurant across from us. As the disgraceful words were escaping the idiot's lips, Hugh head-butted him, sending the dumbass over the rail and onto a table in the restaurant. Security broke up the altercation before the foul-mouthed racist could get what he deserved from Hugh, who—amazingly—resumed the show with no sign of what had just happened.

Around that same time, I created a problem for Hugh when I was on one of my rampages over Terrell Owens during the wide receiver's 2005 holdout. Owens was scheduling daily media updates from the front lawn of his home in Moorestown, New Jersey, and—as usual—making a spectacle of himself. Even though he was a Super Bowl hero earlier in the year, we slaughtered him verbally for weeks.

When he returned to the team, having accomplished nothing by holding out, I was still ranting, calling Owens every insulting name I could conjure while Hugh sat quietly. Douglas was nothing if not a loyal teammate.

Then Hugh made a mistake I never would, either because of my intelligence or, more likely, my cowardice. He appeared in the Eagles locker room after the show, and T.O.—no threat for membership into MENSA—attributed everything I had said to Douglas.

They squared off, there was a brief skirmish, and then word leaked out that Owens had gotten the better of our co-host. Please. Owens was a spindly wide receiver. Douglas was a muscular defensive end. No contest. Douglas would have squashed T.O. like a bug.

Hugh learned an important lesson that day.

"I had no business being in that locker room," he said.

Duh.

I would like to report that I got some great Hollywood stories from the stars who appeared on our show in the early 2000s, but most of them were interested only in promoting their current project. I did get Debbie

Gibson (who was one of the nicest celebrities I ever met) to sing her huge hit "Electric Youth" a cappella, I got Mark Wahlberg to tell the story about how Vince Papale taught him how to return kickoffs for the movie *Invincible*, and I got Janet Leigh to acknowledge that doing the famous shower scene in *Psycho* haunted her for years afterwards.

What most people find hard to believe, even now, is that two U.S. presidents appeared on our show. (In fact, there were three appearances by U.S. presidents on the *WIP Morning Show*.) The first was a cameo by Donald Trump as he was storming through the lobby at the Trump Marina during a remote broadcast we were doing there.

He sat down for a few minutes to talk about how wonderful all of his properties were in Atlantic City, but all I can remember was his charisma. By this time, I had sat with Muhammad Ali and Wilt Chamberlain, and I had some sense for special people. Trump was definitely one of those. He exuded a confidence that was undeniable, whether you liked him or not. (I am not a fan.) I was mesmerized that day.

Far more impactful were two visits, on back-to-back weeks, by a basketball enthusiast who also happened to be running for president, Barack Obama. As was too often the case, I turned what was supposed to be a big coup for our show into an awkward mess. Hey, it was his idea to call *us*.

With the state of Pennsylvania deemed critical in the 2008 Presidential race, Obama's handlers called us one day to book the presidential hopeful. We jumped at the chance. What we didn't know then was that Obama was doing a radio tour of sports stations to talk about the NCAA basketball tournament. (We were the only sports station that didn't get the word.)

So I prepared an interview heavy on politics, while Obama was planning to talk mainly about sports. This was a recipe for disaster, on both ends of the call. Sure enough, the trouble developed quickly when I asked the candidate about a speech he had given about race at the National Constitution Center in Philadelphia the previous night. In that address,

Obama said his White grandmother had some of the same concerns many White people had when she encountered a Black man on the street.

He responded on our show: "The point I was making was not that my grandmother harbors any racial animosity. She doesn't. But she is a typical White person who, if she sees somebody on the street that she doesn't know, there's a reaction that's been bred into our experiences that don't go away, and that sometimes come out in the wrong way, and that's just the nature of race in our society."

The story went viral, of course. Obama got clobbered for using a racial stereotype, and I got crushed for not following up on his answer. I still don't understand what he said that was wrong. He was just sharing an honest impression. And as for me, well, I just hope none of my Columbia professors was listening. I was totally out of my element in that moment. I should have stuck to sports.

Later the day of that interview we learned that I had not followed the pre-interview instructions to talk hoops, not politics. So—in a bizarre twist—I was punished for my mistake by getting a second interview with Obama one week later. (I can provide no other example of my stupidity being rewarded like this, ever.)

The second time, Obama made his Sweet 16 picks, and everybody seemed much happier. I know for sure Obama was.

Now I need to make a political confession. My father was the biggest Democrat in Rhode Island. He would have voted for a serial killer if the candidate were a Democrat. We never moved out of Ward 5 in Providence because my dad had political connections with the people who ran our neighborhood.

I was more a Republican than a Democrat in 2008 when I had one last brush with Obama before the election. Do I have to tell you how it all started? The usual way, with a call from Mayor Ed Rendell, of course. I was driving back from the Borgata late one Friday morning when my flip cell phone rang. It was good old Ed.

"What are you doing tomorrow?" he asked.

"Whatever you tell me to do, Ed. You just have to ask."

"Good. I need you to host a rally for Obama on the [Ben Franklin] Parkway. He won't be there, though. Bruce Springsteen will be."

My first thought was to fake a bad cell and not answer any more calls for the next day. My second thought was I owed the mayor for putting WIP on the map. Plus, I have always been a huge Springsteen fan.

What the mayor neglected to tell me before I arrived at the designated time was that this was a big event, and not because I would be attending. My guess is between 75,000 and 100,000 showed up on that warm fall afternoon, and the schedule was, shall we say, a bit fluid.

No one was sure when Bruce would be appearing, and the idea of putting him in the middle of all those people was unimaginable, so I watched an elaborate plan unfold in which the singer arrived in a fancy SUV with tinted windows, and it was carefully parked door to door with a tour bus located right behind the stage. In the snap of a finger, Springsteen slipped from the car into the bus.

Now we were on the clock. I had to start the speeches, coordinate how long everyone talked, and then clear the podium the minute I got word from Springsteen's people that the singer was ready. I had to start things off with my first political speech, in front of all those Obama fans.

"This is a time for change," I boomed. (I read that message off one of the signs. I had no actual preparation for this assignment.)

Realizing you should always leave the audience wanting more, I got off the stage very quickly and proceeded to introduce a parade of politicians, all of whom appeared thrilled to be speaking in front of such a loud and welcoming audience. Then Ed Rendell appeared, and I whisked off the previous speaker to make way for my friend.

Rendell never met an audience he didn't love, and he was savoring the moment when, a couple of minutes after he began his speech, I got the word that Bruce was ready. In fact, Bruce was standing outside the bus now, strumming an acoustic guitar. I tried to give the signal to Ed, but he was in a trance, bellowing words of undying support for the city and for Obama.

After the third sign that Bruce was ready—the singer clearly was getting irritated—I stood on the stage and did everything but bear-hug the mayor. He finally gave up the mic, reluctantly, and Springsteen did a terrific set interspersing some of his biggest hits with messages of support for Obama.

The crowd slowly dispersed after the last number, and I was gathering my notes when I heard the mayor's familiar voice.

"Come over here, Angelo," he said. "I want you to meet Bruce."

As always, I did what Rendell said, and I got to shake the hand of Bruce Springsteen.

Then I couldn't help myself.

"Sorry I couldn't get you on faster," I said. "I couldn't get the mayor to stop talking."

We all laughed.

I am not at all sure Mayor Rendell thought it was funny.

Bruce Springsteen never actually appeared on our show, but a soulful singer named Billy Paul did, and he provided the perfect olive branch for Laura Jones after Jonesy's inauspicious debut. One day during our Famous People phase in the early 2000s, Billy called our show to set us straight about the Eagles. Then he dropped a bomb.

"You probably know me for 'Me and Mrs. Jones,'" he said nonchalantly.

Hello? I have loved that song since it became a No. 1 single in 1972, never knowing that the genius behind that R&B classic was on the phone with us right then. His real name was Paul Williams, and he was a Philadelphia native. I have no idea why he was listening. Maybe he was a sports fan. Who knew?

After Billy Paul's first call, he became a contributor, calling from time to time with some entertainment nuggets from his extraordinary career. And it took very little coaxing to get Billy to sing. He loved launching into song, and was still terrific at it, well into his seventies.

Then one of us—I can't remember who—got the brilliant idea of what we could do to woo Jonesy's wife back into our good graces. What if we got Billy Paul to sing to Laura?

Not only was Billy a willing participant, he agreed to rework his classic song to accommodate the occasion.

Thus "Me and Laura Jones" was born.

Since I was never that thrilled with sports accomplishments—except for the two championships, of course—I will place what happened next in my Top 5 of favorite moments ever on our show, as the great Billy Paul serenaded Laura Jones with a new version of his song.

"Laura, Laura Jones...Laura Jones, Laura Jones, Laura Jones..."

(Sorry. Those are the only lyrics I remember.)

Laura swooned at the end of the performance.

All was forgiven, she assured us. This made up for the terrible joke. Laura loved us again.

I'm pretty sure that was the last time Laura ever listened to our show.

My final brush with Hollywood came in 2019, when the Borgata gave me the chance to host a special night for Chevy Chase, a major star of TV and movies whose fame had dimmed with time and controversy. Chase was the biggest name in one of my favorite films, the first *Vacation* movie. He was also my favorite star in the first season of *Saturday Night Live*.

Chevy was just starting a tour to promote the 30th anniversary of another of his huge hits, *Caddyshack*, and he had agreed to sit for an intimate interview after a showing of the classic film in the big room at the Borgata. The one doing the interviewing would me. Gulp. Chase had a reputation for creating awkward situations, and I was the master of awkward. Disaster seemed inevitable.

In fact, in the radio interview a day before his Saturday-night show, he was scarcely tolerant of me or my questions. At one point he felt I had asked the same question twice, so he snapped: "Asked and answered." Silence, followed by me stammering, followed by more silence.

All I could think in that moment was how I could squirm out of the show the next night, when I would be facing Chase right there, alone, on that big Borgata stage. Surely, I could cultivate a flu in the next 36 hours, no?

No. Chevy showed up a few minutes before the show and sat with me for a quick prep-talk. He appeared to have no knowledge of our "asked and answered" conversation the previous day, and he seemed interested in neither my gushing praise nor my lame wisecracks designed to loosen him up.

When we got out on the stage, he received a terrific ovation from the half-filled venue, and I began asking questions about *Caddyshack*. We were not five minutes into the Q&A when a woman in a red dress stumbled down the aisle and started screaming at Chevy, asking repeatedly that he "stop being so boring."

Never deviating from my surefire plan to panic in times of stress, I started screaming: "Security, security, security!" My wit eluded me once again in a big moment, but Chevy Chase had no such trouble. He knew exactly how to handle the woman. Recalling a trademark line from SNL, he calmly referred to her as an "ignorant slut."

It was the highlight of the show.

No thanks to me.

Chapter 13

Finally, a Championship

The 2008 Phillies season started like most of the 132 we had during our long run at WIP. There were predictions of greatness, of course, but we didn't take them seriously for a very long time. At that point, our Philly pro teams had failed exactly 100 consecutive times without a single championship between 1983 and 2008. (We were 0 for 68 on WIP.) Why would this season be any different?

We had learned a lot by then about what the listeners cared about, and what they didn't. For example, hockey. When I began doing the show full-time in 1990, I treated all four pro sports equally. Tom Bigby quickly cured me of that misimpression. The Eagles were kings. The Phillies were princes. The Sixers were dukes. And the Flyers were peasants.

I fought against that prejudice for my first seven years until the Stanley Cup Finals in 1997. The Flyers had a huge star, Eric Lindros, they had some thrilling victories, and they were the talk of the town, or so I thought. This was the year when coach Terry Murray said about this team when they fell behind 3–0 to Detroit in the Stanley Cup Finals that it was "basically a choking situation." We crushed him for that.

Our show went wall-to-wall covering the Flyers that spring, with Al Morganti out front analyzing and pontificating on the finer points of playoff hockey. We even did a show at the top of City Hall, the day when the statue of Billy Penn was adorned with a Flyers jersey. Then the ratings came out. We always took pride in how consistent our numbers were, but they were down dramatically in the second quarter of 1997.

Bigby said (not directly to me, of course) that we needed to stop talking about the Flyers, immediately. We took his advice, and never turned over a show to them for the next 26 years. The Flyers had a niche following in the 1990s; it wasn't 1975 anymore, when the Broad Street Bullies ruled the city. Hockey could never carry WIP. We learned that, for sure, in 1997.

Then, in 2001, the Sixers got their chance to steal the spotlight, behind the latest Philadelphia sports hero, Allen Iverson—a brilliant performer on the court and a troublemaker off it. Perfect. Allen would dazzle everyone with his wizardry in games—starting with his brilliant crossover move against Michael Jordan as a rookie—and then he would get wrapped up in squabbles involving him and his problematic posse, Cru Thik.

Allen would often hang out with this group at the TGI Fridays off City Line Avenue just outside Philadelphia. He even had his own reserved table, and they had a selection of board games for him to play with his friends. TGI Friday's on City Line Avenue became chic back then because of Iverson, who often would end up there after a night of wild spending at local strip clubs.

He was perfect for Philly, in body and spirit. And then everything came together for him in 2001 when his charismatic boss, team president Pat Croce, and Hall of Fame coach Larry Brown combined forces to give him the best roster of his career. George Lynch, Tyrone Hill, Aaron McKie, Eric Snow, Theo Ratliff, Toni Kukoč, and, toward the end of the season, Dikembe Mutombo, all snapped snugly into place right behind Iverson.

When they made it all the way to the NBA Finals, the 6-foot point guard with a prison record—at 17, he got into a brawl in a bowling alley and served four months—took over the city. He even led the team to an improbable first-game victory over the Shaq-Kobe Lakers in the Finals, before the magic quickly ended with losses in the next four games.

The Sixers passed the test for WIP's popularity in that season—far better than the Flyers four years earlier—but Iverson actually gave us a bigger ratings bump the following year when he had an incident involving his wife, a gun and—believe it or not—poom-poom pants. Allen was charged with 14 counts—10 felonies—for making terrorist threats against a 21-year-old man named Charles Jones, who favored cut-off shorts called "poom-poom pants."

Allegedly, Iverson was looking for his wife and encountered Jones, who claimed that Iverson waved a gun in his face and threatened to shoot him. Charges were filed, but Iverson's wife—who would divorce him years later—refused to press charges and Jones' credibility was compromised by his fashion choices. In the end, all charges were dropped.

Everyone was referring to the situation as a circus, so we decided literally to make it one. We recruited from our callers a clown and a juggler, who camped out with the reporters while they were waiting for the latest update at Philadelphia police headquarters. The best part was when news stations went live, and there were our goofballs right in the background, making faces and juggling balls.

What we learned in that time period was that winning sells, but big controversies are even better business for sports radio in Philadelphia. After that, we favored more of a tabloid approach. When Eric Lindros nearly died in a bathtub, when Terrell Owens wouldn't show up at training camp, when Michael Vick signed with the Eagles fresh out of prison, when Joel Embiid traveled to Qatar to get his broken foot treated, when Carson Wentz balked at the signing of Jalen Hurts, and so many more controversies...we went to 24/7 coverage of every comment, every twist, in their stories.

It was a winning formula, tested over the final decade of the *WIP Morning Show* with consistently high ratings. In those years, our show moved well ahead of KYW's news approach, and occasionally threatened—but never really beat—the No. 1 show in our 25-to-54 men's demographic, Preston & Steve. They won for two reasons. Like Stern, their show had a broader appeal because it wasn't locked into the sports format, and they were really good at their jobs. Really, really good. They deserve all the success they have had in Philadelphia.

One of the few times we managed to challenge Preston & Steve was the summer and fall of 2008, when we finally got to celebrate a championship. Yes, WIP will always be known more for its negative style, which I will always say is a direct reflection of the fans. But we proved we could cheer for our teams just as passionately, right up to and including the parade.

I was never as comfortable getting behind that Phillies team, despite its star power with Jimmy Rollins, Chase Utley, and Ryan Howard, because I never liked Charlie Manuel. Yes, technically I was wrong about him being a disaster when the Phils hired him since they did win a World Series. But I watched all of the games, and it still seemed he was overmatched most of the time against other managers.

What I learned late that year—and never forgot—was that my opinion had very little effect on what the fans thought. Generally, Phillies fans were no more thrilled than I was when the team opted for a hayseed (Manuel) over a mastermind (Jim Leyland). The difference was, the fans warmed up to Manuel. I never did.

Looking back, the turning point for the fans probably came when Charlie threatened to beat up Howard Eskin.

The team was struggling in 2007 when Howard suggested Manuel abandon his soft disciplinary approach and throw a tantrum in the clubhouse. Manuel thought Eskin was challenging his manhood, so he said he would prefer to "knock out" Eskin. The 63-year-old manager then moved menacingly toward Howard before being halted in his tracks by two assistant coaches.

Nothing appeals to Philadelphia sports fans more quickly than a throw-down, and doing so with Eskin was doubly beneficial to Manuel. Manuel's popularity skyrocketed after that incident.

But not with me. I declared that I was on Team Eskin, and I may have even predicted that Howard would win a fight on a first-round knockout. No one cared what I said that season, nor did they a year later when the Phillies raced all the way to the World Series.

Not to beat a dead horse, but the Phillies won that season despite Charlie, not because of him. He had three stars in their absolute primes (Rollins, Utley, and Howard), a starting pitcher who rose to the occasion (Cole Hamels), and—above all—the best relief pitcher in baseball (Brad Lidge). The closer was so good that season (48 for 48, including postseason) that he made the Phillies Charlie-proof. When Manuel waved for Lidge, the game was over.

In the World Series, the Phils caught another break by avoiding the powerhouse Red Sox and Yankee teams and facing the Tampa Bay Rays, who had neither the money nor the fan base to compete with the big-market Phillies. When they got to the clincher in Game 5 at Citizens Bank Park, the fans were all delirious with anticipation—and only more so when there was a two-day rain delay in the middle of the deciding contest.

Never before at WIP did we get to explore, in the middle of a game, the next strategic move by Manuel, the next pitching change by the Rays. Those 48 hours were pure, glorious torture. And then the Phillies won, players pouring onto the mound and piling onto (and apparently injuring) Lidge after the last strike.

WIP was not ready for this brand-new experience. How do we behave when our team has finally won a championship? Our station had one of its best months in the history of our sports format, because we were smart enough to just open the phone lines and allow the fans to share their joy. For a week or two after that championship, the fans did our jobs for us. It was amazing.

The parade was joyful for all of us (except me—see next chapter), as millions of red-garbed revelers clogged every inch of Broad Street. The rally at the ballpark was extraordinary. It actually spilled over to Lincoln Financial Field across the street, where Charlie Manuel took a lap before heading to the ballpark. Rollins whooped. Howard laughed. Utley swore. It was spectacular.

The fact that that Phillies team never got to celebrate another championship, despite having the best roster for the next three seasons, will always temper my memory of that milestone. But at the time, I assumed (negatively, of course) that it would probably be my only chance to see the fans party after the ultimate sports accomplishment.

So I took it all in, thankful that at least someone won something on our watch. Little did I know something even bigger and better lie ahead for us.

Of course, nothing comes easy for Philadelphia sports fans, so I cannot end this chapter on such an upbeat note. Discriminating fans realize the 2008 title also represented a far greater opportunity squandered. Welcome to 2009, 2010, and 2011.

With Lidge returning to his human ways—he was 34 for 45 in save opportunities the season after going 48 for 48—the Phillies had to rely more on Manuel's bullpen management, a sure recipe for failure. Making 2009 even more snake-bitten was the fact that many conspiracy theorists (starting with me) attributed some of Lidge's 2009 struggles to the celebration on the mound in the moments after the Phils won the World Series.

Study the tape again and you will see catcher Carlos Ruiz arrive first, enveloping the closer with an awkward hug while Lidge is kneeling in front of the mound. Then Ryan Howard, all 250 pounds of him, bowls over both of his teammates with a frightening splash, followed by the rest of the team. Arriving last from center field is Shane Victorino, who truly was The Flyin' Hawaiian as he threw his body onto the top of the pile. None of these actions were conducive to Lidge's continued good health. He needed two procedures on his right knee in the next several months.

Even worse than the closer's struggles was one of the worst days in WIP history, and in the long tenure of our show. Harry Kalas, the beloved broadcaster who proclaimed: "The Phillies are the world champions of baseball!" on October 29, 2008, died of a heart attack six months later in the press box at Nationals Park in D.C.

Name the greatest Phillies of all time—Mike Schmidt, Robin Roberts, Steve Carlton, the three more recent stars (Chase Utley, Jimmy Rollins, and Ryan Howard), and Harry's partner in the booth for many years, Richie Ashburn—and it is safe to say none of them received the love that Harry did. All these years later, he is still the most popular Phillie of all time.

And with good reason. On one of our memorable early shows, we welcomed to our studio the voices of our two most popular teams, Harry and Merrill Reese of the Eagles, and they were both generous with their time and endlessly deferential to the fans. Harry even took it a step further. He sang for us.

With almost no provocation, I asked Harry for a quick rendition of his signature song, "High Hopes." He nailed it.

Kalas did Phillies games for 39 years, his voice becoming the soundtrack for so many summers down the Jersey Shore. In my own four decades in the Philly media, I heard not one single negative word ever about Harry Kalas. And remember, this is Philadelphia, a city that suffers no fools and takes no prisoners.

So it should come as no surprise when I remind everyone how sad, how desperately somber, that entire week was after Harry's sudden passing. Fans who never called our show were openly crying, telling stories about what he had meant to them. So many of them had run into Harry somewhere over the previous four decades, and inevitably they had heartwarming stories to share about their encounters.

The critics who couldn't wait to remind everyone about the thuggery of Philadelphia sports fans got no fuel for their fire that week. What they heard, if they were so inclined to listen, was a city in pain, a city whose passion takes many forms. Philadelphia has a heart bigger than the Liberty Bell. Yes, we boo big. We grieve even bigger.

Harry Kalas got the sendoff he deserved, by fans who will embrace his booming voice and engaging smile for the rest of their lives.

If anyone was looking for bad omens, Harry's sudden passing and Lidge's balky knee were a good place to start. But the Phillies of those years were so good; they still made it back to the World Series. This time the opponent would be more formidable—the New York Yankees.

This presented a unique situation for me, since I was a Yankee fan all my life—a fact Al never missed an opportunity to mention.

So I decided to take a stand just before the first game of the 2009 World Series. I would call in a police officer whose primary job was to use a lie detector on prospective criminals. If I could prove I was rooting for the Phillies in that World Series, would everyone finally lay off all the criticism?

Now is a good time for full disclosure. I was still a Yankee fan back then, though I saw that a Phillies win—and another parade—would be far more beneficial for WIP and our show.

Live on our show, the officer strapped some wires to my chest and had me sit on a pad. He asked me a few introductory questions just to gauge how I reacted, and then he asked me which team I was rooting for in the 2009 World Series. It's hard to explain why, but silly, contrived situations like this one often created a real sense of drama.

"The Phillies," I said. "I want the Phillies to win."

There was a pause while the officer read the results. Then came the final verdict.

"He's telling the truth," the officer said. "He's a Phillies fan."

I made quite a spectacle of myself at that point, yelling and screaming and demanding an apology from Al and all the doubters. Of course, the first reaction was that I had fixed the test, given my dubious background with stuff like this. Once that accusation passed, the next emotion was shock. Even though I still carried a Mastercard with a Yankee logo on it (long story), I was a Phillies fan at heart.

The most shocked person there that day, I can now confess, was me. I did not fix the test. Through no special technique or trick, I beat the lie detector. I guess this is why the device is not admissible in court.

And since I'm making some big confessions right now, I must also say my son, Neil, and I attended the decisive Game 6 at Yankee Stadium—the one where Manuel stupidly passed by his best starter, Cole Hamels, for a washed-up Pedro Martínez. We sat just a few rows behind Phillies owner John Middleton, right behind home plate.

And when Hideki Matsui of the Yankees hit a big double in the fifth inning, pushing New York's lead to 7–1, I stood and cheered. I am not proud of that moment, but my love for my dad—who had died five years earlier—transcended anything else at that moment. The next day I had no trouble expressing the emotion of frustrated Phillies fans, but a part of me was, in a way, faking it.

I always told myself Philadelphia sports fans would understand, since their love for their teams is so bonded by generations of own their families. Of course, I am kidding myself. I will lose some fans over this. I understand that. But if I don't tell the truth now, when will I?

Go, Phillies. And go Yankees, too. I just hope they never face each other again in the World Series.

The biggest injustice in that extraordinary five-year run by the Phillies was not 2009. It was two seasons later, when GM Rubén Amaro put together the best starting-pitching staff in the team's history: Hamels, Roy Halladay, Cliff Lee, and Roy Oswalt, supported by Vance Worley and Kyle Kendrick. Charlie Manuel's legion of defenders have never had a good explanation for how that team couldn't win the championship.

Rhea Hughes does, though. Before the final weekend of the season, with the Phils sitting at 99 wins and having clinched home field for the playoffs, Rhea introduced a term that would become common with the 76ers just a few years later. Rhea said the Phils should *tank* the final three games in Atlanta to deny the hottest team in baseball, the St. Louis Cardinals, a chance at a wild-card spot.

Manuel had other ideas. He wanted the Phillies record for most wins in a season, and he got it—102—with a sweep. He also got the Cards in the NL Division Series, and after splitting the first four games, the teams faced each other in the decisive final game of the series at Citizens Bank Park.

No one ever listened to our show for its intricate expertise, but the morning of that game, we worried for four hours about Halladay facing St. Louis in the first inning. Roy was in his prime at the time, but he had one tiny imperfection. It usually took him a few batters to find his rhythm. With Chris Carpenter pitching for the Cards, it was essential that the Phillies escape unscathed in that initial at-bat.

They didn't. Rafael Furcal hit a leadoff triple and scored the only run of the game. Carpenter pitched a three-hit, complete-game shutout. The best regular season in Phillies history was over. Even worse was the final out, when Ryan Howard's last swing produced a benign grounder to first. The slugger spun his wheels out of the batter's box and then crumbled in agony, his left Achilles tendon snapped.

Howard would never be the same.

Neither would the Phillies.

They didn't have another winning season for 10 years.

Chapter 14

Trouble with My Bosses

One of my favorite movies of all time is *Private Parts,* the hilarious story of how Howard Stern became the biggest radio star in the world. My favorite sequences are when Stern depicts his bosses as money-obsessed, morally challenged incompetents. (Paul Giamatti actually comes across as more adept than one or two of my higher-ups.)

For much of my tenure in radio, I did feel that way. (Don't lose sight of the fact I left journalism because of my editor, David Tucker. The problem could be me. I'm just saying.) I can't estimate the times I told my fellow workers at WIP that the biggest enemies in radio always work in your own building. Even now, after a final period of relative job peace, I cannot look back over my career without feeling a boiling rage over some of the outrageous things that our bosses did.

The biggest disgrace, by far, requires us to go back to 2008, when, after a 28-year drought since we started the *WIP Morning Show,* our station and our city had an honest-to-goodness championship to celebrate. (We never counted college sports, which barely registered with our audience.) It was a time to rake in the ratings numbers and the advertising money.

Unfortunately, that Phillies title came at a terrible time economically for the country and especially for radio. The Great Recession caused by the mortgage-lending crisis overwhelmed most budgets in of all U.S. media. For WIP, that World Series became a life raft in an ocean of red ink. Everybody wanted to pay a premium to run ads that would link their product to the best team in baseball.

When we arrived at the historic Union League early on the morning of the Phillies championship parade, October 31, 2008, we were in a state of delirious disbelief. I was so excited about finally ending our long wait, I actually shelled out $1,500 of my own money to buy scalped tickets for the decisive and rain-delayed Game 5. I was 57 then, and I honestly believed it would be the only championship I would ever experience in my radio career.

The show started with no inkling of what was about to happen. We opened as scheduled at 6:00 AM, did 10 minutes of happy radio, and then went to break—where we stayed for 6, 8, 10 minutes. The station, with no input from any on-air people, or any warning, had oversold the show, which had always adhered to a maximum 16-minutes per hour commercial limit.

By the time we returned to our live coverage of the parade—our perch hung right over the parade route on Broad Street—we were already bumping up against the next break. On what should have been the happiest day in the history of our show, and WIP, I was faced with the impossible task of chirping happily on the air about the Phillies and howling miserably off it about my stupid bosses.

When our new program director, Andy Bloom, arrived at the Union League in the seven o'clock hour, I wasn't the only one trying to figure out how to do a show when we were off the air more than we were on it. Rhea Hughes and Al Morganti—yes, even Al—were getting as upset as I was. I unloaded on Bloom, who pleaded innocence and promised to check immediately with our GM, Marc Rayfield.

A consummate salesman, Rayfield had worked his way up the ranks at WIP from the sales department—where he prospered—to a top management position. After the turmoil during the dual departures of Tom Bigby, Rayfield emerged as a new power broker at WIP. This was a good thing because he really understood sports, but also a bad thing because he came from sales, where money ruled.

Marc ended up getting a big promotion to New York a few years later, but back then I was rarely buying whatever he was selling. Technically, he had power over the content of our show, even though I had helped to invent the product over the previous generation. Why would I listen to a guy whose main job was selling ads? I didn't.

And then, on parade day, all hell broke loose. For the eight o'clock hour, I got out my trusty Tag Heuer watch—Yeah, I know, I could have used my cell phone—and I timed how much of the hour we were actually doing. The split was 36 minutes off the air, 24 minutes on it. I cannot get anyone from those WIP years to admit to those numbers, but hey, I timed it. And I lived it. I'm still outraged.

For this book, Rayfield said he thought the ad-content mix was 30–30 that day, which he readily acknowledged was "disgusting." His rationale was that no listeners would be tuning out the day of the parade, regardless of how many ads we ran. And, as I speculated, the station really needed the money. Of course, none of these explanations were acceptable to me then, nor are they now.

Whenever you hear that successful radio hosts are prima donnas, please keep this in mind. We were trained to be so, in many cases. To believe what you say is important enough for thousands of people to listen every day, you need a big ego. No, make that a BIG EGO. Often that ego will come into conflict with bosses who want to take more credit for your success than you think they deserve. At least, that's usually how I saw the situation through most of my years at WIP.

By 2008, I was earning more in annual salary than the people were making above me on the company tree. They knew it, too. The way I looked at it, WIP was paying me to make the decisions every day on what was important to the listeners and what wasn't. So I tuned out all of my bosses, all of the time, when it came to the content of our show. This approach did not encourage peace between me and the higher-ups.

I guess you can imagine my reaction when I looked down at the parade on that long-awaited day in 2008 and saw the man we believed had sold WIP down the river, Marc Rayfield, riding in a float. That's right. Our boss was actually in the parade. At that point we still had no explanation for why our show was stolen from us that day, but there was our GM waving to the crowd, in a bus behind Ryan Howard, Chase Utley, and Jimmy Rollins. It is still a miracle to me that I didn't have a stroke at that moment.

I finally got my chance to confront Rayfield later that day when I showed up at the rally to do a simulcast with the brilliant afternoon host on our sister station, WPHT, Michael Smerconish. I even took a photo with Bloom and Rayfield from up there in the press box at Citizens Bank Park, and I am amazed that my hands are not around either of their necks. I cannot recall what Rayfield told me to calm me down in that moment, but hey, I never said he wasn't a terrific salesman. I must have bought it then.

After the second shift of my double duty that day, the indignities just kept on coming. If WIP listeners wanted to hear my voice that afternoon, they were far better off listening to WPHT, because WIP kept bailing on our simulcast to jam in more commercials. In those two shifts combined (seven hours), in arguably the biggest day in my first 28 years at WIP, I was on the air less than my usual stint in the morning.

What Rayfield said to me years later did make me laugh. He acknowledged the absurd number of breaks all day at WIP, but what he lamented the most was the fact that, against all odds, both WIP and WPHT were on the air live when Chase Utley violated FCC standards by shouting "World Fucking Champions!" at the rally.

Levity aside, that Phillies parade will always remind me not of the first championship we experienced at WIP, but of the way we blew a chance to reach ears that might never otherwise have checked in on our show.

Even after Bigby was gone, my issues with bosses remained a major obstacle to my overall mood, if not our success.

Months before the parade, when Bloom made his first appearance, I was skeptical about how we would co-exist because he was not like anyone I ever encountered in radio, before or after. He would show up, often right at the end of our show, in custom suits, tie hiked right up to the collar. His claim to radio fame was bringing Howard Stern to Philadelphia, setting into motion a network of stations that sent Stern's voice into all corners of America.

Not long after Bloom arrived, I was told—by several people—that his plan to build up WIP started with me leaving. This news didn't shock me. Andy had a big reputation in radio before he had left for four years to work as a political operative in Washington. He did not return to the career where he had his greatest success to sit on the sidelines.

Still, I was not prepared one Monday when who should arrive at the start of our show but Bloom himself, resplendent in an impeccable suit and brandishing a yellow pad and a pen. He said he planned to sit in the producer's cubicle and quietly take notes. At some point he would share his ideas with us.

Sure, boss. No problem.

Big problem.

We were the No. 1 sports morning show in Philadelphia, by a lot, and were among the most successful and enduring sports-radio shows in America, and this guy was going to tell us how to do a morning sports show in Philadelphia? Really?

Our relationship didn't get any better when Bloom called me after a game early in his first Eagles season at WIP and told me to back off my criticism of the team. He didn't say he was trying to protect the business relationship between our station and the Eagles, but that was my immediate interpretation. I told him I would offer my honest opinion every day, regardless of the repercussions. Then I'm pretty sure I threatened to quit again. (Like I said, this was a very common occurrence.)

To my relief, Bloom backed off. He was not Bigby. From that point on, our relationship improved dramatically. For most of his eight years with us, Andy became our loudest and proudest advocate in management. At the end of my run, he even wrote an incredibly generous story about the ways Stern and I were similar. It is one of the most positive appraisals of my work anyone has ever offered.

To me, the thing I shared the most with Stern was not talent or work ethic. It was a deep distrust of my higher-ups. For example, there were at least two occasions when management came to me during the early 2000s and said our producer, Joe Weachter, was making too much money. (He was not.) I told them they were in no position to judge his contribution to our show. I may have then also told them to go to hell, an all-too-common response to management intrusion.

I learned only while doing research for this book that Rhea was in their crosshairs, too. Bloom didn't like her tone, which she learned from me. When a boss suggested something we knew wouldn't be good for our show, we were not diplomatic in our response. Until Spike Eskin and Rod Lakin, our last two program directors in my tenure at WIP, I can recall no executive ever making a creative suggestion that actually helped out show.

In my last days before the Bigby clause, he would call me into the office and say I shouldn't talk about this or that. I would listen quietly and then reply with: "Okay, Tom. What should we be talking about then?" He always said that wasn't his job. Then I had him.

I would say he was right. It wasn't. Butt out.

Bigby trusted the hosts so little, he even installed a clock in the studio that counted down the amount of time every caller was on a show. It went from green to yellow at 1:30, then to red at 2:00. Every day, I unplugged the clock while we were on the air. My argument was, what if a caller confessed to a murder at 1:50? Should we tell him to call back tomorrow?

Actually, we couldn't do that under Bigby's leadership either. He had a rule that no caller could appear more than once a week on a weekday, and once more on the weekends. (No one, including the boss, ever actually kept track.) Even more worrisome were Bigby's rules about which callers were to appear on WIP. He instructed producers never to post two women callers back-to-back, and to avoid similar-sounding callers in succession, too. (He never said what that meant, but we took it as racially and ethnically insensitive.) We ignored these rules, too.

In my final words before retirement, I said I was a jerk for a major portion of my time at WIP, because I was. What I didn't say is that I never thought I had much of a choice but to act that way. When a boss tells you not to talk about Mike Tyson biting off part of Evander Holyfield's ear, what are your choices? Sabotage your own show and do what you're told, or do what is best for the audience and feel the wrath of your higher-ups?

Toward the end of my time at WIP, I must have mellowed. There's no other explanation for how I handled one of the most offensive ideas I somehow agreed to adopt during the far-less-contentious rein of Spike Eskin, son of the legend.

Despite my utter contempt for Andy Reid, Spike said he was going to hold an Andy Reid Appreciation Day at WIP, even though Reid had failed to win a championship in all 14 seasons in Philadelphia.

Instead of fighting back, I went along with the plan, in my own way. The first four hours of Andy Reid Appreciation Day became Andy Reid "Depreciation" Day, and I accepted calls mostly from people who hated him the way I did.

Bigby would have recoiled at my insubordination. Spike laughed. I had fallen right into his clever trap. All Spike was doing was creating a dynamic on his station during a quiet time. That's what actual creativity can do for a show. My hat's off to Spike.

Only by writing this book did I realize how Spike reined me in so effectively. Just as I had the clause to control Bigby's excesses, Spike had a not-so-secret weapon, too.

He saved my life.

Now, I don't mean that in a figurative way. I mean, he literally saved my life.

Early in Spike's tenure, around 2016, there were at least a dozen WIP personalities posing for a promotional photo in the waiting area just outside the studios. I was handed a cold, greasy cheesesteak, and my role in the photo was to take a big bite when the photographer yelled, "Smile."

I did as instructed, and then—when we were told the shot was perfect—I had a mouthful of gristle. What to do? Should I chew and swallow, or spit it out? I was caught in between. Part of the dry meat slipped into my throat. I couldn't breathe.

At this point I did what everyone would have predicted. I panicked. I remember making a guttural sound as I gasped for air, and then I began to stumble frantically down the hall to the office area, away from the only people who could help me. Soon, I couldn't breathe at all.

I'm pretty sure there were at least a few people in that photo shoot who would not have minded if I met my untimely demise that day, but Spike Eskin apparently wasn't one of them.

Calmly, he approached me as I was walking, grabbed me, and applied a Heimlich maneuver. The first attempt did nothing, but his second squeeze from behind me sent a chunk of nasty meat flying out of my mouth and onto the floor 10 or 15 feet in front of us.

Gail and I got a perfect score in a one-time remake of *The Newlywed Game* on Comcast SportsNet with the original TV host, Bob Eubanks. Revered (and then reviled) columnist Bill Conlin said we cheated. *(Photo by Comcast-SportsNet)*

After Buddy Ryan went silent on me for half a season when I covered the Eagles, we got along much better in our later years. It took me a long time to appreciate how he inspired a new wave of fan love for the Eagles. *(Photo by Cindy Webster)*

My wife, Gail, rarely visited the studio, but she made an exception when Jon Bon Jovi visited. (I wonder why.) *(Photo by Gail Cataldi)*

One of the best friends of our show was Senator Arlen Specter. We helped convince him to launch a congressional investigation into Spygate after the Eagles lost the Super Bowl in 2005. *(Photo by Gail Cataldi)*

Thanks to Senator Specter, I got to meet some very powerful people in Washington. A few years after this, one of these people became president. *(Photo by Gail Cataldi)*

Keith Jones (left) became a major reason for our success because of the cerebral nature of the listeners he attracted. This is one. Now Keith is the president of the Flyers. *(Photo by Cindy Webster)*

We had most of the biggest Philadelphia sports stars on our show over the years, like this visit with Allen Iverson, but the real stars were the callers. *(Photo by Cindy Webster)*

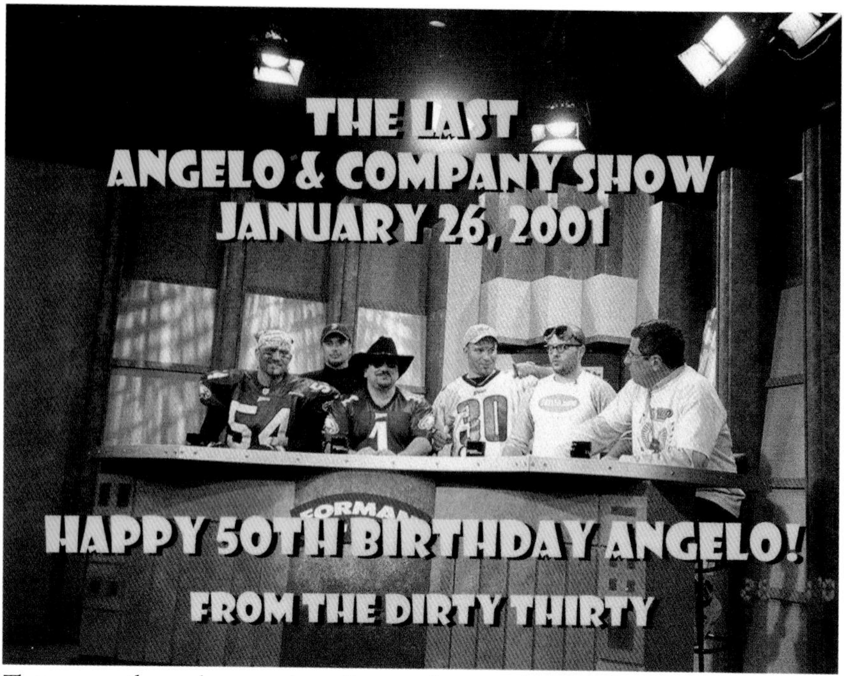

These were the real stars—the callers—who were honored on my final TV show. To my immediate right is a rare shot of the elusive SuperPhan. *(Photo by Comcast-SportsNet)*

A special day at Beloved St. John's in North Philadelphia. That's Eagle Shirley; my wife, Gail; Pastor Clement Lupton; and his wife, Brenda. *(Photo by Beloved St. John)*

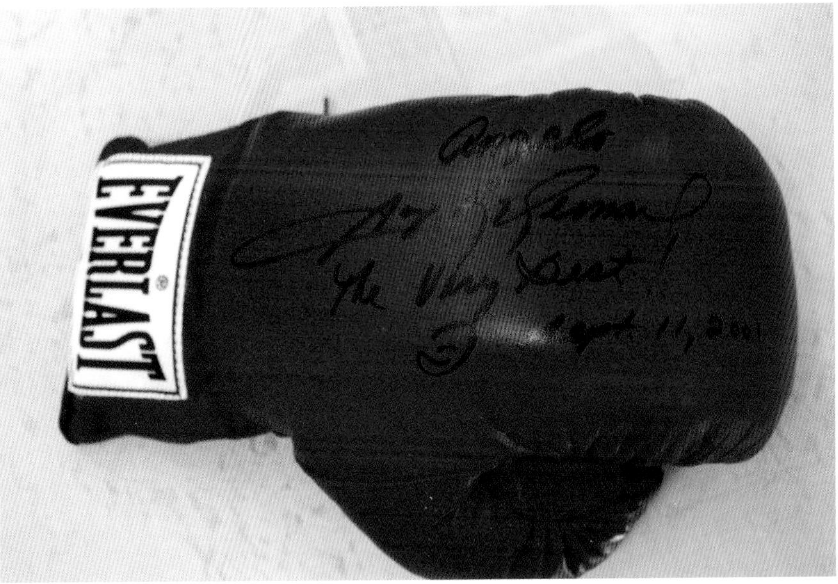

Just a few minutes before the horrific events of September 11, 2001, Sugar Ray Leonard was an in-studio guest on our show. I am still haunted by his inscription. *(Photo by Gail Cataldi)*

After 28 years on WIP, we finally got to celebrate a championship. This photo was taken just before we found out that management had sold more than half our show for commercials. *(Photo by Cindy Webster)*

The day of the Phillies parade in 2008, I missed out on a great chance to strangle my boss, Marc Rayfield, after he oversold our show. I'm confident talk-show legend Michael Smerconish would have helped me if he knew what was going on. *(Photo by Cindy Webster)*

The Eagles championship in 2018 and the parade was the highlight of our 33 years at WIP. Here's PR wizard Cindy Webster with my wife and our daughter Caitlyn at the start of the parade. *(Photo by WIP)*

Thousands of callers won prizes over the years, but the biggest winner was Kenny Justice. He got a kidney. *(Photo by Melissa Justice)*

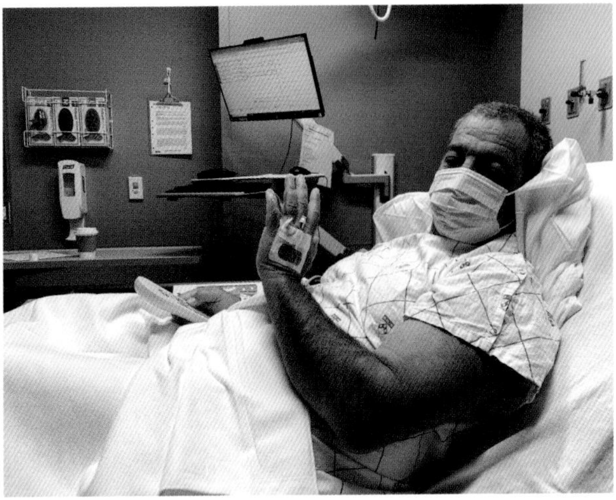

One of my biggest regrets was covering for governor Chris Christie after he fell on his rear end just before an interview in our studio. We ended up showing the video on the big screen a month later at Wing Bowl. *(Photo by Cindy Webster)*

A special night at Borgata turned into a shouting match when a heckler began screaming at the legendary comic. I panicked. Chevy saved the event with a classic taunt. *(Photo by Gail Cataldi)*

The Phillies invited me to throw out the first pitch on a 106-degree day in June of 2022. I fired a strike to legend Larry Bowa. (Unofficially, the pitch was 85 mph.) *(Photo by Cindy Webster)*

The two great parents in this photo are my mom and my son Neil. Ida died during the COVID pandemic in 2021 at 98. We never got to say goodbye. *(Photo by Gail Cataldi)*

There are really no words to describe the feeling of utter relief when your windpipe opens back up and brings life-saving air into your lungs. I was speechless for at least a minute, and then I shook Spike's hand. (I think I went in for a hug, but he backed off. At least that's the way I remember it.)

I believe I never again contested Spike's suggestions or complaints, including his dumbass Andy Reid Appreciation Day. He never once reminded me of his heroic act in all the days that followed, but I never forgot.

The perspective I took from that experience is that none of my endless previous battles with WIP management were life-or-death issues.

All it took for me to see this was an actual life-or-death experience.

Like Spike, his replacement, Rod Lakin, understood how to help the talent instead of getting in the way. One time our sales department sold the worst giveaway I had ever seen, a beer can under glass. It represented a big sale with a top beer company, and the grand-prize winner would take away this monstrosity of a prize, a big glass cube with a beer can propped up in the middle.

Twenty years earlier—maybe even 10—I might have thrown the prize against a wall and told my bosses to give it away piece by piece the next day. Not this time. The new people in charge knew there was more than one way to win this conflict. They were creative themselves. They were actually helping our show.

When I said this gift was garbage, Rod agreed. Then he told me it was fine if I trashed the giveaway on the air as long as I didn't rip the beer company in the process. So I did. Win-win. We got some fun radio out of criticizing our own sales department, and the beer company got plenty of mentions for their product.

So what's the lesson of my 33 years of insubordination? It's simple, really. Either you believe in yourself or you don't. Either you value your own judgment more than the people who have power over you, or you're merely a victim of their clueless whims. I did what I believed in every day, at every job, going all the way back to my start in Narragansett, Rhode Island.

Now this is where I would have Joe Conklin launching into a stirring rendition of Frank Sinatra singing *My Way*.

Unfortunately, Conklin is not collaborating on this book.

And unless Conklin is doing my voice, I can't sing.

Chapter 15

And Now for a Word from Our Sponsors

Jim Naughton wasn't just right about my jarring conversion from journalist to commercial shill. The top *Inquirer* editor who predicted my inevitable commitment to commerce actually understated what would happen to me when I switched from newspapers to radio.

Over the next 33 years I would do commercials for teddy bears, pajamas, both alcoholic and non-alcoholic beer, two forklift companies, four different car dealerships, a sports bar, three jewelers, restaurants, lawyers, soap, a tailor, a snack food company, a rehabilitation center, a cable-TV network, two cell phone outfits, a weight-loss business, and a golf school.

Listeners may not believe this, but I always considered myself very discriminating in which products I would endorse. And of all the business associations I had, one stood above the rest because it saved my career.

The closest I ever came to leaving WIP—even closer than my flirtation with Boston in the early years—was in 2012, when, for a fleeting moment, WIP and I had agreed to part ways. It was the week of Thanksgiving, and my contract ran out at the end of the calendar year. Our parent company,

CBS, was still happy with our ratings, but it was inflexible when it came to company edicts. And the very top of CBS management had put a freeze on salaries, just at a time when my deal was running out.

I was 61 at this point and had begun to think about when I should walk away from the best job I ever had. Getting up at 2:30 AM is never something a person wants to do forever. I had a deal with my agent, Steve Mountain. The first time WIP offered less in a contract proposal than what I was already making, I would leave. It would be a sign that I was over the hill, no longer at my peak, cooked. And if the offer was identical to my current one, I would consider that a pay cut as well because of inflation.

All I asked for in that 2012 deal was a cost-of-living raise. All CBS would offer was exactly what I was already making—a cut, in my eyes. I said no. They said no. There was a month to go before I was done, and no sign either side would move. (I know I wouldn't.)

Somehow, my longtime sponsor friend Steven Singer heard what was happening, and he was far angrier than me. An exceptional jeweler and an even more talented marketer, Steven was the most generous and loyal sponsor in our show's long history—and we had lots of very loyal sponsors. Not only was he the title sponsor for many Wing Bowls, but we did one of the weirdest promotions ever with him for more than a decade—The World's Largest Bubble Bath.

Every spring, Steven would fill his entire store at 8th and Walnut Streets with bubbles. He actually invested in a $10,000 bubble-making machine, he trained a Russian man who spoke no English how to run the Zamboni-like contraption, and he covered every inch of his counters and floors with protective wrap. Then the machine would grind out millions of bubbles, covering every corner of the store. We would sit right at the counter, inhaling the bubbles and the exhaust from the machine.

It was even more ridiculous than it sounds. Listeners would call in for a chance to strip to their bathing suits and crawl on the floor of the jewelry store through the bubbles in search of jewelry. Every once in a while, someone would find a diamond engagement ring, at which time we would strongly urge the person to propose right there. I even officiated at a wedding amid the bubbles one year, though I seriously doubt that the union is legal. (I obtained an online minister's license for $39.99.)

Steven and our show had a long and productive history together, as he did with Howard Stern and other successful radio shows. Steven also knew something I would never understand—business. He was prosperous enough to command the attention of other people in his community, and my imminent departure from WIP was, at least to him, a stupid business decision by CBS.

I have no explanation for what happened next, except to report that it gave me back the last decade of my radio career. Steven got in his car one day, drove to New York, found the office of CBS Radio president Dan Mason and talked his way into a seat right across from one of the most powerful people in radio.

I have only Steven's side of the discussion, but I know for sure the jeweler wasn't buying the salary freeze or any of the other corporate-speak that was prevalent in that era of CBS Radio. Steven was on the attack. He said he was pulling all advertising from CBS radio stations, and he was organizing a boycott by our other advertisers of WIP.

(I know Steven. This was no bluff.)

The following Monday after Thanksgiving, the CBS salary freeze had melted, thanks to Steven Singer. Dan Mason agreed to our last offer, and soon the papers were signed on a new five-year deal. During the span of that deal, CBS would sell its radio division to Entercom, which became the current owner, Audacy. It was the last dispute with our parent company I would ever have. The new people understood radio a lot better than the old people.

In the last month of my career, Singer asked for a minute of airtime to say goodbye. He actually took eight and a half. In it he expressed a bond with our show and with me that transcended our business relationship. My only response was to remind him that my last 10 years were only because of him.

Would I really have left WIP?

Yes, I would have.

Would I have walked away from radio at 61?

Probably not.

But I would never have felt the same way about any station except WIP, where I grew up, where I screamed and laughed and occasionally even shed a tear. It was the only radio station I ever worked at. I have a lot of people to thank for that (later in the book), but one who I can't wait that long to acknowledge.

I do *not* hate Steven Singer. I love the guy.

Thank you, Steven.

Not every sponsor developed the bond that Steven and I did. In fact, two of my very first commercial-spokesman deals blew up in my face, one because I was too good a representative and the other because I wasn't nearly good enough. The journey for commercial shills is a bumpy one indeed.

In my first weeks at WIP, the sales department made me an offer I couldn't refuse. A weight-loss company wanted me to go on their program. Now, I was not exactly Doughboy at this point, but I could definitely tighten things up, especially because I was working with a world-class athlete, Tom Brookshier. I said yes, went for the weigh-in, tipped the scales at 250 (I'm 6'4", people. Back off.), and I began a regimen that included eating their prepackaged food and working out regularly.

The goal was 225, a 25-pound loss. Perfect. Now one thing I'm pretty good at is reaching goals, so I threw myself into the program. Sometimes I wouldn't even finish the small portions they offered, enhancing the results. I lost seven pounds the first week and kept losing at a remarkable rate. Every week I would do ads saying I was four pounds lighter, three pounds lighter. And it showed. In a matter of weeks, I went from being a fat nerd to a skinny one.

I reached my goal weight of 225 within six weeks, an achievement that delighted the company, WIP, and me. At my weekly meeting, I asked the counselor if I could change my target weight to 220. Why stop now?

I lost those five pounds in a week and was back at my new goal weight. Now it was time to go on Maintenance, where the goal became staying within a pound or two of 220. I weighed in the next week at 216. The counselor was perplexed. Was I eating more? Was I following the maintenance plan?

No and no. I was still locked into losing as much weight as I could. I was in a zone. Don't stop me now. You can see the photos of those early days with Brookie as I began to resemble a telephone pole. I was at 213 the second week on Maintenance, 210—10 pounds (really 15) below my target weight—after three weeks.

That's when the boss at the weight-loss office was waiting for me upon my arrival after the fourth week. I weighed in at 208. This was not good. She pointed out that I was no longer following the program. I was getting too skinny. I was making the company look bad.

They were right. The program was excellent. I was not. They said I couldn't go any lower. I had a week to at least level off around 210. I had one week to hold onto the account.

The next week I was 205. The last thing I remember the counselor saying was, "You have a problem. You may have an eating disorder."

I can't really explain what I was thinking back then, but even losing the account didn't discourage me from my new single-minded quest. I did not have anorexia; I was still eating. It's just that I was so conscious of everything I put into my mouth that I was not eating nearly as much as a 6'4" man needed to nourish himself.

How low did I go before sanity prevailed? I know I was under 200 pounds for a while there. In retrospect, the weight-loss company—which I would still endorse today—did me a huge favor by dropping me. With the goal of bragging about my weight-loss gone, I slowly began to eat normally again. Within a year or so, I was back to being a fat nerd.

Now I just have to find a way to get rid of all of those awful photos.

The first tip I received after I announced my retirement was to take up golf. It kills lots of time, it gets you out into the fresh air and it is fun activity for people of all ages. I would just nod when some well-intentioned person made this suggestion. I didn't want to tell them about my one unfortunate dalliance with golf.

Again, this was my first year working full-time at WIP, a calendar filled with charity golf tournaments featuring my beloved partner, Tom Brookshier. When a new golf school was looking to create a model player, it wasn't long before they turned to me.

The school would assign their top golf pro to me, and using the latest computer technology, would make me into a respectable (or better) golfer. I got some used clubs, a new golf shirt or two and even those weird shoes with the big spikes on the bottom.

By most accounts, I showed great promise in the lab setting. Whacking balls into a plastic flap from about 20 years away, I was Arnold Palmer—or so I thought. After failing at all physical endeavors, I was actually believing that maybe I had found something I could do well athletically.

Then I went out for my first round at the public course in Northeast Philadelphia, with a bunch of pals who I can assure you would never admit they were there that day. On the first green, I drove the cart right onto the green and up to the hole. This is not proper golf etiquette. When informed of this infraction, I sheepishly drove back off the green, leaving behind me an unfortunate ridge from the tires.

I quit that day after nine holes because I ran out of golf balls. Playing on an actual course is not at all like slamming balls into a plastic flap. I can't remember a single drive that landed in the fairway, and my putting was not good either—despite a history of success in miniature golf. (The ridge on the first green didn't help.)

The people at the school laughed off my first pratfall and said I was a work in progress. I intensified my instruction at the golf center, continuing to excel on the computer. They prepared me diligently for my next venture onto an actual golf course, something they called a scramble tournament. Each foursome featured a "celebrity," and three pour souls that day got stuck with me. The rules of the tournament called for each team to use two drives from each player.

Earlier in the round, I actually hit a decent shot in the fairway, and the serious golfers were smart enough to use my drive. Unfortunately, we got to the 18th hole tied for the lead—I had nothing to do with the solid score, believe me—but they still hadn't used my second drive. So the other three golfers sat in the golf carts and said, "Hit a good one. We have to use whatever you hit."

Gulp. If I just got the ball 150 yards or so out onto the fairway, these guys could bring us in, for sure. They were really good golfers. I harkened back to months of instruction, took several very impressive practice swings, and swung mightily.

I skinned the top of the ball, causing it to trickle off the tee, roll along the wet grass and settle onto a barren patch of grass that I later learned was the women's tee. We lost the tournament by one stroke.

Undaunted, I kept at my lessons religiously until the school said I was ready for my final exam. I would go out with the top pros from the place for a full round of golf at Ron Jaworski's course in Sewell, New Jersey.

To be safe, I took 18 balls with me that day—just enough to get me to the second shot on the eighth hole. When I shanked that final ball hopelessly into the woods, I remember turning to the golf pro who had invested many hours in my development and posing a simple question.

"Can *anybody* learn to play golf well?" I asked.

"Well, not anybody," the pro said. "There are exceptions."

"Do you think maybe I am an exception?"

"It's very possible."

With that, and with no balls left to hit, I grabbed a ride back to the clubhouse, left my old golf clubs in the locker room and drove away.

I have never picked up a club again.

The golf school went out of business.

I would be remiss if I didn't offer a minor digression here to explain my unusual connection to one of the greatest golfers who ever lived, the aforementioned Arnold Palmer. We shared a moment that both reinforces the name of this book and also symbolizes perfectly my disconnect with the best of the best in sports.

In my early days with Tom Brookshier, we did a bunch of remote broadcasts at swanky country clubs throughout the area, usually on mornings before Brookie was a celebrity in the charity tournament later that day. One time, we were at a senior tournament featuring Palmer, by far my dad's favorite golfer and one of the pioneers of the sport.

Arnold came over to our small tent and shared a few words with Brookie—I stayed far away from that one—and then he left to work at the putting green a few yards from the site of our broadcast. Brookie and I moved on to other topics, and before long I was bellowing out some nonsense on a topic long forgotten. Then we heard a thump.

"What's that, Brookie?" I asked.

"Maybe a bird?"

We resumed our discussion, and I raised my volume again.

Thump. Thump. Then a ball missed the tent and rolled past us.

We were under assault, and the assailant was Arnold Palmer.

Apparently, he didn't agree with my style of sports talk, especially when he was getting ready for a tournament. He was throwing golf balls at our tent. (By the way, Arnold had a great arm for an elderly man.)

I never had the guts to tell my dad, who was still angry about Rocky Marciano.

Now back to our regularly scheduled programming....

I gained a reputation, in my prime years, for selling anything and everything, as that list above suggests. But I will insist until my last breath that I held the people I represented to a high standard. The best example I can offer is the time I cost WIP a $500,000 deal with a prominent car dealership because, well, the business wasn't even smart enough to take reasonably good care of its spokesman. Namely, me.

Car dealerships are, by nature, a precarious sponsorship because not all of them are as customer oriented as they say in their ads. In all four car places I represented, I became a customer the moment I agreed to do the deals. This meant whenever I needed a vehicle, I would use the dealer I was supporting in my ads.

One day my stepson Brendan's car broke down for the last time, and he desperately needed something better to go to and from work. He just wanted a reliable used car. Nothing special. So I called our sales rep, and she made an appointment with a top salesman at this dealership. Brendan went there, found a car, got their unqualified assurance this was a terrific vehicle for him, and signed the paperwork.

To say that Brendan got a lemon would do a disservice to all produce. Apparently, the meticulous checking system applied to every used car on the lot was ignored in the preparation of a car being bought by the son of the company spokesman. Let's just say this dealership had not mastered its attention to detail.

When one of the tires started to wobble soon after Brandan got the car, we had it checked. All of the bolts holding in all four tires were loose.

A couple were missing entirely. Does it get any more basic for a dealership than tightening the bolts on the tires?

I posed this question to a representative of the dealership—not an owner or GM; just a guy—in a manner that was neither calm nor professional. I was told that they couldn't imagine this were true, and no one was about to take back this lemon. They were willing to tighten the bolts, though. It's not like they were being unreasonable.

Of course, I asked to speak to the manager, or the owner, or the president of the United States. On the line hopped a jerk who wouldn't even provide his name, and he made it clear he didn't care if I was being told to go on the air every day and lie to the listeners.

"In that case," I said, "You can take this car and shove it up your ass. I'm done with you people!"

Then I called the WIP sales rep and told her I was withdrawing my support of the dealership. She was incredulous. Did I realize this was a $500,000 account?

I'm proud of my answer. I said, "Do you realize these people expect me to lie to our listeners every day? And if they're screwing their spokesman, what are they doing to everybody else?"

Of course, the dealer dropped the account, and I was persona non grata for a while, at least with the sales department. But I did the right thing. It only happened a few times—and none more dramatically than this case—but I would drop a sponsor if I was no longer comfortable representing them.

In the list of businesses I represented, the biggest shockers are the two forklift companies I represented. The idea of me operating a forklift is ludicrous. I can barely drive my car. And the fronts of my shirts are proof that I am not even adept at lifting my own fork.

But late in the 1990s, a local forklift company with a president who liked our show approached the station, and we did a deal. The whole pitch was: I may not know anything about heavy equipment, but I sure do know a good business when I see one.

The owner turned out to be a guy with similar interests to mine—namely, sports and Hollywood. I have often said I have no close friends—and it's true—but we actually went out to dinner with our wives a couple of times and even took in a movie or two.

Against logic, the sales campaign was working even better than our relationship. People were buying the pitch, and the forklift company was prospering. Everybody was happy.

Until the company started falling behind on its payments to the station. This is the only time I recall actually being informed by my bosses that I may have to drop a sponsor before they drop me. So I figured there would be no harm in using my friendship with the owner to resolve the issue. This would prove to be a huge mistake.

The owner clearly was embarrassed by my call, and he ended the discussion by firing me before WIP could let go of him. At the end of the call, I did something that was totally unprofessional, and extremely enjoyable. I told the guy he was such a phony, I was going to jump to his biggest competitor at the time. He laughed. What other forklift company would want to join forces with a doofus like me?

The name of the company was MHS Lift, and within days we began a 20-year relationship that brought honor to me, to WIP, and, I hope, to them. Owners Bob Levin and his sons, Andy and Brett, had heard my commercials for their rival, and they were sorry they hadn't thought of it first.

I was doing live reads for MHS Lift within a month from getting dumped by the other forklift company, and no one even knew the difference—until MHS Lift became the most powerful and successful forklift company in North America. Now I'm not saying their association with WIP caused this upsurge in business, but it definitely didn't hurt.

As for the other forklift company, I have no idea what happened to them, nor do I care.

At our second-to-last show, I got Andy and Brett on the show, and I asked a question about something I had been promoting with great relish for over a generation.

"Hey, guys," I asked innocently. "What the hell is a pallet jack?"

Chapter 16

My Love Affair with the Callers

Because I never adhered to Tom Bigby's edicts about how often callers could appear on WIP or how long they could talk, I developed deeper connections with them than the other shows. At least that's what I have always believed. My biggest reward for my blatant insubordination was the quality of our many regular callers.

Unlike Tom Brookshier, who was happiest when a big name like Bobby Knight or Frank Gifford was booked, I was in my best mood when I looked at the computer screen and saw Eagle Shirley, Butch from Manayunk, and Arson Arnie waiting to get on. Especially Arnie.

Our association with this South Philly cab driver began during one of the most insane radio promotions in our history—maybe even more insane than Wing Bowl—when a beer company offered us a $10,000 prize. The main requirement was that we recruit listeners by asking: "What are you willing to do for $10,000?" The company also asked that a representative of the firm be one of the three judges.

We rented out a bar, scheduled the contest for the early evening—it was not even a part of our morning show—and invited callers to propose their feats. The more ridiculous, the better, of course. The three biggest contenders would all be rejected immediately by WIP lawyers today, but this was well before the scrutiny of the later Wing Bowl years.

The first stunt was a man who vowed to lick clean his entire car. That's right, after a light rinse of his old junkheap, he would take his tongue and run it across the entire surface. Who wouldn't want to see that?

The second finalist was a very attractive woman—clad only in a swimsuit—willing to dip herself in a vat of warm chocolate. Again, there were no dissenters.

Arnie was third. He wanted to shave his head, and then take all the clippings and season them with gobs of hot sauce. Between gulps, he would attempt to swallow 61 live goldfish. We made Arnie a finalist largely because of his warped ingenuity. No one actually wanted to see him do this.

Sure enough, the guy did wash his car with his tongue. In fact, to enhance the appeal, he often stuck his tongue out to prove he was picking up lots of grime. Still, it was actually boring to see a guy spend two hours doing this, so he didn't get the judge support he expected.

The surefire winner, of course, was the woman, who was even more appealing than her photos, attired only in the skimpiest of black string bikinis. After her handlers rolled out a vat of thick chocolate, she lowered herself seductively into the sweet nectar. The crowd went insane. The $10,000 was hers, no doubt.

But then something happened that took all of us by shock. She stood up and asked the drunk, primarily male audience if she could get a few volunteers to lick the chocolate off her. I asked her again to make sure I had heard her right. Yes, she wanted guys to come up and lick her. (If memory serves me right, even the guy licking the car took a break to help this damsel in distress.)

Unfortunately, one of the first volunteers was the beer-company representative himself, who clearly had been sampling his own product all night. He leaped over the judging table, tongue hanging out, and aimed himself right at the woman. The moment his tongue touched her thigh—which it did repeatedly, by the way—the judge was disqualified, and so was the young woman. She had expanded her stunt, a transgression not allowable by the FCC-sanctioned contest rules.

The crowd was not happy—nor were the 61 doomed goldfish—when Arnie then completed his far less exciting stunt and was awarded the $10,000. What we didn't know then was, our first star was born. Arson Arnie—named after the hot sauce—became must-listening on our show for the next 30 years.

Arnie's fame was well-earned. If my goal was to turn up the volume in the most passionate sports city in America, then Arnie was my best ally. He was perfect casting as a loudmouth South-Philly cabbie, with the thick dem-dese-dose accent and the tough talk. Any time there was a Dallas game coming up on the schedule, I knew I could count on Arnie to take the first shot.

Arnie hated the Cowboys so much, he would publicly pray for their plane to crash—something Rhea Hughes constantly made him take back—and he would mean it. One time he called from the Cowboy offices in Plano, Texas. He said he was standing right next to the Dallas Cowboy logo in from of the main building.

"Can you hear that?" he said.

"Hear what?" I relied.

"I'm pissing right on the logo. Can you hear it?"

He was.

Now, granted, this might not seem the kind of thing that would appeal to the upper class in our audience, but somehow even they embraced his antics. He became the darling of one of our early Wing Bowls when he agreed to box a Philadelphia lawyer named George Bochetto, who, we later learned, was an actual amateur boxer. Arnie got slaughtered that day. The crowd loved it.

After Arnie gave up his cab because of the increased violence in the city, he had more time to go out on assignments for us. One time a cat got trapped in the same tree Tony had trimmed a few years before, right in front of our studios at 5th and Callowhill. Arnie said he would climb up the tree and rescue the feline.

While teetering on a weak branch far above the street, Arnie called and instructed us to seek help from the callers. Immediately, a man who identified himself as a "cat expert," breathlessly advised Arnie: "Whatever you do, don't poke the cat with a stick!"

"Who is this *cat expert*?" Arnie barked out. "What do I look like, an idiot? Don't poke a cat with a stick? That's your advice?"

Arnie's final years were poignant for him and for the rest of us. He developed a serious neurological condition requiring delicate brain surgery that could impair him, or even kill him. So we honored him a couple of weeks before the major operation at Wing Bowl, where he was inducted into our Wing Bowl Hall of Fame and given a standing ovation.

He survived the operation, and for a year after that he would cry at the first sign of emotion. Over time, he recovered from that issue, too. In our final days, however, I often told him he was my all-time favorite caller, and he would quickly put a stop to the platitudes. Those last few shows were a test of all of our emotions.

When I saw his name on the screen in the final moments of our last show, I knew there was only one person I had to hear from before I left. Arnie ripped the Eagles for losing the Super Bowl and said goodbye to 30 years of the best radio drama a host could ever hope for. I ended the call by telling him I loved him.

He said the same back to me.

At that point, Al Morganti appeared to throw up in his mouth.

Although Arnie was there with us through our many transitions, the final decade of our show was more about the callers than any of our 20-plus years before that. It took me that long to realize the listeners wanted to hear from their favorite fans—some of whom they loved to hate—more than us, our expert hosts, or anyone else.

One of our first breakout stars was a mysterious character named Tyrone Johnson, who started calling because he loved the Wing Bowl (before it got seedy). Tyrone embodied those early years of our biggest promotion with an innocence and joy. He even wrote a song, "Wing Bowl Happy," that was a mainstay at our event for several of its formative years.

What we never really talked about on the air was who Tyrone was, where he came from, and what he did for a living—if anything. He would dodge any questions about his background, and we didn't press him because, well, he wasn't, ah, overly smart, let's just say.

At his peak, Tyrone was so popular, callers would ask where he was if he missed a single week. They would boldly request another rendition of "Wing Bowl Happy," or just his ecstatic announcement that "It's Football Friday!"—sometimes even when it was Wednesday.

And then, poof. We never heard from Tyrone Johnson again. For many years, we asked listeners to help us find him, but no one knew who he was even before his sudden burst of fame. All I can say is, thank you, Tyrone. You were a shooting star in the WIP galaxy.

Tyrone wasn't the only caller over the years who was unconventional in his style. Like him, the captain of the Dirty Thirty, Jason, was not the most eloquent, or even coherent, caller, but he developed a following that was astonishing by the end of our show.

Jason called in religiously for at least the last 20 years we were at WIP, often asking to address his fans directly. Reading from notes, he would then launch into a speech that featured his assurance—"no doubt about it"—before every Eagles game that they would win easily, always ending his pep talk with a rousing E-A-G-L-E-S cheer.

I had no idea how popular Jason had become until the COVID pandemic, when he ended up in a hospital, on a ventilator, with the potentially fatal virus. It was only then that I learned Jason had other medical issues that increased dramatically his risk of dying. The situation grew even worse as he fought for his life. He suffered a stroke while at the hospital.

For weeks, his brother and friends would call with medical updates. At one point, his brother asked our audience to pray for Jason—never a good sign. But Jason made it, slowly at first and then with more momentum. Eventually he went home, and his first call after the medical emergency was a source of tears for many of our most devout listeners.

Then the damnedest thing happened. Jason became a far funnier, wittier, snarkier caller than he had ever been before the stroke. His words slurred a bit more now, but they were all golden nuggets. For the first time, he did impressions of other callers, barked out catch phrases and attacked Eagles naysayers with a renewed vigor. No one at our show ended more strongly than Jason from the Dirty Thirty.

By far, Jason's best impression was of another regular caller who developed his own following, Big Rube (Reuben Harley), an entrepreneur who worked in the sports apparel, photography and restaurant businesses. By the time we took our final bow, he was the chef at a Manayunk, Pennsylvania, restaurant that featured ribs drenched in his famous Baby Mama sauce.

Because he had taken on so many jobs in his career, Rube ran into hundreds of famous people, and he was not shy to share his brushes with Beyoncé, Jay-Z, Rihanna, supermodels Naomi Campbell and Tyra Banks, and pretty much any other Black star at the time. Toward the end, I started throwing out names, and inevitably Rube would have a story about meeting them.

Did he really meet all of those famous people?

Does it matter? I was not in the journalism business anymore, and Rube's stories were entertaining. Most of the listeners couldn't get enough of Rube, and neither could I.

One concept so many talk-show hosts seem to miss is the inclusion of colorful regular callers. What I learned after a long while was that they bring more value to a daily show than the biggest names in sports, because they are there all the time, offering opinions and—above all—bringing the passion that embodies sports fans, and especially those in Philadelphia.

No matter how hard a host screams, how loud the reaction is after a big win or bad loss, nothing compares to a fan emoting live the morning after a game. Eagle Shirley was better at that than anyone I ever encountered. She is even featured in a 2020 documentary called *Maybe Next Year* on Amazon Prime, where she is shown calling us from her kitchen, howling and chanting before she headed out to work. If Shirley didn't come on the air after an Eagles game—something that happened very rarely—the listeners wanted to know if she was okay.

We discovered Shirley in 2004 after she appeared in some hype ads for the Eagles during their "You Can't Script This" campaign that season. I saw them and put out an alert to have her call in. She never stopped after that, for the next 19 years. That's loyalty.

I got so close to Shirley that she invited me to go to church with her in 2017, at a lovely old Evangelical place of worship called Beloved St. John in North Philadelphia. This was the kind of church often depicted in movies, with parishioners dancing and singing and a fiery pastor preaching with an infectiously rhythmic cadence. I was a fallen Catholic by that time—long fallen—and I was swept up in the spectacle.

The second time I went, during my final Eagles season in 2022, the pastor, Clement M. Lupton, actually had me get up in front of the gathering and speak. I had 35 years of experience in front of a microphone at that point, and yet all I could say was that I was no match for Pastor

Lupton. Before that day, I thought I was a sports evangelist. Not true. You want to hear real passion? Go listen to Pastor Lupton. Wow.

During those final years, when the callers took center stage, my co-hosts were ambivalent, as were my emailers. And I understood, to a point. Some of the regulars were more charming on the air than off it. A case in point was Butch from Manayunk, whose claim to fame was using the melody to *The Flintstones* theme song to pen sports-related ditties. Butch perfectly fit the model of so-bad-it's-good, both with his gravelly, off-pitch voice and his tortured rhymes.

Butch was a master of getting free stuff, so he would always appear when we had a remote broadcast in hopes of treating himself to a free buffet, product giveaways, and anything else that wasn't nailed down. He went over the line many times, but never more so than when we did a broadcast at a file-shredding business in southern New Jersey.

That morning, Butch needed to go to the bathroom, and he wasn't fussy about where to do it. There were restrooms right near our broadcast table, but Butch chose to relieve himself out in the parking lot—just as the owner of the business and his mortified wife were arriving. (I wasn't an actual witness, since I was doing the show at the time, but I was told he was using someone's rear tire as a urinal.)

We were never invited back to that place.

One of Butch's final appearances came at Borgata in Atlantic City, where he would often arrive in those final years with a regulation NBA basketball. We never knew why. During breaks he would bounce it, run layup drills, and generally annoy all of the other people around him (especially Rhea).

Still, I wasn't about to turn my back on a loyal caller that late in our tenure, so I put him on the air one day late in 2022. Big mistake. Butch was plastered. He started by talking about the great luck he had gambling the previous night at the Hard Rock, the biggest Borgata rival. Not good. Then he started slurring his words so badly, I had to ask.

"Have you been drinking, Butch? It's 8:15 in the morning."

"Yes, I have."

"Then I have to ask you to put down the mic."

We didn't hear from Butch for several months after that. He finally contacted me via email and said he was going through a hard time. He was clinically depressed. I gave him as much insight as I could from my own experience, and he recovered enough to come back for one final (sober) appearance at the end of our run.

He even wrote us a special song.

To the melody of *The Flintstones*, of course.

Arson Arnie would often say that listening to our show, in some small way, saved his life. I doubt it. But we did play a significant role in saving one of our most dedicated and beloved callers, Kenny (Justice), a charter member of the Dirty Thirty. In fact, Kenny placed his first call to our show in 1996. For 27 years, he never stopped calling.

Although he was a charter member of the Dirty Thirty, Kenny had a life away from WIP—a very productive and successful one. He couldn't make the infamous trip to New York to cheer for Ricky Williams, but after years of trying to explain his absence, he just started saying he did go, adding some fake anecdotes along the way.

In many ways, Kenny was the best friend our show ever had, always there whenever we needed something, no questions asked. We all learned how valuable he could be when, on a flight from Philadelphia to Clearwater in April 2020, Joe Weachter collapsed. I was up in first class (big shot), and I heard a commotion midway 10 or so rows back. Then I saw our producer's body lying between the rows, his head and shoulders blocking the aisle.

This will shock no one who has managed to stick with this book for 16 chapters, but my first instinct was to panic. Though we were still in the air—cell phone use was strictly prohibited—I started calling people. The first call went to Kenny, who was already in Clearwater and had always been my go-to person in crises.

"I'll meet you at the gate," he said. "I got this."

Joe regained consciousness a minute or two later, but he needed more room to make it through the rest of the flight. He was incredibly lucky that a nationally renowned expert on emergency medicine from the University of Pennsylvania was on the flight and making all the decisions.

One of the first things Joe needed was more room. Hey, Cataldi has a first-class seat. Perfect. A flight attendant asked me if I could switch with Joe. I was happy to help.

But I wasn't as enthusiastic about changing seats as I let on. Just a week earlier, when I went home to see my mom, I had a panic attack shortly after I boarded a small airplane for the return flight from Providence to Philadelphia. I knew I was in trouble the moment I had to duck my head to get down the aisle to reach my seat. (The plane was so small, it didn't have first class.) Moments before takeoff, I jumped up and ran for the front exit, where I was stopped by a flight attendant named Karen Hebert.

"I've got to get off!" I yelped. "I can't do this."

"Yes, you can," she said. She sat me in the front seat, and she talked to me for the entire 45 minutes back to Philly. At the end of the flight, she even gave me one of those little buttons with wings on them that are usually reserved for little kids. Thank you, Karen.

Karen came on the show the next week, and I made a public appeal for her to get a big raise. (I don't think she got one.) I rationalized the episode by saying the aircraft was the problem, not me. Once I got on a big plane, with lots of room in first class, my claustrophobia would not be an issue. Uh, oh.

Now with Joe getting treatment in first class, I was in a middle seat in the middle of the plane, the walls of the plane closing in on me again.

(This is where, during a show, Rhea would point out that stories like this would always end up being about me. Sorry.)

More than once, I felt the urge to bolt from my seat again, but I got through it because I kept reminding myself to be there for Joe, and because I knew Kenny would be waiting to take over as soon as our wheels hit the tarmac at the Tampa airport.

Sure enough, there was Kenny. He and I accompanied Joe to the hospital, where Joe stayed one long night for observation. (He was fine. Just dehydration.) Kenny was back for our show early the next morning, and then he drove me back to the hospital to visit our recovering producer.

In the interest of full disclosure, I must now offer a brief confession. We were still very concerned for Joe—extremely concerned—but at one point when the doctor was checking him out, we were told to stand outside the door of his hospital room. It was the first week of the COVID outbreak, and all of the hospital personnel wore masks. Suddenly, our worries about Joe took an unscheduled break. Here's how Kenny described it:

"Like the men we are, suddenly we couldn't have cared less about Joe's condition when the most incredible, most beautiful, well-endowed nurse sat down at the computer station right in front of us," he recalled for this book. "I don't really remember much about Joe or his diagnosis for the next few hours—nor did I really care. In the end, Joe was fine—but not nearly as fine as that nurse."

Unfortunately, Kenny was back in the hospital the following year for a far different reason. He was fighting for his life. Kenny had been hiding from us for years a kidney condition that had reached the point my father got to late in his own life—dialysis or death. I had learned about it via email a few weeks before, and I was haunted by the idea that Kenny would face my father's fate all too soon.

Kenny called us on his way for a dialysis treatment to discuss the upcoming NFL draft—making no mention of his personal crisis—but then I abruptly asked him about his medical condition. He was surprised I had brought it up, but he described in vivid detail the ordeal he was facing and the one hope he had left—a transplant.

I made a public appeal right there for a donor, and soon we all followed Kenny's journey back to good health. Twenty-eight listeners stepped up that day to help Kenny, proving once again the amazing humanity of Philadelphia.

Bob Wright from Bucks County made the incredible sacrifice, and while he wasn't a perfect match for Kenny, his kidney donation led to Kenny receiving one on November 3, 2021. Kenny is back to full health now, a dedicated husband and a terrific dad to a daughter and son.

To me, Kenny has always embodied the consummate Philadelphia sports fan. He has owned season tickets to all four major sports, and he has made his presence known with boos and catcalls at every opportunity. (The first words he taught his son, Roman, were "Dallas sucks.") But underneath the crust is a soft, warm core.

As soon as Kenny was back healthy, he created an organ-donation charity called Kidneys for Kenny. In the first year, the foundation raised $30,000 dedicated to helping people going through the end-stage kidney disease and kidney transplant process. Kidneys for Kenny provides moral support, as well as financial grants, to worthy kidney-disease candidates in the Delaware Valley and nationally.

In my last days at WIP, Kenny kept saying I saved his life by talking about him and the foundation every chance I could get. He was wrong. All I did was speak into a microphone. The sports fans of WIP are the ones who did all the work. They went through the testing, endured the surgeries and reached deep into their pockets to support a great cause.

I wrote this book because I want America to see the Philadelphia I lived in, and benefitted from, for the past 40 years.

Snowballs at Santa, my ass.
How about Kidneys for Kenny?
When will that story get national coverage?

I will end this chapter about my favorite callers—sorry I can't mention all of you—the way we ended our Football Friday shows for so many years, including the last. Yes, it's time once again for SuperPhan.

Our association with this, er, unique talent started when we received a low-budget movie written, directed, and starring Vince Mola, a local filmmaker who had developed a alter-ego named "SuperPhan"—which was also the title of his debut flick. It was almost impossible to differentiate where Vince ended and SuperPhan began, but most would agree he conceived a caricature of the Philly sports fan that was cartoonishly accurate and highly entertaining.

Shortly after we started talking about his film, Vince called in—as SuperPhan, of course. (In hundreds of calls that followed, he never appeared as Vince Mola.) He had a distinct formula for his calls. He would always announce at the beginning that he was "coming out hot today." Then he would belittle the opponent, predict an easy Eagles win on Sunday and would end with a chant that included a rrrrrr that sounded like someone starting a lawn mower, then a loud "Shaka," and finally a piercing howl. You had to be there. It was awesome.

It's safe to conclude that Vince's film career had its ups and downs, as evidenced by his disappearance for at least a decade before his triumphant return for our last Eagles season in 2022–23. We all loved Vince's first movie, but it was not a roaring success, nor was his follow-up, *Bald.* The failure of his second film is easier to understand. He included many of us in it, as unpaid actors.

With WIP's promotional power behind the film, he even held a premiere on the campus of Penn, inviting all of us, including a few of our bosses. It was only during that premiere that WIP management learned

Vince had used our studios, and especially our sales department, as sets for the film. (We didn't ask for permission because we knew what the answer would be.)

Bald got a huge ovation when the credits rolled, but not by our bosses. The next day, we were all grilled about how much we knew about Vince using WIP for his sets. We all played dumb.

Let's just say we gave a better performance in those meetings than we did in the film.

Chapter 17

A Boost from the Experts

One of our many early battles with Tom Bigby was over interviews with sports figures or self-proclaimed experts. Unlike Brookie, who would routinely schedule six or more guests a day, we usually held to three, at least until Bigby had made his final exit and we could book a show based more on need than quotas.

John Marzano was an early breakout star, setting the career track for many more ex-athletes who started with us before expanding into television. A former big-league catcher, John was a native Philadelphian, equipped with the South Philly accent and the corresponding attitude. John was a natural.

No one adapted to our show faster that John, who loved to shout me down on any opinion he thought was stupid. And it wasn't just about baseball. John made no secret of his disdain for my knowledge on all four major sports. He was funny, in a locker-room way, and also smart. He knew when to engage and when to back off, the hardest things for co-hosts to grasp.

To say that John Marzano was a godsend to our show is an understatement. He brought us content, humor, and—above all—acceptance among other athletes. The Phillies still hated me, but probably a little less so now that John was there to set me straight.

Actually, I met John years before he joined our show. Early in my tenure at the *Inquirer*, I was assigned a trip back home to New England to interview the pride of south Philadelphia, John Marzano, who was a backup catcher with the Boston Red Sox. He was brash, smart, and fun right from the beginning. As you might imagine, we felt a special bond because of our shared Italian heritage.

John's career in Boston and later in Seattle was typical of a journeyman backup catcher, never rising to a starter but also bringing solid work on the field and in the clubhouse. His claim to fame was a hit that came with his right fist, not his bat. Constant whiner Paul O'Neill was complaining about a strike call in a 1996 game between the Yankees and Mariners, and John had heard enough. He threw off his mask and landed a right cross right onto O'Neill's jaw. A huge brawl ensued, causing five ejections and thrilling every tough Italian in South Philly.

After John's major-league career wound down, he was looking for a chance to break into broadcasting, doing guest appearances on the Phillies postgame show. We liked what we saw there, so we invited him to sit in for a few shows. He was a perfect fit, so we signed him as a weekly studio contributor.

John was becoming a broadcast star by the early 2000s—so much so that he joined us for our annual spring-training visit to Clearwater, Florida, spring home of the Phillies. We were heading back from a show one morning, me at the wheel. Rhea Hughes had already warned Marzano not to drive with me; she has sworn off the exercise after a near-accident earlier in her time on our show. John laughed off her warning. He was tough. He could handle me.

Unfortunately, as often happens when I'm behind the wheel, I got lost on the drive back to our hotel, and I made an ill-advised split-second decision to pull a U-turn on a major thoroughfare, not realizing that the traffic coming in the opposite direction was getting there faster than I anticipated.

Cars roared by us on both sides as I straightened the car, missing us by inches. When we were out of danger, John just glared at me. If looks could kill.... He then told me to pull over. At that moment, I know exactly how Paul O'Neill felt just before the punch. I did as John instructed. He drove the rest of the way back in total silence.

John never got in a car with me again.

I wish this was the end of the story. It isn't. A year or so later, John died in a most improbable way, at 45, when he fell down the stairs of his apartment on Passyunk Avenue in South Philly. It was, by all accounts, the flukiest of fluke accidents. Just like that, he was gone. The wake for him was one of the saddest times in all of our lives, attended by hundreds and hundreds of the family and friends whose lives he had made so much better.

I am writing here of John in the past tense, but I can tell you he has been alive in my mind for the past 15 years. He passed away on April 19, 2008, the first month of a season that would end with the Phillies winning the world championship.

Man, John would have loved that season.

It seems hard to believe so many years later, but Stephen A. Smith honed his $10-million-a-year ESPN broadcast style on the *WIP Morning Show* in those early 2000s. Al Morganti and I argued often—usually off the air—about how effective a guest Stephen was. Al thought he was more bluster than substance. I said substance was overrated. I thought Stephen was a star in the making. (Hey, for once I was right.)

Stephen picked up what works in broadcasting faster than anyone I have ever encountered, even though back then he was a far more influential basketball writer at the *Inquirer* than he was a talker. He was born to express strong opinions in a compelling way. That was all it took. The fact that he could also work in some humor made him that much more memorable.

For the final years of Iverson's reign in Philly, Stephen was our go-to reporter and analyst. We shared a connection through our *Inquirer* roots, and he would call regularly, both on and off the air. I wish I had recorded our private calls. The man gets paid more per word than any sports commentator in history, and yet back then he was equally bombastic for free.

I loved the guy then, and I still love him every bit as much today. Most of the other big mouths on network TV now—Colin Cowherd and Skip Bayless, for starters—are just in the business of hot takes. Stephen is wired to think that way. He believes everything he says. He was destined for greatness long before he became such a valued contributor to our show.

My favorite story, I must admit, is one I can barely remember. All I can recall is that, through some odd twist of fate, Stephen happened to be in our studio on 5th Street at the same time when Sixers GM Billy King was also visiting. It's safe to say they were suffering through a rocky patch in their relationship.

The incident happened three years before Iverson's iconic "Practice? We talkin' about practice?" rant, but it was an issue even then in 2003. As was his job, Billy was defending Allen, and Stephen was suggesting the star of the team should be a better leader. The volume of both their voices was growing with each exchange. The looks they gave each other were even more ominous.

Here's how Kenny Justice (who was a witness that day in the studio) remembers the incident:

> *I immediately told Joe [Weachter] I was going into your studio, and I positioned myself between the two of them, just behind them. I was worried; while at that time in my life I was strong and in shape, Billy was huge and Stephen A. was/is crazy.*

> *They kept going back and forth, edging closer and closer to each other.... I've bounced in enough bars to know the signs when a fight was about to break out. I planned on getting between them and pushing them apart or, if I had to, I was going to get between you and them and protect you.*
>
> *Al Morganti was on his own, but he was closest to the door. Remember, that studio was very small. Thankfully a combination of Morganti's snarkiness and a commercial break allowed the men to take a pause and calm down.*

I find it embarrassing and hilarious that Kenny's first reaction was to protect me. If ever there were an indictment of my ability to protect myself—in a fight that didn't involve me, no less—this is it. But the story does have a happy ending. Billy and Stephen are no longer poised to throw fists at each other.

Kenny brought up the incident years later when Billy King had joined us as a guest co-host. Billy immediately recalled the intensity of that discussion, though he doubted it would have ever become physical.

It wasn't long after Stephen's early days with us that he became a superstar at ESPN. He was so loyal to us—and so powerful at ESPN—that he regularly violated the ban against ESPN broadcasters coming on WIP because of a contractual agreement with our rival Philadelphia sports station.

As someone who has known Stephen A. Smith for 25 years, I need to say here that no one deserves his success more than him.

I am positive he made our show better.

I am far less positive that we made him so.

Hollis Thomas shared a bond with John Marzano, though I doubt they ever met. Like John, Hollis lived every day to the fullest. And like John, it was best if you never challenged him physically. Ultimately, a single lapse cost Hollis a terrific career at WIP.

One of the most likeable people I have ever met, Hollis never got angry. Never. He had no love for Joe Banner or Andy Reid—both of whom he claimed lied to him at the end of his career with the Eagles—but he never raised his voice in the five years he was with us. Whenever he wanted to rip his old bosses, he summoned his mom, Caroline.

Caroline visited our show in person one time. Unlike Hollis, she was normal-sized, but her fingernails were not. They curled and swirled for a foot or two beyond her fingers. In front of the mic that day, Caroline was tentative, often answering questions with only one or two words. She reminded me of Ron Reid. Some people change when they appear in front of a microphone.

But when she called, wow. She was a protective mom who supported her kids in a way that was both charming and hilarious. She suffered no fools, including me. You never would have thought that tart-tongued lady from St. Louis was the mom of such a low-key man like Hollis Thomas.

This Day in History was a segment Hollis insisted on doing every day he was in. I didn't find out until years into his time with us why he was so persistent about doing that daily exercise. It was his way of keeping his brain functioning well after 13 years of absorbing punishment as a nose tackle in the NFL. Hollis was worried about CTE before we knew about CTE, the brain disease often triggered by the violence of professional football.

Caroline loved to talk about Hollis' appetite for food, and especially for sweets. Hollis had siblings with a comparably insatiable hunger, and Mom loved to describe what her family could consume at one of her famous dinners. The woman could cook.

At 350 pounds, minimum, Hollis loved to eat even when Caroline wasn't the one working in the kitchen. We found this out one time when we all went out with some callers for a lunch we had auctioned off as part of our annual Radiothon. It was Rhea, Al, Joe Weachter, Joe Conklin, and Hollis Thomas all at a fancy restaurant with some fans who had paid thousands for the privilege.

Hollis ordered an appetizer and a main course (I believe it was a big piece of meat). When his plate arrived, he cut the order exactly in half and wolfed down 50% of the lunch. Then he asked for a doggie bag. I assumed he was on a diet of some kind, until the waiter asked if we wanted dessert. We all said no—until the waiter got to Hollis, who ordered two.

We already knew Hollis had a sweet tooth because his first appearance with us came at a tent show in 2003 when he was out of action for the season with a torn left bicep. He asked to be paid in snack food, so we handed him a shopping bag filled with Tastykakes, Devil Dogs, and Twinkies. (Hollis wasn't fussy where he got his sugar fix.)

The day of that unforgettable lunch, we all sat as Hollis polished off both desserts, then grabbed his doggie bag and left, a smile plastered on his face. Hollis Thomas is bigger than life—and I'm not talking about his physical size.

Hollis left us during the final year of our show because of an incident that was atypical of him. He lost his temper one day. Hollis infuriated Spike Eskin when he unwittingly appeared live on one of our rival morning shows during a trip to England with the Eagles. I argued that Hollis just didn't know how to say no. There was no evil intent.

But then the situation got beyond the point where I could repair it.

He had been affiliated with a travel agency that was in conflict with a new one started by WIP, and Spike informed Hollis that he had to make a choice. During the ensuing disagreement, Hollis suggested that he would settle the dispute with a tire iron.

I tried a few times in that last year to weasel Hollis back in the picture—it's not as if he would ever actually wield a tire iron—but he was banned for good a few months before I retired. I still speak to him regularly. I still feel I owe him something for all of his contributions to our show.

Maybe I'll send him a box of Tastykakes.

Of all the ex-athletes and sports figures who helped us with our shows in that final decade, one actually became a viable candidate to replace me. That was Ross Tucker, a journeyman NFL player for seven seasons who was much more than that in front of a mic. His exposure on our show for over a decade helped earn him the chance to become an analyst for Eagles' preseason games, a job he performed brilliantly.

A graduate of Princeton and a native of Reading, Pennsylvania, Ross does everything well in broadcasting. He's analytical, eloquent, funny, and a compelling speaker. The only reason he should not go further in radio is because he's also very good-looking. TV is his medium, if not movies.

It was inevitable when I started talking about retirement around 2015 that WIP would look into Ross as a permanent replacement for me. When Spike Eskin broached the topic with me, I immediately appointed myself as an intermediary in discussions between WIP and Ross. The move had my full endorsement, though I hadn't decided yet exactly when I would leave.

The discussions got serious enough around 2018 that salary numbers were exchanged. By then, Ross was working for several other media outlets, a star in the making. For a week or two that year, I believed Ross was going to be my replacement, but he couldn't commit to the commute every day from Reading. His priority was to be there when his kids headed off to school.

In my final year, Ross worked two hours every Wednesday through a remote hookup from Reading, and he reminded everyone what a great choice he would have made—not only illuminating everyone on the intricacies of the Eagles, but even singing some Taylor Swift songs along the way. Ross truly can do it all.

There was only one guest we had who was a carryover from my days covering the Eagles at the *Inquirer*. He was Garry Cobb, the linebacker who somehow misplaced the "arry" in his first name after he retired from the NFL. He became just G. Cobb.

When I covered the Eagles, G. was the best quote in the locker room. He said when the team sucked, corrected me when something I wrote was wrong and was absolutely unrivaled in his ability to provide a quote that summed up every game, win or lose. When he jumped over to WIP, he became the most underrated host at the station.

G. made only one mistake in his highly successful career after football. He decided to run for Congress in New Jersey. He never had a chance. There is no place in politics for a truth-teller like Garry Cobb. G. didn't know how to lie. That's why I reveled in his attacks on Jonathan Gannon in that final season, and all of the other honest, informed opinions he shared for the 40 years of my media career.

Through it all, there was one thing G. liked to do more than talk sports. He loved—really, really loved—to eat. Al tells a story of his early days at WIP when he was co-hosting a weekend show with G. at Chickie's and Pete's in Northeast Philadelphia. In the middle of a segment, the waitress appeared with a heaping bowl of King Crab Legs.

They smelled amazing—so much so that G. couldn't wait for the next break. So he reached out for a leg, cracked it right on mic—Crrrrunccccch!—and never paused as he finished his point and then sucked down the sweet crab.

G. Cobb is the coolest person I have ever met.

The most unpredictable of all the ex-athletes who worked with us in that final decade or so was Mitch Williams, the player who handled adversity best in my time at WIP. Mitch threw the fatal home-run ball to Joe Carter that ended the championship quest of the 1993 Phillies, but he was not a goat for long. He answered every question, took every insult, with dignity and humor.

He also did a brilliant job of skewering me, depicting me as a nerdy loudmouth with far less knowledge of the sports I was talking about than I believed. His homespun Texas humor was a winner every day he worked with us.

So why did he disappear in the final year of our show, at a time when he was doing his best work? No, it wasn't because of his scrapes with youth sports leagues, a series of events that unjustly cost him his job at the Major League Baseball Network. It was, simply, politics.

Mitch was a vaccine denier during the COVID pandemic, adamantly refusing to get the shots required by our parent company, Audacy. As a result, Mitch was not allowed into our building. Things did not end well with us because Mitch started sending me propaganda about the vaccine, and I finally asked him to stop emailing me.

But I really don't care about politics. Mitch Williams will always be one of my favorite people.

The worst job to have at WIP, based solely on criticism, was general manager of one of the three top pro teams, so it was more than a little strange when two of the most reviled GMs crossed the line and joined our show as co-hosts. I hated pretty much every GM of every team for 33 years, but I did not feel that way after I worked with Billy King and Rubén Amaro Jr.

Billy was a gentleman in an ungentlemanly city. He was the Sixers GM in the years when the head coach, Larry Brown, had most of the power over personnel. What we know now that we didn't know back in the early 2000s was that Brown was impulsive and emotional, to the point where he would tell Billy to get rid of a player whenever someone did something that set off Larry's hair-trigger temper.

Still, Billy caught the brunt of our daily attacks because Allen Iverson was such an extraordinary talent who suffered constantly from a lack of complementary players.

"Dammit, Billy. Get some better players in here for Allen!"

We must have made that plea 100 times in the Iverson years. Neither Brown nor King could find those players—if indeed Iverson was capable of sharing the ball with anyone. Back then, we assumed Allen just needed his Shaquille O'Neal, like Kobe Bryant had in Los Angeles.

Billy's best story is about what happened when Larry Brown finally left the Sixers. There was a news conference on May 26, 2003, to announce that Brown was leaving after six seasons with the 76ers—for the vagabond coach, a relative eternity. It was emotional for everyone, including Iverson, who had battled the coach for most of those six years.

Then a strange thing happened. Larry kept showing up to work. He was even looking at tape of prospects for the next season. Billy compared it to the *Seinfeld* episode when George Costanza quit his job and then just started showing up the next week as if it never happened. In the end, Billy had to tell Larry Brown to leave before owner Ed Snider changed the locks.

Billy agreed to join our show in 2019 if we made two key concessions. One was that he would leave as soon as he got a good job offer (he'd been ousted as GM of the Brooklyn Nets before we hired him), and the other was that we didn't get too personal. I had painted Billy as a ladies' man when he was GM of the Sixers, but he was happily married now, with kids.

I fulfilled my part of the bargain until one day when I was an innocent victim of a situation that led to Billy taking a brief hiatus. He had told us about how he once did a commercial for a candy bar while he was a student at Duke, and he even got us a copy of the tape.

Now, it's important you know we did not play that old recording without Billy's total approval. The fact that we played it over and over—especially the part that was rather sexually provocative—is probably where we went wrong. But, hey, what did he expect? We were never known for our restraint.

It took us weeks to get Billy back into the studio after his family reacted negatively to that candy-bar commercial, but it was worth it. No one understood the inner workings of the NBA better than Billy, and no one was better at explaining the real story behind roster moves.

In the end, Billy left us when he got a big job as an executive in corporate America.

We were sorry to see him go.

His family was not.

The funniest person who ever contributed to our show—with the possible exception of Joe Conklin—was Dom Irrera, a professional stand-up comedian who left the big city of Philadelphia for the riches of Hollywood, where he prospered both as a comic and as a character actor. He is best known as Ronnie Kaye, the prop comic on *Seinfeld*, and as the chauffeur on *The Big Lebowski*, but he made most of his acting money in animated films and TV shows.

Dom observed no boundaries on stage or on our show. I watched him do a long bit on the death of Pope John Paul II in a live show the week after the pontiff's passing that toed the line perfectly between hilarity and desecration. On WIP, he had no reluctance to ridicule our sponsors.

One time, at our annual Philadelphia International Airport show on the day before Thanksgiving, I had to read a live ad about a famous soup company's newest product, canned steak. Dom couldn't help himself.

"You know," he started, "some people like their steak on a grill or at a ritzy restaurant. I prefer mine in a can. Hmm, mmm."

Dom doesn't know this but we kind of uninvited him to our last couple of airport shows because he was making uncomfortable the many travelers we would stop on the busiest day of the year at the airport. Our interns were instructed to find the most attractive people—preferably women—and we would interview them.

Once Dom got there around 8:00, the tradition often went from funny to awkward. Dom was not above asking a young couple when they first slept together, or whether a hot young woman had ever tried an older man (implying himself, of course). I happen to love awkward humor, but I was outvoted. Instead, Dom would come in the Tuesday of Thanksgiving week. We never told him why.

I'm pretty sure Dom won't read this book.

The most successful person who ever appeared regularly on our show was best-selling author Mitch Albom. Since he penned the iconic *Tuesdays with Morrie* in 1997, everything Mitch wrote has topped the best-seller lists, fiction or non-fiction. Though he grew up right over the bridge in South Jersey, Mitch became a superstar in Detroit, where he had a phenomenally popular sports column and a terrific sports-talk show. He was also a regular contributor on ESPN's *The Sports Reporters.*

In other words, Mitch did everything I did, only much, much better.

Also unlike me, Mitch decided early on to share his success by getting behind countless charitable efforts, and that's what led me to join him in 2009 at a religious benefit in Philly called Have a Little Faith. Appearing with me would be Bob Costas and Tony Bennett. (Okay, I was appearing as a tiny footnote to those big stars.)

To generate sales for the event, I even made a lame attempt at singing Bennett's signature song, "I Left My Heart in San Francisco," on the show that morning. It was predictably hideous.

If I recall this correctly, I was doing Mitch a big favor appearing and promoting his event, but that didn't stop the famous author from dragging me out onstage, and then having Tony Bennett himself appear right there, live, to listen to a tape of my rendition that morning.

I was mortified, of course.

What's worst, I'm pretty sure Tony genuinely felt insulted by my version of his song.

I don't not recall ever agreeing to another charity appearance after that night.

Thanks, Mitch.

I apologize to all the other contributors I didn't get to in this chapter. Sorry. Thirty-three years is a very long time, and my memory is fading quickly. But thanks. You know who you are.

The best way to end is with a nod to two of the best sportswriters in Philadelphia history, both of whom made a seamless transition to the broadcast media and to our show—namely, Ray Didinger and Stan Hochman.

When we were all writers on the Philadelphia sports pages, I was in awe of how beautifully crafted every column by Ray or Stan was—words perfectly selected to describe the same event I was laboring to recreate. Ray took hours to pound out a column, often finding himself alone in press boxes all across America. Stan needed less time but was no less eloquent.

Ray's memoir, *Finished Business,* is the model for this book, believe it or not. I'm certain I'm going to finish a distant second to him again.

Listeners to our show actually know Ray better both as an Eagles analyst on the postgame Comcast SportsNet and NBC Sports Philadelphia regional networks, and on our shows every Monday and Thursday.

Ray spoke the language of Eagles fans better than anyone. His formula was simple. Tell the Eagles to run the ball, blitz the quarterback, and do it all in honor of the early days of the franchise. He even wrote a play called *Tommy and Me* about his first sports hero, Eagles wide receiver Tommy McDonald. Ray didn't just write *The Eagles' Encyclopedia.* He *was* the Eagles' encyclopedia.

My favorite Ray Didinger story came from Ray himself—much to his own regret. He was a young writer for the *Daily News* covering a big boxing match when he ran into supermodel Christie Brinkley. (He did not include this story in his own memoir, so I'm stealing it.) Ray and Christie were both single at the time, and both were in their physical primes. It was a perfect match.

Things were going so well with Ray and Christie that she suggested—I repeat, Christie Brinkley suggested!—that they continue their conversation at lunch. As Ray told the story, he paused for a moment and then declined, saying he needed to write a story and didn't have time.

Now the story has a happy ending, I guess. Ray got married and has remained so with a wonderful woman he met at the newspaper, and Christie got married, too (several times, in fact).

But still....

Who says no to a date with Christie Brinkley?

Before he joined our show as the Grand Imperial Poobah of Philadelphia Sports, Stan had a spectacular media career that included his extraordinary column, a delightful biography of baseball clown Max Patkin, and regular stints as a TV sports anchor and a food critic. He was great at everything he did.

So it wasn't exactly a brainstorm when I asked him one day as he approached 80 years old—and still going strong—if he would like to serve as a judge on the *WIP Morning Show*.

"What do you mean, a judge?" he asked.

"We fight all week," I answered. "I need you to declare who won."

I promised to send him a list of all the debates we would have the first three days of every week, and he would appear on Thursday at 8:00 AM to review, with his soaring wit, the arguments and declare the winner.

He quickly agreed, and then—after a few weeks of invaluable contributions—he decided to ask for some money. We had never thought of that. Our sales people quickly found a sponsor, and Stan was now a paid (not much) expert on our show.

One of the greatest compliments I ever got was when Stan told me I gave his career a third act—after newspapers and TV. I laughed. I gave him nothing. He provided to our show an infusion of much-needed class, and what we call in radio "appointment listening." People made sure they had our show on every Thursday at 8:00 to hear The Grand Poobah.

Stan's amazing wife, Gloria—he also had a perfect marriage—recalls the last appearance her husband ever made on WIP. It was classic Stan, skewering idiots with wit and compassion. She said I ended the conversation by telling him I loved him.

I had no inkling that Stan's gravelly voice would never be heard by our listeners again. He suffered an attack of pancreatitis soon after that call, landed in a hospital, and lost a courageous battle for his life a month later.

Gloria told me Stan consoled her right to the end. She was crying one time in his final moments, and he told her to dry her tears.

"We had a wonderful life," he said.

Indeed they did. We are all so lucky Stan Hochman shared it with us.

Chapter 18

Final Rulings on the Big Debates

In the spirit of The Grand Poobah, it's only right that we declare the winners and losers in the biggest debates during our 33-year history. After all, the *WIP Morning Show* was known more for its disputes than anything else. It's about time we settled them, don't you think?

Now, in a perfect world, Stan Hochman would still be here to render final verdicts, but in his glaring absence, I will attempt to channel the Poobah and provide the necessary closure. At the risk of leaving out lots of knock-down-drag-out disputes, here are the some of the biggest arguments we had over more than three decades, plus a topic we debated only off the air.

Andy Reid vs. Doug Pederson

Maybe it's my own obsession with Reid, but this debate overwhelmed the last half-decade of our show. Even now, it seems incredibly stupid to me. Pederson won one Super Bowl in five years. Reid won none over 14 years with the Eagles. The fact that Reid receives so much support in this argument is insane to me.

This analysis goes way beyond the numbers. As stated earlier (more than once) Reid lapsed into robot mode whenever any important questions came up. He gave lots of lip service to the fans, but he offered them nothing when it mattered. Also, Reid went on to win two Super Bowls with Kansas City (thanks to the coach's savior, Patrick Mahomes), but his work elsewhere should not be a factor in this debate.

Meanwhile, Doug Pederson was the most honest, and honorable, Eagles coach, by far, in the too-short five seasons he coached the team. I told him when we had him back in my final year, after he had signed to coach Jacksonville, that he was the best coach I ever talked to after games because he actually answered my questions.

My favorite story about Doug's honesty came after a perplexing tie against Cincinnati on September 27, 2020. Known as a gambler, Doug was totally out of character when he punted with a few seconds left in overtime, ensuring the tie. I asked him the next day why he didn't try to win the game.

"Looking back on it, I would have probably gone the other way and maybe taken a shot down the field and put the ball up in the air," he said. "Looking back on it, with clearer eyes this morning, a lot of things could have happened—DPI (defensive pass interference), illegal contact, could have been an offensive holding, could have been a sack. There's a lot of things that go into those plays. That's probably what I would do."

I was delighted by Doug's candor. Al Morganti was mortified.

After the interview, Al ripped into Doug for sharing his innermost thoughts. Clearly, after 40-some years, Al was still struggling with his role as a media member. Our job was to get the truth for the fans, and Pederson handed it to us right there that day, live, on WIP.

By no means was that answer as shocking as Al made it seem. Doug was honest in good times and bad. He never pointed the finger at individual players, but he got the message across. For example, later in that same 2020 season, the coach said if he ever benched Wentz in favor of rookie

Jalen Hurts: "I think you're sending the wrong message to your team. The season is over."

Hurts wasn't ready, he was saying, and Wentz would check out mentally if he were ever benched. Without saying it, Doug was telling fans that Carson couldn't handle being a No. 2. Pederson was right, of course, as later developments confirmed. (Two weeks later, Wentz was pulled from the starting lineup, never to return there as an Eagle.)

But the real question is, how would Reid have handled the same situation? I have the answer. He wouldn't have. He would have said he needed to do a better job, that Carson was a fine young man and an excellent quarterback, and the *sun will come up tomorrow,* blah, blah, blah.

So let's see. The bottom line is, Doug was a winner who respected the fans unfailingly for five years. Reid was a loser and a liar.

Winner: Doug Pederson.

Should Pete Rose Get Inducted into the Hall of Fame?

Although I am not an objective observer in this three-decade debate, I am prepared to render a surprising verdict.

In my first week at the *Inquirer,* while my knees were still knocking in fright at the challenge of the big city, I was assigned to do an in-depth interview with Pete Rose for a newspaper supplement that would come out the morning after Rose got his 3,000th hit. The one problem was, no one told Rose I would be asking for a half hour of his time before a game. I had to show up and make the request. Good luck, kid.

When I got to Veterans Stadium very early, around 4:00 for a 7:00 PM game, Pete was there in the locker room, a few years away from being crowned the most prolific hitter in baseball history. I tentatively approached him, explaining not just my assignment but my obvious discomfort. Rose could not have been more accommodating.

We went out to the dugout, and he sat with me for at least 45 minutes talking about his favorite topic—hitting. This was not pulling teeth like with Larry Bird; this was a seamless, lively discussion from the master of the base hit.

Pete was great that night. I was not as great, but good enough to show I could do the job. I felt a debt to him that would expire a few years later when I was assigned to interview Pete again, under far less glorious circumstances. I was part of the *Inquirer* coverage of allegations that Rose had been betting on baseball—a capital offense.

No one actually got to talk to Pete then; we were all stuck with his lawyers. In the end, he was banned from the game that was his life, because of unassailable proof that he had indeed violated the cardinal rule of baseball. All these years later, Pete is still trying to get back into the game, and finally gain induction into the Hall of Fame, where his statistics would normally be a free ticket to immortality.

I would love to repay the favor Pete did for me that first week at the *Inquirer*, but his conduct since then has made it impossible to look the other way—even as baseball has entered into a new era of acceptance for sports betting. Pete's attitude has aged no better than his reputation. He proved this sad fact in his visit back to Philadelphia to celebrate the 40th anniversary of the 1980 championship was appalling.

Reports had surfaced of a relationship Rose had with a "14 or 15-year-old" girl in the 1970s when he was a member of Cincinnati's Big Red Machine, and he was asked by a woman reporter about it during his one-day dispensation to appear with his Phillies teammates in 2020.

"No, I'm not here to talk about that," he told Alex Coffey of the *Inquirer*. "Sorry about that. It was 55 years ago, babe."

There an old saying attributed to Abraham Lincoln that Pete should have followed in the last 30 or so years of his life: "It's better to keep your mouth shut and appear stupid than to speak and remove all doubt."

Sorry, Pete. No Hall for you.

Michael Jordan vs. Wilt Chamberlain

In my three-and-a-half decades on the radio, I doubt there was a single time when I missed the chance to correct our uninformed younger callers when they referred to Jordan as the greatest basketball player of all time. I would simply refer them to the NBA Record Book, where Chamberlain still owns most of the individual milestones a quarter-century after his death.

Earlier in this book I described how spellbound I was when I watched him play in Providence one night and then met him years later in Philly. Wilt actually took this debate less seriously than I did. I fully understand Jordan has the benefit of recency bias, and the tough-to-beat argument that he won six NBA titles to Wilt's two.

Because I rate players on honesty and accessibility, Jordan comes up short there. He was shy early in his basketball career, and then quickly became entitled and discriminating in whom he talked to and when. He had his own media bobo in Ahmad Rashad (like Aaron Rodgers these days with Pat McAfee), and he was, basically, a jerk the minute he reached the pinnacle of his profession.

On the other hand, Wilt was moody but engaging. He made his own rules, but he never excluded the public. Heck, after his 100-point game in Hershey, Wilt returned to his home in New York City—that's right, he lived 100 miles away from Philadelphia when he was still a Warrior and a Sixer—in the back of a limousine with some female fans. He was fun. He was entertaining. He was Wilt.

In the end, I'm ready to concede a debate that raged on our show for all of our time there. Wilt was the greatest individual basketball player ever—the numbers don't lie—but he was not the greatest team player of all time. I cannot be a hypocrite now. Winning is the most important thing.

The greatest NBA team player of all time was...Bill Russell.

He won 11 championships, almost double Jordan's total.

Al was right. The guy with the most rings wins the debate.

The answer to the debate, Jordan versus Chamberlain, is Bill Russell.

Is Hockey a Major Sport in Philadelphia?

Since our show employed two of the top hockey analysts in North America, it was inevitable that we would have to address this issue. It is more than a little ironic that Al Morganti and Keith Jones never pressed to discuss the sport they knew best, and loved more than football, baseball, or basketball.

Earlier, I mentioned that we abandoned hockey after 1997 because our ratings took a dive during the Stanley Cup Finals, but the issue was more complicated than that. For example, what happens if a member of our show is suddenly honored by the Hockey Hall of Fame? What do you do then? Is it still a major story if the sport is minor?

The answer is yes. Al's honor was really the biggest prize any of us won in our time at WIP, and we ignored our unofficial restrictions on hockey talk during that time. We even thought we could bamboozle Al—the consummate prankster—with a little trick of our own. We got word from Frank Seravalli, a longtime hockey insider who had a lot to do with Al's selection, that he would like to announce the honor live on our show.

He said Al had no idea, so we could get a rare chance to see some genuine emotion from the least emotional man in North America. As the hour drew near, Rhea Hughes and I were cautiously optimistic that Frank could spring the news on Al. We were delusional. Al got a text about an hour before the announcement. The word had leaked in Canada.

But the story of Al's honor is a perfect example of how we handled hockey in the last 20 or so years of the *WIP Morning Show*. If there were a big story that transcended the sport, yes. When former Flyer Jeremy Roenick was fired by NBC after making some inappropriate remarks about the female host of his pre-game show, we covered it. When goaltender Carter Hart was out a month with an injury, it was mentioned only in the sports updates.

The only time I ever got any complaints about this demotion of hockey as a major sport was in email. And those people, for the most part, didn't fight back. They knew the Flyers had become a patsy in the NHL since the death of owner Ed Snider, and they accepted their fate.

If the Flyers ever have a chance to win another Stanley Cup, will they reemerge as a major sport at WIP?

I doubt it. Actually, soccer has a better chance now than hockey. If a show employs two hockey experts and it still never talks about hockey, it's safe to say the time has passed from those glory years of the 1970s.

Was the Process a Success?

Sam Hinkie was not the inventor of basketball. He just thought he was. When the Houston Rockets stat nerd was hired as GM of the 76ers, fans were warned that they were about to embark on an experiment that could change the world of sports. Their team would fail spectacularly, on purpose, in order to succeed with equal grandeur at an appropriate time in the near future.

The Sixers would tank—try to lose to improve their draft position, to be in an optimum position to draft the very best college players, and to improve their "optionality," one of Hinkie's favorite words.

Hinkie served as the assistant GM in Houston with GM Daryl Morey, and he was like no other sports executive, past, present, or future. He was equal parts hermit and professor. He poked his head out about as often as the rodent on Groundhog Day, and when he did, he spoke a language contoured specifically for the Dork Patrol.

Oh, yeah. He was also gutless. When a huge controversy erupted after top pick Jahlil Okafor was caught on tape in Boston during a street fight, Hinkie accompanied the team for a game at Madison Square Garden but refused to address any questions about a major crisis on the team. Their record at the time, by the way, was 1–18.

In the first three years under Hinkie, the Sixers were extremely successful at only one thing—losing. They were 47–199 under a clueless head coach, Brett Brown, and the largely invisible Hinkie.

Still, Hinkie had his admirers. And it was our misfortune at WIP that one of them was our boss, program director Spike Eskin. Spike formed a club of unconventional Philadelphia sports fans named "The Rights to Ricky Sánchez"—a reference to a scrub who was part of an obscure Sixer transaction back in 2012. (Yes, they were nerds.)

Spike's group represented an army of Hinkie's minions who saw him as the supreme being of the NBA, a sage who was both ahead of his time and behind the eight ball. If only dummies like us could see the wisdom of Hinkie's plan. Unfortunately, one of the people who was not impressed was the commissioner himself, Adam Silver, who pressured the Sixers into firing Hinkie near the end of the third season of tanking.

All this decision did, of course, was turn Sam Hinkie into a martyr. The fallen GM then added to his curious allure by releasing a 13-page manifesto that used up all the words he had stockpiled by keeping quiet for three seasons. The manifesto precisely mirrored Hinkie and his followers. It was somehow both delusional and indecipherable.

All of these years later, the discussion about The Process—a term popularized by the one truly great player the Sixers got by tanking, Joel Embiid—rages on in Philadelphia, kept alive by the Hinkie cult.

Here's the final verdict on The Process: The purpose of all that tanking was to win a championship, not finish in the middle of the NBA pack every year. Since the Sixers returned to their winning ways in 2018, they have been decidedly middle of the pack. At press time for this book, they have made it to zero Eastern Conference Finals. Zero. They won nothing after sacrificing season after season for Hinkie's plan.

Was The Process a success?

In honor of Hinkie, I refuse to answer that question.

Okay, I will.

No, no, no.

Joe Paterno: Legend or Criminal?

A decade after his death, Joe Paterno is still a god to some people and a disgrace to others. You can place me securely into the latter category.

What has always amazed me about the horrors that went on at Penn State is the idea that somehow the most thorough and dedicated coach in college football history could have missed for 30 years the molestation of children right under his nose—by his longest-standing and most trusty assistant, Jerry Sandusky, no less.

I know they still call it Happy Valley, but please. Joe Paterno employed a monster for three decades, and he never thought anything suspicious was going on? And here's another obvious question: When the news of the Sandusky's nightmare finally exploded into America's consciousness, was Paterno more interested in suppressing the truth or dealing with it?

After the story broke in 2011, I lost my mind for close to a month dealing on the air with the Penn State apologists. Part of my response was tied to the one time I met Paterno myself, during a ceremony at the Governor's Residence. (Yes, I was invited by Ed Rendell. Who else?) Ed was honoring Paterno and Franco Harris of the Pittsburgh Steelers, and I was there to take in the ceremony.

Upon my introduction to Paterno, he immediately made mention of our ethnic connection. The conversation went downhill quickly after that. He came across to me a miserable old grump, complaining about everything from the food to the weather to sports-talk radio. I have met a lot of people with charisma, starting with Muhammad Ali. Paterno had none, at least not that night. He carried himself with an air of stifling entitlement.

So, I must admit I was no devotee of Paterno even before the Sandusky scandal obliterated his legacy. That's one reason I eagerly booked Joe's son, Jay, when someone from Penn State asked that we present the other side of the Paterno story. I knew I could never do it myself.

When Jay called in, I felt only sympathy. He was going to stand behind his father regardless of the absurdity of the defense. I'm pretty sure I would have done the same thing for my own father. But a son's blind loyalty doesn't give back the lives of all of those children who were sexually assaulted under Paterno's watch.

I pushed back a little when Jay was making comments that conflicted with the facts, but mostly I just gave him a chance to speak uninterrupted about how much his loved his father.

Joe Paterno knew what Jerry Sandusky was doing to all those children for all those years. I will always believe that. To preserve his reputation and that of Penn State, the coach remained criminally quiet.

The verdict on Joe Paterno is in.

Guilty.

Bill Conlin

The greatest baseball writer of all time (Can I still even say that?) became persona non grata both in Philadelphia and on WIP the moment he resigned in 2011 from the *Daily News* after allegations that he had sexually abused three women and a man back in the 1970s, with one of the accusers being Conlin's own niece.

How should a city that revered Conlin for his bold and enthralling coverage of the Phillies over 46 years react to a sordid ending like that?

We didn't. His name was barely ever mentioned in my last 12 years at WIP. There were no meetings that preceded this stand, but I'm sure each host debated with himself how to react on those rare occasions when Conlin's name came up on the air. It may be the only example in my long tenure at WIP of avoiding a topic that was being discussed in hushed tones all over the city. My job was to talk about that stuff.

Still, the accusations were so horrific, so outrageous, that it was best not to go near them. I did try a few times, to no avail. Having nothing good to say about someone or something had never stopped me before, but I had no idea how to approach the topic. As a result, at least on our show, the name "Conlin" became the eighth obscenity you could never say. (The other seven were provided by legendary comic George Carlin in his famous bit.)

Before Bill Conlin's name became a dirty word, he had an extensive history with our show. The weirdest twist was that he was our unofficial weatherman for a couple of years, calling in with forecasts based on his independent analysis of the radar readings. He did it all with aplomb, as was his nature. He even told me one time off the air how much he appreciated the forum for his other big interest, meteorology.

Of course, with Bill, there was always another shoe about to drop. When Gail and I were pitted against Bill and his wife, Irma, on Comcast SportsNet's version of *The Newlywed Game*—hosted by the actual star of the legendary game show, Bob Eubanks—Conlin publicly accused us of cheating. (Gail would never cheat.)

And when it came to sports, Bill was not shy about heckling us for our inferior knowledge. He had become a columnist after decades of covering baseball, and he was as acerbic as ever back then.

But after his abrupt exit because of the allegations, and then his death three years later in 2014, people have been wrestling with how to feel about him now. (I know I have.) How should a city that loved Bill Conlin's work remember him? And what should the Baseball Hall of Fame—which honored Conlin in 2009—do about a man who never offered an aggressive defense against those horrific accusations?

I was as big an admirer of Bill Conlin as anyone when he was the embodiment of a Philadelphia sportswriter—knowledgeable, opinionated, and often downright antagonistic. But it's impossible to ignore the other side of what happened in his mysterious life.

Bill Conlin's name should not be in the Hall of Fame, nor on the lips of Philadelphia sports fans ever again. He sacrificed the privilege. That's my final ruling.

Chapter 19

The Holy Grail

It's so easy looking back to see the early signs of my slow decline as I reached beyond my sixties, but back then I assumed I could do the job forever. Then came the first warning sign, one that still makes me shudder a decade later. For a few hours in late January 2013, my brain stopped working.

It was one week before Wing Bowl 21, and I was feeling fine as I pulled my yellow legal pad out from my bag and began jotting down the script for the show that morning at Borgata Hotel Casino and Spa in Atlantic City. I wrote just a couple of lines before an uneasy feeling washed over me. Why couldn't I remember names?

I put my pen down for a minute or so, and my mind was blanker than the pad. I couldn't recall who the No. 1 starting wide receiver on the Eagles was (DeSean Jackson). Soon, I couldn't remember anything. What happened next is an account developed exclusively through others who were there. The next three hours remain missing to me.

When I realized I couldn't do a show if I couldn't remember anything, I told our engineer who had just finished setting up the equipment for our show, David Uram, that I was having a major problem thinking clearly. He looked shocked, but his first thought was to call for medical help. Maybe I was having a stroke.

I either didn't hear him or just didn't compute what he was trying to tell me, so I very matter-of-factly gathered up my belongings and walked calmly toward the exit of the Borgata. This was a major sign I was in trouble because my usual reaction in a crisis like that would have been to panic.

Before anyone could stop me, I was in my car and on the Atlantic City Expressway. Then the situation got downright bizarre. In the course of those few minutes, Dave had called Rhea Hughes, who was still on route to the casino. (I may have even passed her on my way home.) Gail tried repeatedly to contact me, but I wasn't picking up. Instead, my clouded brain decided to take a different route back to our home in Medford, New Jersey.

I veered off the expressway at Exit 28, drove through downtown Hammonton, and then jumped onto Route 206 and headed on the back-roads that I rarely used to get home. If my condition worsened on that ride, the chances of getting help would have been much smaller than if I had stayed on the main roads.

What was I thinking?

I wasn't.

Gail was waiting for me when I pulled up our driveway in Medford, and she led me by the hand directly to her car and began the drive to Virtua Hospital in nearby Voorhees. She said she tried to talk to me along the way, but I was not present mentally.

When we got to the hospital, I was rushed right into an area inside the emergency room, and a male nurse started asking me sports questions to determine how well my brain was functioning. I flunked. When he tried to get me to remember DeSean's name, I still drew a blank. Al Morganti arrived at the hospital later that morning, thinking (I'm pretty sure) that it was hard to believe I could be even more clueless than usual.

Gail said Al took over at that point, grilling the medical people about what I had just experienced. He was a lot better in crises than I was.

The only way to find out what was going on inside my skull would be to give me an MRI. Now Gail and I had an understanding that if any doctor ever proposed an MRI, she was to inform the authorities that I would prefer to die. (I have serious claustrophobia.)

She did not follow my instructions. In fact, when the hospital staff said they would take me down to the MRI machine to show me how safe it was—at this point I had regained my faculties enough to know I was not getting into that tube—she stopped them.

"No," she said. "Drug him first."

Despite her lack of medical training, Gail stood there while the nurse handed me four Xanax tablets and watched me swallow them before rolling me on my gurney down to the MRI lab. By the time we had arrived, I no longer feared the tube. At that point, I would have shrugged at a zombie apocalypse.

Still, one of the nurses stood right next to me as I rolled into the tube, blindfolded and drugged to the max. I had no recollection of how long I was in there. I just know the MRI was no problem for me. (I still have no intention of ever getting in that tube again.)

Hours later, when my brain was back to normal, the hospital released me with no firm diagnosis. It was definitely "an episode," but they couldn't explain why it happened or what it meant. The next week I underwent an entire day of testing. The doctors at Pennsylvania Hospital studied my brain extensively. They found nothing. (Ha, ha. I couldn't resist.)

In the end, the head doctor told me what I had was fairly common—I can't remember what he called it—and assured me that it would never happen again. (He may have said that so I wouldn't live the rest of my life in fear.) The best guess was it was a reaction to the stress of having to do Wing Bowl 21 the next Friday.

I still have no recollection of those first few hours, and I have no idea why I literally lost my mind that day. All I know is, I was actually relieved when the Eagles released DeSean Jackson at the end of that season.

Now I would never have to remember his name again.

Of course, six years later, the Eagles brought him back.

Then I figured out a way to remember his name. I ripped him every day in 2019.

Once you have a bout with clinical depression, you learn very quickly that it could come back again at any time. For me, it took 20 years.

In April of 2015, 15 months after my brain episode, I stopped sleeping. There was no easy explanation for why this happened. My best guess is, I had just turned 64, and I was dealing directly, for the first time, with the end of my career and, yes, even the end of my life. All I knew back then was, I was helpless. Doing a show at 44 while battling insomnia is a lot more manageable than at 64.

I batted back tears in the office of my family doctor—the same one who pulled me through my 1995 crisis—as she reluctantly let me try a sleep aid again, this time Lunesta. It was a miracle drug to me, despite the inescapable threat that I would get hooked. I got through the next eight years with the drug, never using it other than on work nights. It did everything Ambien didn't—no nightmares, no deeper despair, no side effects at all, really.

There was one other development in my early sixties—a secret I kept until now. I tried marijuana. Yes, nerdy old me decided it was time to fire up a blunt when Gail and I took a vacation to Los Angeles, where medical marijuana was legal. We strolled down the boardwalk in Venice Beach, drawn in by sign after sign urging us to get medical clearance (Within minutes! Everybody qualifies!).

Tentatively at first, we ventured down a dark, sweaty alley behind a tattoo shop, filled out the initial paperwork, and then snaked back up into a tiny waiting room, where we sat for a few minutes with a group of other aspiring potheads.

When our names were called—I kept wondering if a listener might discover our secret when the receptionist yelled out "Cataldi!"—and then we proceeded into an even tinier room where sat the oldest man we had ever seen. He was a doctor—long retired, we assumed. He was wearing a purple baseball cap and a bristly mustache and glasses whose lenses were somehow even thicker than the thatch above his lip.

He asked Gail a bunch of questions, to which she gave the shortest answers possible. Then he started with me. It didn't appear that he could actually hear our answers because he punctuated every response with a sharp, "Heh?"

"Have you had any recent operations?"

"Why, yes, Doctor. Last year I got a colon resection because of a bout with diverticulitis. It all started..."

"Heh?"

I felt a hard thump against my left shin. Gail's expression said it all: *TMI! He doesn't care. Remember? Everybody qualifies?*

The doctor listened to my lungs, right through my t-shirt ("Heh?"), proclaimed both of us worthy of a medical-marijuana license ("Heh?"), and sent us on our way to a nearby dispensary ("Heh?"). Less than an hour after we began the adventure, we had in our possession a few joints and a couple of edibles.

For the first time in my life, I was about to be cool.

The problem in L.A.—now, all pot is legal there—is that acquiring marijuana and smoking it are two different challenges, especially for visitors who are checked into a hotel, where all smoking is prohibited. With my new laid-back persona (even before my first toke), I told Gail I would figure it all out. Later that night, there we were at a construction site adjacent to a strip club a block from our hotel.

Gail lit the blunt and took a deep drag. (Something tells me this wasn't her first time.) Then it was my turn. Since I had never even tried a cigarette, I had no idea how to smoke. I drew in briefly and started choking like I had done with Spike Eskin. At least I didn't require a Heimlich maneuver this time.

Eventually, I got the hang of it and went on a glorious trip to marijuana heaven. It was the most relaxed I had ever felt. I liked the feeling so much, I decided to try the edibles next. I ate an entire cookie. Gail tackled a brownie. This was stupid. Edibles take a lot longer to hit, and we were already high from smoking.

That was the last time I ever tried an edible. I kept seeing a fist punching through the wall above our bed, bugs crawling around us, and, at its worst, I felt the whole room shaking.

When the pot finally began to loosen its grip, we got some sleep. The next morning, I snapped the remote on and got an L.A. news station. At 9:09 PM the previous night, a 5.1-magnitude earthquake had hit the L.A. area.

If ever there was a sign never to try pot again, this was it.

We immediately stopped edibles.

But I have smoked pot pretty much every week since then.

It did not make me any cooler, however.

I can pin down precisely the first time I openly spoke about retirement. It happened in October of 2015 on a trip with Gail to New York arranged by my trusty friend at WIP, marketing director Cindy Webster. Back then, Jimmy Fallon was dominating the late-night TV landscape on the *Tonight Show*, and Cindy managed to get us three tickets through the keyboard player on The Roots, Kamal Gray.

For a TV aficionado like me, it was a wonderful day. We stood in the hallway backstage and watched a horde of crazy people dressed as hobgoblins who were appearing across the hall on the *Meredith Vieira*

Show. Then Kamal showed up, got us into great seats, and treated us to a mini-concert by the Roots before the show. (If you haven't seen them in person, you need to very soon. They are spectacular.)

When I heard that a special guest on the show that night was supermodel Kate Upton, I briefly sidled over to her dressing-room door, hoping for an up-close look. Gail and Cindy finally coaxed me back to my seat, convincing me that stalking was not a good way to pay back Kamal for the tickets.

I did get to bump fists with Jimmy when he raced up the aisle, and we had a rollicking good time. (Except I lost my wallet—and medical marijuana card—in what I claim was a pickpocketing incident on the subway. Gail does not agree.)

We were waiting in a small, disgusting sandwich shop inside Penn Station when I told Cindy I thought these were my final years at WIP.

The brief return of my sleep problems was the first sign. The second was, I was tired after 25 years of the rigors of morning radio. And third, we had the gala Wing Bowl 25 coming up in 19 months.

"What if I did what Brookie did? What if I said nothing and then just announced that I was retiring at the end of Wing Bowl 25 in January of 2017?"

"Seriously?" Cindy said.

"You're going to keep a secret for 19 months?" Gail added skeptically.

It was just a passing thought back then. Gail was right about me keeping the secret. From that point until I did retire eight years later, I talked about it so much, on and off the air, that there was zero chance I would ever be able to replicate Tom Brookshier's classy departure.

But I was thinking about it.

If I followed through with that plan, I would have missed the best year of my life at WIP.

At the beginning of the 2017 NFL season, there was no reason to believe the Eagles were going to do anything special, and certainly nothing as improbable as winning their first Super Bowl. Coach Doug Pederson and quarterback Carson Wentz were both starting only their second seasons with the Eagles, and both carried with them many legitimate concerns.

Wentz had taken over the starting job during a 7–9 season, but he was a long way from a finished product, and the injury worry that he carried with him at North Dakota State was still there. Pederson was widely rated as the seventh-best choice among the seven new NFL coaches in 2016, and he had done nothing at that point to win over the doubters.

No one could have guessed that Wentz would play like a Pro Bowler from the first game, throwing dimes through tight windows, scrambling with abandon for big first downs and leading with a confidence well beyond his 25 years. And no one could have imagined that Pederson would become Big Balls Doug, redefining when teams should go for it on fourth down.

Something amazing happened after the Birds split their first two games that season. They didn't lose again for two months, winning nine straight behind Wentz and a brilliant roster of veterans and young players who adopted the underdog theme of their blue-collar city. Only in Philadelphia can two offensive linemen become folk heroes the way center Jason Kelce and right tackle Lane Johnson did that year.

Then came a tough loss in Seattle, that win that felt like a loss in L.A. when Wentz tore his ACL, and the feeling of inevitable defeat that hung over a city that can't have nice things. The Eagles hadn't won a championship since 1960, and 2017 wasn't going to be their year, either.

Doug Pederson was under contract to come on our show the morning after every game, and he was the first voice to rise above the incessant whining after Wentz's injury. Nick Foles was an able backup, the coach assured everyone. This season was not over.

Yeah, sure. It was the familiar lament of a loser, a rationalization heard often during the 57-year championship drought.

The Eagles managed to squeeze out two unimpressive victories before Pederson rested the starters in a regular-season 6–0 loss to Dallas, finishing with a 13–3 record and the home-field advantage for the playoffs.

Fans looking back on those weeks before the playoffs have rewritten the narrative. What I remember was a city bracing for another disappointment. Other than the usual few optimists, most fans didn't really believe in the team when the playoffs began.

The precise moment when fate appeared to switch to Philly's side came near the end of the divisional playoff game against Atlanta—favored by 2.5 points despite playing on the road—when a fourth-down throw to the great wide receiver Julio Jones appeared to zip right between his sure hands in the corner of the end zone. He had been wrestling with cornerback Jalen Mills, actually slipped twice while Matt Ryan bought time in the pocket, and then was in perfect position to catch the ball with 58 seconds left. The Eagles won, 15–10.

How did Julio Jones miss it?

Was this THE YEAR after all?

The documentary *Maybe This Year* on Amazon documents better than I ever could in these pages the emotion in Philadelphia right after that ball eluded Jones. Fans exploded in living rooms throughout the Delaware Valley, jumping and screaming and crying. One man whose father was dying of cancer said the win was "better than any chemo treatment he's getting."

It takes very little to encourage Philadelphia sports fans, and that win detonated a surge of optimism that had been missing since Wentz's injury. Before the next game against Minnesota, one man in the documentary pulled down his pants, turned to the camera, and announced, "The Vikings can kiss my ass."

That flicker of a hope before the Atlanta win became a five-alarm fire when Foles led the Eagles to a 38–7 slaughter of Minnesota, who had received a reprieve the previous week after New Orleans safety Marcus Williams whiffed on a tackle that gave Stefon Diggs a 61-yard touchdown on the final play of the game.

The Vikings, who were favored by three to beat the Eagles, were supposed to be the miracle team of 2017. That play was called "The Minneapolis Miracle." Heck, the Super Bowl was in Minneapolis in two weeks. How could the Eagles, minus Wentz, be going there instead of the Vikings?

Still, the greatest quarterback in history, Tom Brady, was waiting for the Eagles, as was the NFL's greatest coach, Bill Belichick. This matchup was worse than the one in 2005, when Brady and Belichick were much younger and when the Eagles starting QB, Donovan McNabb, was healthy.

The sense of anticipation for that Super Bowl was like nothing I had ever encountered before at WIP, or since. This time, nothing could temper the emotion—not Brady, not Belichick, and not even the 4.5 points the Patriots were favored by. Though by then I was preaching a gospel of hope, deep down I couldn't stop thinking we were all getting set up for one more crushing blow.

In the documentary, a young man talked about how, on his death bed, his father promised him this was the year the Eagles would win the Super Bowl. That was the theme all week before the big game. Families bonded by their love for the Eagles, including fans who died in pursuit of the Holy Grail. It is unimaginable to me, six years later, to think any city ever craved a victory more than the Philadelphia did that day.

And then they won the greatest Super Bowl of all, 41–33—the game with the most yards, the most points, and the most excitement in Super Bowl history. It ended with a Hail Mary by Brady falling ceremoniously to the ground after a tangle of desperate hands lunged for it.

Eagle Shirley cried. So did Arson Arnie. And so, too, did thousands more. It was not just the greatest victory in Philadelphia sports history, it was also one of the greatest in American history.

The city known for its passionate fans finally received its just reward. For a short time, at least, the sick were healthy again, the depressed euphoric, the poor rich.

It's hard for me to imagine any sports triumph meaning more to a city than Super Bowl LII meant to Philadelphia.

Every street for blocks and blocks was overflowing with jubilant people the night of the win and three days later for a parade that drew at least two million fans. (Mayor Jim Kenney estimated 700,000 were there that day. Obviously, he wasn't one of them. There were 700,000 in a three-block radius just around his office in City Hall.)

What followed the parade was, in my not-very-objective opinion, the greatest rally in sports history, highlighted by the greatest sports speech of all time by Jason Kelce. Dressed proudly in a Mummer's costume replete with a massive white, feathery, bulbous hat and a green, spangly cape over a sparkly purple undercoat, Kelce spoke from the heart about underdogs:

> *Carson Wentz didn't go to a Division I school. Nick Foles don't got it. Corey Clement's too slow. LeGarrette Blount ain't got it anymore. Jay Ajayi can't stay healthy. Torrey Smith can't catch. Nelson Agholor can't catch. Zach Ertz can't block. Brent Celek's too old. Brandon Graham was drafted too high. Vinny Curry ain't got it. Beau Allen can't fit the scheme. Mychal Kendricks can't fit the scheme. Nigel Bradham can't catch. Jalen Mills can't cover. Patrick Robinson can't cover.*
>
> *It's the whole team. The whole team.*

The speech lasted over four minutes, and it covered a lifetime of suffering for Eagles fans. I am happy to report WIP broadcast all of it, uninterrupted. Unlike the Phillies-parade debacle, the station's new management team did not shortchange the listeners or the hosts. It was a normal ad load that day, which was almost as big a miracle as the Super Bowl victory itself.

When I look back on the answered prayer of Super Bowl LII today, I no longer see it as the greatest day in Philadelphia sports history. Because it wasn't just a day. It was a month, maybe two, before the fan base reverted to its cynical ways.

Oh, there was still plenty of the old Philadelphia nastiness. More than a dozen callers advised Tom Brady to kiss their ass, and that was just on our show. Bill Belichick is crusty enough; if he had listened in the weeks after the Eagles won that game, he might have sought the refuge of retirement. As for Patriot owner Robert Kraft, let's just say he's very lucky his adventures in a Florida massage parlor happened a year later.

Did the Holy Grail change Philadelphia? Did winning the biggest game, by our most important team, give fans better perspective—maybe even a kinder, gentler approach?

Not really. But it definitely changed the way I saw the world I had covered for more than half my life.

And it definitely made me feel much more comfortable about planning my exit.

Chapter 20

A Change in Plans

Tom Brookshier died in 2010, but he was still with us in spirit when WIP—and the world—faced a crisis in 2020 like none in our lifetimes, guiding me and my co-hosts through a medical calamity that still defies belief. One of my first lessons on what to do when the sports world shuts down came from Brookie in 1991 during the Gulf War.

When I got to the studios that morning, Tom made it clear that this would not be an ordinary day, not with American troops launching an aerial attack against Iraq called "Operation Desert Storm." Somehow, I had survived two years part-time and my first year with Brookie unscathed by world events that required our acknowledgement on a sports station.

Even though we were in the final stages of an NFL season—the Eagles were long-gone, of course—Tom said we would be a news station at least for the first day of the war. He told stories of his own involvement with the U.S. Air Force from 1954 to '56,, and he welcomed calls from soldiers, past and present, and anyone else feeling a pang of patriotism that day.

There's no way that show should have worked, even with Brookie at the controls. Our primary rival back then, KYW, was designed for a crisis like that, and the news-talk shows were far savvier about the political implications of the situation. But it is still one of the shows I am proudest of, though my own role was minimal.

I used the template of that show many times in the three-plus decades to come. It was a simple formula that worked every time. Make the crisis personal. Get people to humanize the crisis. Ignore the station's format in favor of something far timelier and more engrossing.

The biggest decision in times like this always was when to break format, when to prioritize world events over our secure little world of sports. This led to one of my worst mistakes—at least according to my co-hosts—on September 11, 2001. Long before the planes crashed into the World Trade Center and the Pentagon, we were having a show for the ages. That's my best explanation for what happened next.

The marquee in-studio guest that day was boxing god Sugar Ray Leonard, who was every bit as good a storyteller as he was an athlete. We were spellbound when he described what it was like to see Roberto Durán scream out *"No más!"* during their title fight, or how he felt about one of the most controversial decisions in boxing history, his narrow defeat of Marvin Hagler in 1986.

We felt as if we were in the ring with Leonard for those iconic matches, and I was despondent when the hour was up at 9:00 AM and he had to leave. He presented me with a pair of boxing gloves, and autographed them right there, just before 9:00. He even did something I have rarely seen; he wrote out the date next to his name: September 11, 2001.

Soon after the nine o'clock break, we had our favorite returning guest, Sixers president Pat Croce to talk about Allen Iverson, his team, and expectations for the upcoming season. As usual, Pat was dazzling with his positive energy and his inspiring message when Rhea Hughes saw something on the TV monitor in the newsroom. A plane had flown into one of the towers at the World Trade Center, and smoke was billowing from a gaping hole near the top of the skyscraper.

Within seconds, Rhea started gesturing for me to say goodbye to Pat and go to her. I never put on the monitors in the main studio—I found them distracting—so I ignored her for a few precious minutes, thinking, "What could possibly be better for our show than this interview?"

When Al Morganti went out to see what had happened, he came back into the studio with an alarmed look that sealed the decision. Something more important than the Sixers president was happening. I finally said goodbye. Then Rhea described what she was seeing—maybe a full five minutes after most other stations were into their coverage of the assault on American freedom.

Moments later, we got a call from a then-close friend of our show, Larry Mendte, who was the top anchor at the NBC affiliate in Philadelphia, Channel 10. Before a scandal involving Mendte and his co-host, Alycia Lane, torpedoed his news career, Mendte was a first-rate news person, and he adeptly took us to the end of the show with observations and speculations that were far more factual than we ever could have delivered.

Back then, we often went five or 10 minutes past 10:00 AM, so we were still on the air when the South Tower collapsed. I can still remember the sense of nauseating disbelief we all expressed as we went off the air, wondering what was left of the make-believe sports world that normally occupied our every thought.

It didn't take me long to reflect on what Brookie did with Desert Storm. The sports format would be abandoned until people were ready for it again. The next few days, we were a news show—and not a bad one, if my memory is accurate. We talked to people who knew someone touched by the tragedy, and we launched into a discussion of where sports fits into a world under siege.

After a few days, we started taking calls on sports again, and within a week or so, WIP returned to being a sports station. Brookie's game plan for crises had served us well.

One story I wish I had given more time to was the death of my first partner at WIP, Tom Brookshier, on January 29, 2010. He had such an impact on so many people in Philadelphia—Eagles fans who rooted for him, NFL fans who laughed with (and occasionally trolled) him during his CBS career, and the many WIP listeners who have him to thank for the birth and development of our sports format.

Unfortunately, Brookie died after our show that Friday, removing a bit of the immediacy of his loss by the time we returned to the airwaves the following Monday. I do remember spending most of that day honoring his memory, with the highlight being an appearance by his loving widow, Barbara, who recalled some classic stories and expressed her husband's love for people and for WIP.

In the years after Brookie left, he would call the show from time to time, often to castigate me for a dumb opinion I was expressing. (He had a far higher opinion of Andy Reid than I did, for example.) I never got to say goodbye, but I'm sure Brookie preferred it that way. He was a lot like my father in that way—no fan of sentiment, especially if it was directed at him.

But still I wanted to do something to honor him one last time. Then, thanks to Gail, I got the chance.

It was no secret than one of Tom's closest friends, former Eagle head coach Dick Vermeil, was not a big fan of my biting style. He had never been a guest on our show since Brookie left WIP at the end of 1991. But there he was on a summer night, Vermeil himself, at our favorite restaurant in Stone Harbor, New Jersey, sitting with a party of six in a corner table next to the front window.

"Go talk to him," Gail insisted.

"No," I said. "He hates me. I don't need a to make a scene here."

Of course, eventually I do pretty much everything Gail tells me to, so I slinked over, reminded him who I was (just in case), and expressed my deep respect both for his brilliant football career and for his exquisite Vermeil Wines. (He has a winery in Napa Valley.)

Dick was surprisingly cordial—so much so that I even suggested maybe he could come on our show sometime as a special guest.

He didn't say no.

Soon, our sales department was talking to the ex-coach about weekly appearances to discuss the upcoming Eagles games and to promote his many great causes.

When he agreed—starting a six-year association that was a highlight of my time at WIP—I had two thoughts. One was, we got a fantastic guest for our Football Fridays. And two was, Tom Brookshier is looking down right now, smiling.

During his final appearance in my last year, Dick Vermeil said Brookie had told him long ago that he had found the right guy to replace him. Me. It's just like Brookie to tell his friend Dick Vermeil something he never told me.

When Dick said that to me that day, he accomplished something my many enemies failed to do over 33 years.

I was speechless.

Thank you, Dick Vermeil.

Once the Eagles had secured the Holy Grail in early 2018, I knew I was getting closer to my expiration date in radio. I was 67, and I was running out of rage. Doing the show was just as much fun, if not more so, than ever before, but my mind was not as quick, especially with names. My credo was to bring intensity every segment of every show, no exceptions. That's a much harder goal to reach at 67 than 47.

I was always a loud critic of athletes overstaying their welcome. Steve Carlton, Allen Iverson, Michael Vick...the list was endless of players who faced my wrath by refusing to retire after their talents had dwindled. It would have been the height of hypocrisy for me to bleed dry my own career.

People who listened to our show the last five years know it was a major preoccupation for me, so much so that my co-hosts used it to demean me at every turn. Rhea would groan, Al would scoff, and Jonesy would laugh whenever I brought up the topic of retirement.

What would I do with myself if I were not doing this job?

All of those questions were pushed aside indefinitely when the world shut down on March 12—one day before my 69th birthday—in 2020. My blood still heats to a boil whenever I picture Utah center Rudy Gobert touching everything on the table before a news conference on March 11, the night before everything changed.

In fact, Gobert's brazen stupidity was the bridge to three months of conversation that rarely ventured into sports. I had spent most of my career trying to avoid the real world, but there was no escape this time. Sports was gone indefinitely, and we were sailing into unchartered waters. As always, it started with Brookie's template on how to handle a crisis.

On one of our very first COVID shows, we broke a story. I think. The fact that so few media outlets picked it up suggested to me then, and now, that WIP was not seen as a go-to place in those early days of the pandemic even though our ratings stayed respectable throughout the crisis.

Sharing our personal experiences in the first week of the pandemic, a caller said he had seen Mayor Jim Kenney on a street in Philadelphia on March 12, the very same day he asked City Council for millions to support Philadelphia's battle with the virus. The mayor was filming a reality show on CNBC called *The Profit* while the rest of the world was unraveling.

I gave the mayor—a personal friend of Rhea—the same kind of treatment I would offer to an Eagles coach when he blew a big game, but the reaction on our phone lines and in the community was much different. In fact, there really wasn't much of a reaction at all.

The mayor's office did release this idiotic statement when the story finally surfaced in the mainstream news media days later:

> *This will be for a national television broadcast that promotes Philadelphia as a tourism destination, to air months from now. Given the potential impact of COVID-19 on tourism in our city, the mayor deemed this appropriate.*

The most amazing part of the story is that the statement appeared in the *Washington Examiner*, a D.C. political publication. The local newspapers and broadcast media never really reported an extraordinary lapse in judgment by the mayor.

But the sports station, WIP, had it first. Thanks to the callers, who have always been the most important ingredient in our station's success.

Even now, years later, I am often asked how we got through the pandemic. It was easy, really—much easier than it appeared at the time. I just treated local government like I did the Eagles. Mayor Kenney was the head coach. His inept (at least in my eyes) health commissioner, Dr. Thomas Farley, was the offensive coordinator. President Donald Trump was akin to NFL commissioner Roger Goodell. Dr. Anthony Fauci, chief medical advisor to the president, was the starting quarterback.

We ripped them all, of course. And so did the callers. That was the easy part. We knew that world very well.

What we were not prepared for was the overpowering intrusion of politics. I was answering emails every day, and the vitriol on both sides was far greater than anything I had ever dealt with in sports. Routinely, people on both sides of the vaccine issue said they were done with our show because of our political stand.

Ironically, for most of the pandemic, we had no political stand. Unlike most of our audience, we never really changed our work schedule. We still went into work at the studio every day. We did wear masks until we went on the air, and we did test ourselves regularly. But the biggest change in our lives was the content of the show. Even when sports began to return, COVID dominated the conversation.

Obviously, our biggest loss was Mitch Williams, who refused to get the vaccine and was adamant about it. When we all publicly got behind the vaccine, we didn't do it for political reasons. We thought it was the smartest way to get back to life before the virus. And we couldn't understand all of the fatalists who fell victim to the propaganda circulating all over social media.

We lost some listeners during the pandemic, and we picked some up, too. But no one got through those months unscathed. The experience reinforced my decision back when I was 27—45 years ago—that sports was the right path for me.

As far as I'm concerned, the real world is overrated.

I got one final reminder of how I ended up in sports when my sister, Phyllis, called me one day to tell me our mother was sick. Now this wasn't shocking news because Ida was 98 and battling a host of maladies. Still, she was a tough old woman. She was not about to go down without a fight.

My sister was there for my mom every day from Ida's mid-eighties, a loyal daughter who forced me to lament my far-less-apparent commitment 250 miles away. She called with news that sounded like a death sentence for my resilient mom. COVID had spread throughout the nursing home where she was staying, and Ida had tested positive.

Under normal conditions, I would have raced up to Rhode Island and made a spectacle of myself trying to get in to see her, but there was no point. COVID was raging then, and no one—not even immediate family members—was allowed in the facility. (Instead, I called the place and yelled at a few people—as if they didn't have enough to deal with back then. Sorry about that.)

While I was waiting for The Call, instead I got a call. Against all odds, Ida was beating the deadly virus. She was on the path to recovery. For a fleeting moment, I wondered if maybe my mother was immortal. Then something unthinkable—though understandable, in retrospect—happened. My mom was trying to get from her wheelchair to the bed, and when no one responded to her call, she tried to do it herself. Nursing homes back then were overwhelmed. It was no one's fault, really.

She fell, landed on her face, and was rushed to the hospital. It wasn't long before we got the inevitable final word. She had passed away as a result of the fall. Even though COVID didn't kill her, I blamed the virus anyway. From the day of her death—May 21, 2020—until now, I recoil at any suggestion that COVID wasn't a killer pandemic, and that the vaccine was in some way less than a miracle.

I will always remember my mother for something she did when I was 12, an act of selflessness that I thanked her for dozens of times in the many years that followed. My dad was always busy with his bowling leagues, his politics, and his eight brothers and sisters, so he wasn't the kind of hands-on father that is so common today. (I don't remember him ever attending any of my Little League games.)

So when I was talking to my friend Tommy one day, Ida overheard us saying we wished we could see a game in Yankee Stadium someday. By train, New York was three hours from Providence, so this was not much more than a dream—until my mother called us together and said we would be going with her to a doubleheader in New York the very next day.

How she weathered the six-hour round-trip and the six more hours at the games I cannot say. But two things happened that day that had a major impact on the rest of my life.

One was the way it bonded me to sports; I had visited the most famous ballpark in the world (at the time). I was hooked.

And two. I had a mother willing to endure a horrible day just to make her son happy. I had the best mother in the world.

I still can't believe I never got to say goodbye.

Chapter 21

The End (Almost)

By the start of 2021, the world—still masked, of course—was slowly coming back to life, and I was free now to plot my retirement. It was overdue. I reached 70 on March 13 of 2021, and I could feel the ravages of age creeping up on me. By then, the real backbone of the show was Rhea Hughes, not me.

I still did the planning for every show, but Rhea emerged as the force behind that process every single day. She came up with most of the guest ideas, she booked those people, she scoured the internet for stories we could use, she was a liaison between us and all the teams, and, in her spare time, she put out every fire.

I still had some energy left, but I was compromised. Names did not come to me as quickly as I needed them. She was usually there to rescue me. One weird thing that started happening was, I would temporarily lose my voice. Either she or Al Morganti were right there to buy me some time. It usually cleared up after a couple of anxious minutes.

Whenever I had one of those senior lapses, I felt like Steve Carlton at the end of his too-long career. He was a guest on our show a couple of years before I walked away, and I got the impression that day that he was finally acknowledging that he had stayed too long. If you did a good job in your career, you should never end it by doing something less than that.

It was time for as graceful exit as possible. Of course, I was never really known for my grace.

One of my biggest preoccupations in those days was not getting fired. I made no secret of this major concern. I came from a different radio era, when so much more was allowed. Suddenly, when someone made a racially-insensitive or sexist remark (including me), I didn't just need to negate it; I needed to recognize it first.

Back in the first decade of our show, Joe Conklin featured a few characters who did not make it far into the 2000s because they fell outside the ever-changing boundaries of good taste. One example is Hector, a caricature of a Mexican who was known to make references to theft or drugs. Another was Spike (before Spike Eskin), a gay stereotype. There was even a Black member of the Sixers named Ira Bowman, whom Conklin made into an old Jewish man. Ethnic humor, embraced for so long by us, was out of bounds now.

In interviews, I often said I didn't know anymore what I could say and what I couldn't. Just in writing this book, I had to change the word "hooligans" that I used to describe Eagles fans; it is an offensive reference to Irish people. "Basket case" is an inappropriate word for handicapped people. "Rule of thumb" is a reference to domestic abuse. I often used the phrase "off the reservation," a slight to Native Americans.

Nobody could ever "throw like a girl" again or be called "whipped" if he was unusually thoughtful toward a spouse. Calling attention to any attributes of a women was verboten, really. The MeToo Era was upon us. (With good reason.)

My all-time favorite question in the early days of recruiting women for the Wing Bowl and Miss WIP contest was: "What are you wearing?"

Today, it would take one complaint to the FCC to get me in serious trouble.

Rhea was there for all of that. She knew where the line was, and she shoved me, many times, back to the safe side. I said Rhea kept me at WIP five years longer than I would have stayed without her. Now that I think of it, I was conservative. It was probably closer to ten.

Al and Jonesy had to adjust to the creeping senility of the main host near the end, too. Al tends to provide short answers to questions. This was not always what I needed, so we developed a shorthand when I needed him to keep talking. I would rotate my right hand, almost like calling a basketball player for traveling, to signal him to keep speaking.

For someone known as a legendary on-ice troll, Jonesy was a main beam in my support system near the end. He would tell me I still had it, even on days when I didn't. He would say it was so much harder, so much different, when I wasn't hosting the show. He made me feel younger than I was.

And Joe Weachter, behind the gruff exterior, changed his game, too. We had more songs, more sound effects, and less me.

We even booked better talkers in those final years. When you asked a question to Mike Lombardi, Brian Baldinger, Ray Didinger, Glen Macnow, Ross Tucker, Ron Jaworski, or Marcus Hayes, you didn't have to worry about asking another one for a minute or so. Those guys could really talk—so I didn't have to blabber as much.

But you can only hide reality for so long, so I finally had The Talk with our market manager—the big boss, really—David Yadgaroff. Unlike every top management person I had dealt with before him, Dave understood the care and feeding of talk-show hosts. Where Tom Bigby would dress down, Dave would pick up.

He would often say: "What can I do to help you?"

Imagine that.

My decision to leave at the end of 2021 came as no surprise to Dave. I'm pretty sure I brought it up at every meeting we had. But he had a problem I wasn't aware of. WIP's program director, Spike Eskin, was about to leave for New York and WFAN, and the timing of my retirement was not good for WIP.

This is where I need a moment to honor the only radio station where I ever worked. WIP gave me the best three decades of my life, it offered me the freedom to express myself that the *Inquirer* didn't, it paid me more money than I ever thought I would make, and it gave me the perfect measure of fame—people knew who I was, but there were no major intrusions. I was semi-famous.

I have never wavered in believing WIP is the best sports station in America and has been since the early 1990s. My rationale is simple. Better than any others—and I have been a guest on most of the big ones—we reflect our fan base. We make stars out of the callers. We honor the people by hearing them out, and then either lavishing praise for their brilliance or smacking them down (playfully) for their ignorance.

The fans have always been the biggest stars of WIP, not the guests and not even the hosts. Just as I lasted longer than any of the sports figures over 33 years, the fans have outlasted me. They are the only constant in our Philadelphia sports world, and they will always be that. WIP understood this relationship better than any other sports station.

I know I always did.

So when David Yadgaroff made one last proposal to me in the fall of 2021, it was impossible for me to say no, despite my difficulties staying at the top of my game after 70.

What he said that day was, "I need one more year."

What I replied was: "Are you serious?"

He was. And then a management person formed the words I never thought I would hear: "What will it take? Just write down a list of what you would need to give us one more year."

My mind raced. I went home to lay out the situation to Gail, and I quickly learned that she was in no hurry to have my friendly face around a lot more. She said whatever I decided was fine with her, but I needed to be absolutely positive when I walked away for good.

A couple of years before I reached this crossroad, I booked one of the all-time greats in our field, Mike Francesa of WFAN, on our show to talk about the Eagles, but he swerved into the topic of retirement, something he had decided to try himself just a month earlier.

Even then, so soon after walking away, I could hear doubt creeping into his voice. He said the same thing, right on the air that day: Be sure before you do it. Be absolutely positive.

A few months later, Mike returned to radio full-time. He was still one of the greats, but I got the sense the audience had changed. The second act for any performer is rarely as good as the first. He walked away from radio for good a year later.

With all of these warnings, plus my allegiance to WIP, rattling in my brain, I decided to put together the list. What did I have to lose?

First of all, I was just as adamant not to take a pay cut, even though I had finally agreed to accept one for a three-month period at the beginning of the pandemic. No pay cut. Not negotiable.

Second, five-day work weeks were becoming too much. My agent, Steve Mountain, had been suggesting for years that I should break the week up by taking Wednesdays off—like some doctors do. Usually, Wednesday is one of the slower sports days of the week, and a slow day makes the job of a sports-talker much harder. Would listeners think I was a wimp if I took Wednesdays off? No worries. They already thought that.

Third, that drive to Atlantic City every week was not just a grind for me; it was precarious for the drivers around me. I would need a driver every week, to and from the Borgata.

Fourth, I wanted one week a month of vacation time. Twelve weeks. Wow. At that point I was just looking for things to put on the list.

And finally, I was still steamed that WIP had let go our marketing director and ambassador of good will, Cindy Webster, so I wanted her reinstated as a paid consultant to our show.

(It should be noted that I got car sick the second time I used the driver and drove myself the rest of the year. Both me and the other drivers on the road survived. Also, I never got to use even half of those 12 weeks of vacation. It was far too exciting a year in sports.)

The answer was a resounding yes on all requests but one. No Cindy. Corporations hate to admit mistakes. Dumping Cindy after 28 years of loyal service was a big one. I told my agent that clause was not negotiable. Eventually, they gave in, and I was back for one more year, ready or not.

It was one of the best decisions of my life.

Chapter 22

The End (Really)

When I was talking to the publisher of this book months ago, he mentioned what a great thing it would have been if either the Phillies or Eagles had won a championship in my final year. Books always get a big boost following a parade. I said nothing in response, but I was thinking that the failures of both of our biggest teams was a far more appropriate ending, for me and for them.

At the same time, I must admit I said often, on and off the air, how lucky I was that I got to see our two most important teams, the Phillies and Eagles, both playing for a championship in the same season.

One last piece of this endgame puzzle had to snap into place before I would get to experience this double-barreled thrill. I was attending a special lunch with my three biggest bosses, Audacy chairman David Field, Audacy market manager David Yadgaroff, and WIP brand manager Rod Lakin. The setting was ideal—the top floor of the Four Seasons Hotel in Center City, Philadelphia.

From up there, 60 floors above the city, Philadelphia was panoramic in its beauty, breathtaking in its scope. At the time, the Phillies were halfway through a disappointing season and the hopes for the Eagles were only slightly better. Very briefly, I said to Rod before the arrival of the others that maybe I should stay until the Eagles season ended.

"That makes sense," he said. "Sure."

It was the fastest negotiation of my radio career, and the weirdest. Why would someone working on fumes at that point in the early fall of 2022 ask for more time? Wasn't I counting the days until I could sleep later and not have the daily challenge of trying to fill four hours of intense radio four days a week?

The answer is simple. I had a feeling about the Eagles. GM Howie Roseman—often a major target of WIP but since the Super Bowl parade, a hero—had a fantastic off-season and the Eagles had a chance to deliver one more championship to our barren résumé.

Before that, though, I got to take my own victory lap.

When I brought back Cindy Webster for my final year, it never occurred to me how quickly she would reestablish good relations between our show and the Phillies. Cindy was a devout Phillies fan, and everybody in the organization knew and loved her. So much so, in fact, that I was shocked to receive an invitation to throw out a first pitch on July 24, 2022, before the game between the Phils and the Cubs.

I could actually picture the Phillies holding their collective noses when they rolled out the red carpet for me, given that they were definitely not big fans during my long run on their flagship station. In fact, I learned only while researching this book they were not happy I was doing a simulcast with Michael Smerconish after the 2008 parade. Even with supporters like president Dave Montgomery and advisor Dallas Green, I was way too negative for most tastes.

But there I was on the mound, on the hottest day in years at Citizens Bank Park, holding a ball and looking down at my catcher, former Phillies great and, for a brief time when he was manager, one of my nemeses, Larry Bowa.

At best, I had a checkered past when it came to athletic endeavors and the Phillies. It is no secret that I had the best chance to catch the first home-run ball at the new Bright House Field in Clearwater when Jimmy Rollins blasted one over the wall in the bottom of the first inning in 2004. I lined up under the towering drive, and clang. It went right off my hands and into the stands.

And then there was the time I got to throw out the first pitch at a spring-training game in Clearwater and instead executed a death sentence for a worm or two a good ten feet in front of home plate.

But this time, with a section of WIP supporters behind me in center field and Larry Bowa gesturing me to hit his glove from about 60 feet away, I let go with my best fastball.

Strike! It was perfect. There was no radar reading when I threw it, but I swear it went 85 miles per hour.

Now I need to repeat an admission that lost me the support of some of our listeners in those final months. I said on the air, and even more so off it, that I was never on the bandwagon that brought the Phillies to the World Series in 2022. I have always been all-in or all-out with our teams, and I could never summon up the joy for the Phillies that took over the city in late September and October.

Look, I have never been a good actor. (Just watch my performance in *Bald*.) I could not fake a sudden euphoria over a Phillies team that inspired only apathy for most of the 2022 season.

Just two weeks before the final regular-season game, Al Morganti saw that the Phillies had drawn over 30,000 fans on the final Hatfield Dollar Dog Night, and he suggested they sell hot dogs at $1 for the rest of the season. There seemed to be no other way to fill even half of the 46,000 seats that had been sold out for every game a decade earlier.

The fans were not excited about the Phillies for most of that season. I feel I'm an authority on the subject, since it was my job, four days a week, to inspire conversation about the baseball team. Until the playoffs, I conservatively estimate that there was one Phillies call for every five about the Eagles, who were off to a great start.

Then something happened that is as puzzling to me today as it was when it unfolded in real time. Day by day, the fans began flooding back into Citizens Bank Park, and onto our phone lines. Nothing like this had ever happened in our long history at WIP.

The 2022 Phillies became overnight sensations. The tipping point for fans was the ninth inning of the first wild-card game, when the Phils exploded for six runs against the Cardinals in the ninth inning and got some long-awaited payback for the 2011 nightmare. They dispatched St. Louis the next day, and—just like that—the city was hooked on baseball all over again.

When the Phillies got home, they found a baseball town that had been dormant for 11 years suddenly alive and screaming. The atmosphere in the stadium was like nothing in Philadelphia history—including the great Phillies run of 2007–11 and even the Super Bowl–championship season of the 2017 Eagles.

The 45,485 who were there on October 23 say the reaction after Bryce Harper hit his go-ahead home run in the eighth inning of Game 5 of the NLCS against the San Diego Padres is the loudest sound from a crowd in the history of Philadelphia sports. What made it even more implausible was that Al was trying to bribe those same fans with $1 hot dogs one month earlier.

The Phillies were going back to the World Series for the first time since 2009, and my preoccupation was still the Eagles. At the risk of leaving WIP on a bad note, I opted for the truth. I cared more about the Eagles, who never lost their fans the way the Phillies had before their sudden return to prominence in the first days of autumn.

My biggest problem was not the Phillies as much as it was the game they were playing. My first love in sports was baseball, but not the current version of a game that was overwhelmed by statistical analysis. To get big moments like the Harper homer, fans were asked to watch extended periods when the ball was never in play. I'll take two doubles every day over a home run and a strikeout.

This preoccupation with analytics really took root during a time when my two least favorite executives were running the team, president Andy MacPhail and his novice GM Matt Klentak. During their infuriating five-year reign, the statistics department of the Phils expanded to 18 members. It was a Goober Brigade.

MacPhail, who hadn't won anything in generations, actually once said of the chances for the Phillies for make the playoffs, "If we don't, we don't." In Philadelphia. I tormented him with that phrase for every day of his tenure after that. Conklin even did a song, "If We Don't, We Don't." It was brilliant.

Meanwhile, Klentak was so bad at his job, even obvious moves were heralded as strokes of nerd genius. After he traded for catcher J.T. Realmuto during a Miami fire sale, owner John Middleton actually compared him to Hall of Fame executive Branch Rickey. Three years later, Klentak's career as a major-league GM was as dead as Rickey.

That era soured me on the Phillies, and no throwing out the first pitch or burst of excitement in the playoffs could bring me back in. Not even a nice old-school guy like Rob Thomson, the new manager after a stat-infatuated Joe Girardi went bust, could bring me back in. Sorry. The 2022 Phillies just never did it for me.

So when they lost the World Series to the evil Houston Astros—whose only previous championship came after they cheated—I felt almost nothing. Hey, at least I admitted it. Oh, I ripped Thomson for managing according to numbers instead of his gut in those final games, but I was already turning the page to the Eagles.

The Eagles were entirely another story. They were going to give me the best send-off ever. My last day at WIP was going to be at the championship parade.

I really believed it.

The first mistake the Eagles made was honoring me before a game against the Pittsburgh Steelers on October 30, 2022. Did they see what happened when the Phillies did it? Kenny Justice loved to call me a mush (pronounced mooosh). I was bad luck.

I hadn't been to an Eagles game in years, but I got to take one last tour of the tailgates and even made a stop at the next generation of the tent shows that I had presided over all of those years ago. There is no tent anymore. It's just a stage on a concourse outside Lincoln Financial Field. It looked a bit like a shooting gallery at an amusement park—a smattering of fans, but no sign of any chainsaws. It made me sad for a world before lawyers and sanity. Where's the 700 Level when you need it?

Inside the building I was greeted by the replacement years ago for Joe Banner, Eagles president Don Smolenski. Don could not be more different than Banner. First of all, he's human. Second, he's humble, though he runs one of the most successful sports organizations in America. And third, he sees the value of people talking about his team, even if the discussion is not always positive. Don gets WIP. Hard to believe.

I looked up in the stands and saw some of the familiar faces of my past. Rocco from the Dirty Thirty was there, a diehard from our very early days and a loyal caller long after the tent went down for the last time. Shaun, another Dirty Thirty member whose actual face has rarely been seen. He has painted it with green and silver before every game for decades. Good old Dave Spadaro, the Eagles insider, was still prowling the sidelines. So was Swoop, the mascot. When did the Eagles cheerleaders get so young?

Of course, some of my favorite people were no longer there to add to the pregame hoopla. I scoured the stands in a futile search for Sen. Arlen Specter or Torchman. No luck. Governor and Mayor Ed Rendell has been battling an illness. We don't see him much anymore. Tom Brookshier is long gone, though he will never be forgotten. I hope he's up there with Iron Man John Zitter, Eagle Joe, Coma Tracey, and all of the other heroes of another era.

When they announced my name, I heard no boos. It was not close to the ovation I would get in a couple of months at Chickie's and Pete's, but it was nice. It made me feel as if I had made my mark in the big city. All I would need now was a big finish.

Tying my retirement to the final outcome of the Eagles decision was a stroke of genius. By then, I had gotten squeamish about the attention my imminent departure was getting, and I figured the focus would be much more on the Eagles than on me. Hey, I was never shy about including my own life in the show, but not when sports were the better option. The 2022 Eagles were pretty much always a better option.

In those last weeks, however, even when the outcome of Eagles games was connected to my departure, callers often deviated from our daily assault of defensive coordinator Jonathan Gannon to reflect on the past 33 years. We encouraged the look back with our Throwback Thursdays, a chance to revisit some of the voices of our past.

Tony Bruno was first. He's a successful podcaster now, and he's the same Tony—full of bluster and fun. I will always wonder how different our history would have been if Tony had stayed longer. His return to our show had an unexpected twist. We booked him for eight o'clock. He was finally on time.

We also invited back the former St. Joe's coach, Phil Martelli, who predicted the outcome of Eagles games for over a decade on our show, even when he was facing criticism for not focusing on his own struggling teams in his final years with the Hawks. We had lots of great coaches contributing to our show over the years. Phil was brilliant in getting inside the heads of the biggest targets of my wrath.

Mike Missanelli was a surprise guest on one of those Throwback Thursdays, telling great stories about his days with a WIP co-host he liked, Steve Fredericks, and one he didn't, Howard Eskin. Mike brought Al and I back to our *Inquirer* roots that day with stories about how improbable our switch was from journalism to sports talk. Mike deserved as big a sendoff as I got. He just ended his radio career at the wrong station.

In those final weeks, lots of people who were part of our show for years, some all the way from the start, were regular guests in our studio. Clifford W. Lentz, our NASA correspondent (yes, we had a NASA correspondent) was there for many of those final shows, giving Jonesy a few more chances to work in jokes about Uranus. Cliff's claim to fame was attending all 26 Wing Bowls. When it came to our show, he was a lifer.

One day all of the star callers were there together—Eagle Shirley, Kenny, Rocco, and Jason from the Dirty Thirty, Butch from Manayunk—and I couldn't help but wonder what would happen to them. The show replacing us would feature Joe DeCamara, Jon Ritchie, and James Seltzer—our very talented midday guys—plus Rhea Hughes and Joe Weachter.

It would be a new show, with mostly new voices. Would they want to bridge the two shows with the same callers? What would I do in that situation? I loved Tom Brookshier, but I didn't want the show to sound the same after he left.

I realized it was the end of an era for the famous callers, too, and I felt terrible about that. But I had no choice. Time marches on. Time waits for no man. Time keeps on ticking, ticking into the future. And so on. There was nothing I could do about it. I got old.

Lots of tears were shed in those final weeks. Cindy Webster, who got a reprieve in our final year, was effusive in her loyalty to WIP and our show. She cried. Steven Singer took eight-and-a-half minutes to say how much he loved our show. Pete Ciarrocchi of Chickie's and Pete's used less time, but no less emotion. Pretty much everybody shed a tear somewhere along the way. (Except for Al, of course. He kept saying: "You're leaving?")

The biggest shock came at the end of a show three weeks before I signed off for the last time at WIP. Gail has never been comfortable in front of a microphone, but Cindy convinced her to say a few words when no one expected it, at the start of the NFL playoffs. Listeners sent me more emails about her final words than anything else that happened in those final days.

Here's what my amazing wife said:

> *I just want to say how proud I am of you. You've given your heart and soul to this job. I laugh when people say you have the best job in the world, that you get to talk sports with your friends for four hours. They don't know. They have no idea that you've given up so much of your life for this job. They don't know the other eight to 10 additional hours a day that you put into this, every day and on weekends.*
>
> *I also laugh when people say I'm a saint for being married to you, because they have no idea. You take the microphone away, and you are the most loving, quiet, family man. You're still really quirky, though. It's just been amazing, but it is very sad. We talk about this and we have the same emotions—we're scared, we're nervous, we're happy, we're excited. I joke around a lot that I want to get out of the house (when you retire), but I really look forward to this next chapter of your life. I'm just so proud. I love you.*

I wish, one time in my 33 years, I was as eloquent as that.

How did I ever get so lucky to find that woman?

Let the record show that, right to the end, I was a nemesis for the coaches and managers of our Philadelphia sports teams. I say that with pride. My job was to hold them accountable, and I did that, with no less energy, right to the very last day.

Nick Sirianni was the young new head coach of the Eagles, and we had an equal measure of our warm moments and frosty ones during our two years together. He hated my incessant criticism of his players, but he really reveled in my positivity when they won. In 2022, all they did, for the most part, was win.

To the surprise of many so-called NFL experts, the Eagles won their first eight games in 2022, thanks to a balanced roster and a ridiculously easy schedule. It was clear to me and to many of our more cynical callers that the team had a serious weakness that remained hidden through long stretches of a dream 14–3 season. The defensive coordinator, Jonathan Gannon, was not aggressive enough, and especially so with the talented players at his disposal.

No one was more frustrated by Gannon's timid approach than Seth Joyner, a member of Buddy Ryan's ferocious 46 defense with the Eagles and now a member of our team in our final season as well. The Eagles would win, week after week, and Seth would come in every Monday and say the defense needed to play up on receivers more, not sit back in a zone defense and allow long drives the way they did in Gannon's defense.

Sirianni ignored the noise from Seth and others who understand football, but he became increasingly frustrated with my criticism of his assistant. The coach finally snapped at a news conference after the Eagles had advanced to the NFC Championship Game with an easy 38–7 slaughter of the New York Giants.

"Sometimes, I have to hear some things about Jonathan Gannon, and I don't know if it's you guys," Sirianni said to the reporters. "It might be more other people. I won't say names—Angelo—but this guy is an unbelievable coordinator. The fact that he doesn't get respect from our radio station blows my mind.... People love to play for this guy. He's going to be a head coach in the National Football League. I can't wait to talk to Angelo on Monday."

There was eager speculation for another verbal blowout like the one I had with Gabe Kapler a couple of years earlier, but I knew that would never happen. Nick had too much respect for the fans. He was just offering his honest truth. The coach just happened to be wrong. Oh, he was right about Gannon getting a head-coaching job. He was just horribly wrong about Gannon being a good defensive coordinator.

The Eagles would have won Super Bowl LVII if pretty much anyone other than Jonathan Gannon had coached the defense. I will always believe that. Once Patrick Mahomes (and yes, Andy Reid) had figured out how to exploit Gannon and his generous unit, the second half was child's play.

The Chiefs ran the same play for touchdowns twice, knowing Gannon would never adjust. They scored a touchdown every time they touched the ball in the second half, except for the last drive, when KC running back Jerick McKinnon wisely slid down at the one-yard line to deny the Eagles offense one last attempt to win the game. Thanks to Gannon, the Eagles were defenseless when it mattered most.

Because my best plan, to leave the day of the championship parade, was no longer possible, I was left with four final shows. The first two were easy. Fans screamed and howled their frustration at another lost opportunity. Nick Sirianni had the option of appearing one last time, no doubt having to deal with a final argument about Gannon before I retired. I was actually relieved when he declined. I didn't have another shouting match in me.

The second-to-last show moved from our studio to a beautiful auditorium just outside our studio, and we welcomed back many of the people who were so instrumental in our success. Marisa, a regular caller from Tokyo, was there, offering hugs. She had flown all the way back to Philadelphia in anticipation of a big Super Bowl celebration. Mrs. Poobah, Gloria Hochman, made a last appearance, too. Once again, she reminded us how special she and her husband were to our city.

At the end of the show, David Yadgaroff asked for a minute and announced that WIP was starting a Hall of Fame, and the first two inductees were Tom Brookshier and me. It was a perfect sendoff. To be together with Brookie one more time was the biggest honor I could ever hope to receive.

For our final show, we did not follow the Brookie model, however. There were not 34 marquee guests. We had three of our favorite people: the Gridiron Genius, Mike Lombardi; former Eagle Brian Mitchell; and—of course—Governor/Mayor Ed Rendell. (He no longer is campaigning for Ricky Williams.)

We talked sports as much as we could. I even made a point of ripping into Jonathan Gannon in my final segment at WIP. We did the same thing on that Friday that we had done for 33 years. We shared the sports world with the most passionate sports fans in America.

There was no Super Bowl parade, but that was okay.

Based on our long history at WIP, it was the perfect ending.

Epilogue

When I'm asked how much I loved being a sports talk-show host in Philadelphia, I usually go back to 2012, when two wonderful things happened to me on the same day. I had successful colon-resection surgery, and Joe Banner left the Eagles.

Joe Banner leaving was the better news to me.

I had been in the hospital for over a week while doctors waited for my latest bout of diverticulitis to abate, clearing the way for surgery. Finally, I got word early one morning that I was ready for what would turn into a seven-hour operation later that day.

Then I got a call (probably from Rhea Hughes) telling me that our prayers had finally been answered. The Grinch of Philadelphia sports, Eagles president Joe Banner, was abruptly leaving the job. His long friendship with owner Jeff Lurie had apparently ruptured under circumstances that have never really been explained. The truth is no one cared why Banner was leaving anyway. They were just thrilled he was gone.

On that morning, with an IV dangling from my arm and red markings on my lower torso (indicating where the surgeon would cut), I called into the *WIP Morning Show* to gloat over the news. I may have even said that if I died on the operating table, now at least I would have a smile on my face. (Well, I hope I said it.)

That's how much I loved being a part of WIP for 33 years. I never for a second regretted leaving journalism. No, not even during the many bloody battles with my old boss Tom Bigby. Talking sports was so much more fun than anything else I have ever done.

Oh, it was a lot of work. Gail was right about that. It required sacrifice, though missing a wedding or two along the way was more a benefit than a detriment. It was a labor of love. Talking sports in a style tailored for the critical ears of Philly fans was an honor I never took for granted.

When you leave after a long time at a job, a few things happen that you won't realize until you experience them yourself. One is, you automatically become a *legend*—which is just another word for *old*. Everybody lines up to tell you how much they love you. Then you get very nostalgic; at least I did. Those tent parties—which I hated the last couple of seasons—were so much fun in my distant memory. And finally, you feel lost. Your job at some point became you, or vice versa. I decided to deal with this challenge by writing a book.

In fact, I wrote all 90,000 or so words in the first six weeks after I retired, both because I wanted everything fresh in my mind and because I needed something productive to do. What I didn't realize when I started is how much clearer in hindsight the past 33 years would become. There were lessons here, for all of us.

The biggest lesson is for sports-talk show hosts trying every day to do the best job they can. Stop catering to the wrong people. Stop worrying about the owners, the coaches, and managers, and especially the players. They are not your friends. Keith Jones taught me this. He used the verb *mold* to describe how he handled the media. He would make them think he wanted them to be his friends.

How many are still his friends now? I can answer that. One. Al Morganti. And that became a marriage of convenience when Al kept helping Jonesy get jobs. (Clearly, Al is very good at that.)

And for the management people dealing with all the complaints, they need to realize that the most important commodity of every host is his or her unfettered opinion. The moment the fans hear a host speaking the gospel of a team every time a crisis erupts, the element of surprise is gone. They already know how a host feels before the On Air light comes on. Soon, they no longer care.

The best advice I got in my life came from Professor Norman Isaacs back in 1976 at Columbia University. I didn't realize this until I wrote the book and kept revisiting his plea to hold the people in authority accountable. Not many lessons in journalism translated to talk radio, but that one did. Hold the people in authority accountable. Never compromise your honest opinion. Tell the truth.

I had a huge advantage over most other hosts because I never wanted to play the sports I covered, because I wasn't worried about offending the people I wrote and talked about, and because I learned early on that the job of the media is to use the forum to tell your best truth. It wasn't always the actual truth, but it was honest. Honesty comes through both in journalism and sports radio.

The next big lesson I learned came from radio, not journalism. The way to win at your job is to add humor. That's why the shows Jonesy did with us every week were always our best. Tuesdays, with Joe Conklin adding his array of fun characters like Chip Snapper and Carmen, inevitably got the most favorable reaction, week after week.

Same reason. They made listeners laugh.

Sports is not nuclear science. It is entertainment. Either find your funny bone or get someone onto the show who can give the listeners a light moment on the way to work in the morning. Al was underrated because he spoke so little, but most of the Line of the Day honors at the end of every show were either his or Jonesy's. Why? Because they were funny. Shows need humor. It is why we never lost the ratings battle against the city's other morning-sports show in all our years on the air. Not once.

Funny was our not-so-secret weapon.

The biggest failure of my radio career was never finding a balance between my private life and my public one. It cost me my first marriage and would have cost me my second if I didn't—by pure luck—find someone who understood my predicament. My ambition overpowered everything else for far too long. I was never inclined to sacrifice my job for my family. That is a regret I will take with me to my grave.

My son, Neil, called our show 15 years ago with one of the greatest moments not just in my radio career but also in my life. On the air, he informed me that I was about to become a grandfather. Twice. He was the first person in our family, for generations, with twins on the way, Chase and Dylan. Wow.

I have watched the sacrifices he has made since then. leaving me wondering why I wasn't wired similarly. My dad was very much like me (but far more likeable). The traditional Italian family of my time in the 1950s had the father with few family-raising responsibilities.

I learned from my father. Work came first. Neil broke the chain. Somehow, he figured out how to become a success as a financial analyst without ever missing one of his kids' games. (In fact, he often coached the team.)

The real success story in my family is not me. It's my son, Neil.

Only by leaving did I learn a lot more about my legacy at WIP, good and bad. Yes, I made it into the WIP Hall of Fame, but at what cost? I was doing an interview shortly before I left with one of my former interns, David Uram, when he asked me a series of questions about why I was so tough on the young people like him who were just trying to learn.

Until that conversation, I had never seen my intense ways like that. I know I tended to panic under stressful conditions—one time I screamed at an intern, "Put down the donuts! We're in crisis!"—but I always thought it was acceptable behavior given our communal goal of doing the best show possible.

When people ask me why I never let up, not for one segment of one show for 33 years, I always blamed my father. He used to say to me, "They're not paying you to goof off." So, I never did. Not once.

As I look back now, however, my intensity was a double-edged sword. Yes, it gave us the best product we could deliver every day, but it also alienated the people behind the scenes, many of those people as committed to success as I was.

The sendoff WIP gave me was more than I deserved. Everyone spoke at length about what Al, Rhea, Jonesy, Joe Weachter, Joe Conklin, and I had meant to the station and the city. No one (other than Dave Uram) added to my résumé the raised voices and the not-so-occasional tantrums. I had to wait until a couple of weeks after I left to get a more honest picture of the people I left behind.

In an *Inquirer* story about the transition to the new show, an unnamed source said: "We're not going to have to worry about tiptoeing on eggshells around here anymore." (The source was talking about me. Duh.)

Wow. I never even saw the eggshells.

Finally, I need to address the most important people in radio. The listeners. One thing I definitely got right was acknowledging from the very beginning that they would be the ultimate judge of my work, not the sports teams and not even my bosses. If they kept listening, I could keep doing the best job I ever had.

And God bless them. They kept listening.

Here's the best example I can give of how important the listeners are. If enough of them were listening—and buying the products our sponsors were selling—a major corporation like CBS would allow a clause in a host's contract excluding his boss from talking to him. That's power. It was power I acquired only because of the listeners.

Back then, at the beginning, the eggshells were on the floor because of Tom Bigby—despite all the good he also did for WIP—and that clause removed them all for me.

Five years before I retired, I looked down at the caller board at the end of a show and saw a half-dozen people still waiting to get on the air. I pictured their disappointment as the line went dead in their ears. What if the next caller had something to say that really added something? How could I fix that?

The next day, I gave out my private email address—Radioman610@gmail.com—and told all of the callers who didn't get on the air that day to feel free to engage me via email. Hundreds of thousands did so over those final years. Not all of the comments were positive, believe me. But they all gave me a much better picture of what the listeners were thinking.

I answered every email personally—still do—because it was a debt I needed to pay back to the most passionate sports in America.

Thank you, Philadelphia, for the best years of my life.

Finally, I started this book with the most famous (infamous?) moment in the history of the *WIP Morning Show*, the booing of Donovan McNabb at the 1999 NFL draft, and I feel an urge to end it there, too.

It was never about you, Donovan.

So get over it, already.

You had the privilege of performing in front of the most passionate sports fans in America.

That's the only thing we ever had in common.

I did, too.

Acknowledgments

Many years ago, my wife and I became infatuated with a show called *Dancing with the Stars*. It just so happened that the show was at its height of popularity around the same time that my son, Neil, was getting married. That's when Gail and I both got the same thought.

Hey, why don't we take lessons so we can dance like that at the wedding?

And so we did. Within weeks, Gail was a model student. I was a statue. Let's just say when the gene for rhythm was being distributed, I got in the wrong line.

Still, we learned how to do a mean salsa, a smooth fox trot, and a scalding rumba. We kept signing up for more lessons, and sure enough, I was boogieing and shimmying for several memorable dances at the wedding.

Then we got the videos back.

I have never danced another step since then. Not one. Just picture Frankenstein trying to shake his hips. That's me.

Without consulting my wife, I began telling people, over and over, about how we had wasted $10,000 on dancing lessons. I'm not sure where that number came from, but I said it often enough that Gail finally got tired of hearing an obvious fiction.

"Where do you get $10,000?" she would ask.

"Okay, then," I would answer. "How much did we spend?"

"I won't tell you. I don't want to ruin your story."

What I'm trying to say here is that I have had a tendency to add a bit of spice to stories, probably because of the nature of my job as a radio performer.

I just want everyone who got this far in the book to know that I kept the spice rack away from my computer. I tried to get every detail as accurate as possible, checking with many of the people who were part of the stories covered in these pages.

If any details are wrong, it's totally my fault. Who knows? My professors at Columbia might still revoke my diploma. I tried to report this story with the honesty and openness our listeners deserve. If I fell short at any point, I apologize.

Now I will attempt the impossible. I will try to thank all the people who helped me reach retirement intact at age 72.

I'll start with my parents, Angelo Sr. and Ida, who taught me to love (and complain about) all people in a world that was not so fair-minded in the 1950s. They also taught me a work ethic that served me well.

She has no idea her name would ever come up (nor, I'm sure, she even remembers me), but my high school English teacher, Linda Youngren, was my first inspiration. She encouraged me to write, and she told me I had potential. I had her for only two classes in my teens, but her impact has stayed with me for the rest of my life.

My first boss, Gerry Goldstein, was the best mentor a person could ever hope to have, especially at a small weekly newspaper like the *Narragansett Times*. Gerry is one of the most talented people I ever encountered—anywhere, at any time. In retrospect, I'm happy I found out the owners were looking to replace him. Leaving that small newspaper gave him a chance to show a much bigger world how great he was.

The people who had the biggest impact on my life at Columbia are easy to identify. First, the application committee. How the heck did you accept me into the best journalism school in the world? Did you have a bad day? Norm Isaacs, my advisor and the man who almost got me to move to Louisville, met with me only a handful of times, but offered lessons I'm still using. And Judith Crist, the movie critic, who showed me how to rip people with grace and wit. (I forgot that lesson quickly, however.)

Next, I have to thank the late executive editor of the *Providence Journal*, Chuck Hauser, for keeping his word and giving me a chance to move into sports. I also want to mention another colleague at the *Journal*, Art Martone. In doing research for this book, I learned that he had passed away in 2022. I am still dealing with the loss. Sometimes you don't realize the influence people have on you until they're gone.

At the *Inquirer*, I need to start with the late sports editor, Jay Searcy. It took him 19 months to call me back, but when he did, I finally got a chance to move to the big city. His replacement, Glenn Guzzo, was a boss I got along well with, for the most part. (He was a rarity.) Glenn was the one who got me to the finals for a Pulitzer Prize. Gene Roberts and Jim Naughton were also gifted editors at an amazing newspaper back in the 1980s. They helped so many of us reach our potential.

Now radio. This book would not exist, nor would my career, without Tom Brookshier. Some people are legends for no good reason. Brookie is a legend for his football career, for his broadcasting career, and for building, from the ground floor, the best sports-radio station in the country. What did he see in me to hand over his show in 1992? I will never know, but I will always be thankful.

Cecil R. (Butch) Forster Jr. was the big boss at WIP during most of the Tom Bigby years. I got a chance to talk to him in researching this book and it gave me a whole new appreciation for how he kept us all going after Bigby had sucked the spirit out of us. One of my favorite moments is when he told me the story of threatening to punch Bigby. Butch truly was a kindred spirit.

Yes, Tom Bigby deserves acknowledgement again here, even though his impact, good and bad, is felt in most of the chapters. He left plenty of scars, but also a foundation in radio that got me through a lot of tense times. When I learned after leaving WIP that there were no more eggshells to avoid because I was gone, I couldn't help wondering if we shared more than a few unappealing traits.

I lost touch with Bigby's boss, Jack Williams, but he helped me tremendously at WIP—often serving as a referee between Bigby and me—and again at Comcast SportsNet when I had my own TV show for a decade. Jack knew exactly when to get involved, and his great sense of humor inspired all of us.

Among the many talented radio performers it was my privilege to work with, the names that pop up first in my mind are Bill Campbell, Steve Fredericks, Mike Missanelli, Jody McDonald, Joe Giglio, Jon Marks, and the incomparable Ike Reese.

Then there was Glen Macnow, who has been part of my life for the past 40 years. He was great at everything he ever did, starting with journalism, continuing with radio and ending with acting. (Check him out as a janitor in *The Arrangement*. Excellent.) He also did a few of his awesome food hunts for our show, willingly gaining five pounds or more while consuming heaps of free food. He's always been a trouper.

Big Daddy Graham deserves a paragraph of his own. When I wrote in the epilogue about humor, I was thinking of this extraordinary man. He did the best overnight radio program in the history of Philadelphia, a nightly sampling of his sports knowledge, his refreshing humor, and his relentless quirkiness. He died way too soon, but he left behind an army of adoring listeners and a daughter, Ava, who inherited his sense of humor and his public appeal. Ava is her father's daughter, which is a very good thing.

On our show, there are so many people who contributed to our success. In the early days, there were Max Vierra, Kris Gamble, Bryan

Ramona, Scott McHugh, Bill Zimpfer, Gordon Thomas, and Jan Gorham. And I won't easily forget John Higham, a great number-cruncher who was thrust into the spotlight every year when he counted the wings at Wing Bowl.

More currently, we had great engineers Ben Hill (the only man I know who loves to visit Rhode Island), Dave Breitmaier, Dave Scopinich, and Lane Massey. (The only times they ever saw me was when I was panicking about a technical issue. I'm pretty sure they still think I'm insane.)

I was trained by Bigby to never talk to salespeople, but I need to thank the few I did get to know. At the top of the list is Jennifer Bernardino, who handled many of my accounts during the middle years and ended up marrying one of the best businessmen I ever met, Steve Bernardino of Montgomeryville Acura and Nissan.

I made it 33 years at WIP because the last eight or so featured the diplomatic executive skills of Audacy market manager David Yadgaroff, and he was smart enough to hire talent-friendly program directors like Spike Eskin and Rod Lakin. And it wouldn't be fair to ignore the major contributions of their predecessors, Marc Rayfield and Andy Bloom. (But I'm still upset about that Phillies-parade show, Marc.)

At the corporate level, we got the indispensable support of Mel Karmazin, Dan Mason, Joel Hollander, Scott Herman, Chris Oliviero, and Jeff Sottolano, who made the jump to New York after a great run with us at WIP. (He thanked me at the end for helping him learn how to deal with demanding employees. Ha, ha. Happy to help.)

Rob Kaloustian was the sales manager for the last decade at WIP, and he's got to be the longest-tenured person in that demanding position over my 33 years. Obviously, he's good at his job. All I can say is, we all got paid, thanks to him.

Our long-time receptionists, Kay DuFrayne and Gerri St. John, were calm, sweet people ideally suited for their roles at WIP. Kay, who passed away in 2016, even looked the other way when Joe Conklin made the announcements about Bigby's black-market cheese.

At times, though it didn't always sound like it on the air, we were educators. First, I did the teaching in the La Salle University classrooms, an honor for which I will always be indebted to the head of the communications department, Brother Gerry Molyneaux. Later, we employed well over 100 interns, some of whom gave up their dream of a career in the media after seeing what it took, and others reaching heights well beyond our own grasp.

The top of that list bears the name of Colleen Wolfe, who is a star at the NFL Network despite our involvement at the beginning of her media career. (She stole the "You're fired!" at the end of each day of our annual Intern Contest from none other than Donald Trump, long before he was president.) That Colleen married John Gonzalez, a former La Salle student of mine and a brilliant writer at The Ringer, is one of life's beautiful coincidences.

Zach Gelb was one of our interns a long time ago; now he's killing it as a national sports host at CBS. (He's just got to stop interviewing Donovan McNabb all the time. Come on, Zach. Did you learn nothing from us?) Kyle Neubeck is a fantastic basketball writer at PhillyVoice.com. When I read his analysis of 76er games, I realize he knew more about hoops than us long before he ever started at WIP. I'm surprised we didn't ruin him. He ended up being our basketball expert for the last few years.

David Uram asked some of the toughest questions when he interviewed me in my final weeks for KYW Radio, where he has emerged as one of their best sports-news voices. I tried many times to get Dave a date during his time with us. On one occasion, he blew it by ordering for dinner, as a main course, a yogurt parfait. That blind date didn't work out, but he ended up not needing my help at all. He's happily married now. (He no longer orders yogurt parfaits.)

And I will never forget Jimmy McKelvie, who got the strangest assignment in the history of WIP internships. I asked him to make out with the ex-wife of Brent Celek, Susie, on the air after a nerd was in a Super Bowl commercial kissing a supermodel. Jimmy gave it his all, and Susie, as always, was a great sport. (You still owe me, Jimmy.)

Our show avoided politics at all costs, but we greeted with joy the calls of Mayor and Governor Ed Rendell, who helped to promote WIP in the early days and who embodies the bold spirit of the Philadelphia sports fan. The late Sen. Arlen Specter was equally aggressive when he made his weekly calls on Monday mornings. (If he were still here now, he would be demanding an investigation into the Eagles losing Super Bowl LVII, I'm sure.)

There's not much more I can say about Jonesy, Rubén Amaro, Billy King, Marcus Hayes, Marshall Harris, Ben Davis, Hugh Douglas, Mitch Williams, and, of course, the late John Marzano. They were athletes and executives who *got* WIP. Not everyone did. Their contributions were invaluable, especially in the last decade or so.

Our army of expert callers over the years gave our show a foundation of knowledge that was otherwise sorely lacking. They included, in no particular order, Mike Lombardi, Dick Vermeil, Ray Didinger, Garry Cobb, Ross Tucker, Seth Joyner, Sam Donnellon, Jack McCaffery, Ron Jaworski, Chad Dukes, John Stolnis, Brandon Lee Gowton, Dave Spadaro, John Brazer, Tom Burgoyne, Derrick Gunn, Michael Barkann, Jimmy and Dei Lynam, Brian Baldinger, Mark Eckel, and Todd Zolecki (who helped me get this book published. Make sure you read his great book, *Doc*).

And while you're at it, check out the only post-WIP job I have continued, my participation with our great TV critic Jay Black and Rhea Hughes in the podcast *The TV Show* on YouTube and PhillyVoice.com. I am a bit player on that show. It is truly a labor of love, talking TV every week. Working with Jay and Rhea is its own reward.

With one notable exception, the public relations departments of all four Philly pro teams saw our show as the enemy. They booked players and coaches only with the deepest reservations—and only after days and days of requests—despite our unfailingly fair-minded interviews over the years. The only one who really understood the PR value of our show was the Eagles' Derek Boyko, who partnered with us for a long run that was mutually beneficial. Why did no one else ever get it? I have no answers.

At the risk of being accused of treason, I also have to thank a caller in our very early days who became a worthy rival host at the other sports station in Philly, John Kincade, who was a major contributor to our show for decades before he crossed over to the dark side. No one ever did Carnacs—a bit he stole from Johnny Carson—better than Kincade. (And that includes Carson himself.)

Usually, an agent is just there to make sure you get paid what you're worth. Steve Mountain was so much more than that. He was as much a firefighter as he was a negotiator. My first call, more times than I could ever recount, was to Steve, who calmed me down and then doused the flames. One of the flames he doused was Tom Bigby, with that legendary clause that gave me unprecedented power over my bully boss.

Cindy Webster is the only person who, solely through the power of her people skills, made the teams like us—or at least tolerate us. She also got the Phillies and Eagles to honor me on the field in the final year, no doubt while questioning their own sanity. Unfortunately, Cindy's return to WIP was short-lived. The bosses let her go again when I retired. I told them they made the same mistake twice. So I hired her to represent me for this book.

And while on the subject of public relations and promotions, I would be wrong not to acknowledge two of the best in those departments, David Helfrich and Bryan Cole. They both hated Wing Bowl, but both were happily willing to take one for the team every year. (Helfrich took an extra one when he got bowled over during that 15-hour pregame show in 1993.)

Despite having no experience in literary circles, Cindy Webster found me a great publisher, Triumph in Chicago, a fantastic director of author engagement, Bill Ames, and a highly knowledgeable literary agent, Stacey Glick.

Joe Weachter was not the happiest guy I ever met, but his smile was luminous every time he fed a line to Jonesy and it connected. Our producer for 30 years, Joe was also the maestro of our show. No one ever has been better at hitting the perfect sound effect at the perfect time. Toward the end, he came up with the "How did we do?" close. It was the best way to end our show, by far.

Al Morganti is responsible for all of this. In fact, if you have any complaints about what we did for all those years, blame Al. He got me my first job in radio, which led to the exodus from the *Inquirer.* He created Wing Bowl. He was a major part of every decision we made for three decades. He is in the Hockey Hall of Fame, because he is a Hall of Famer in life. (He is also the only man I ever saw who looked good with a mullet.)

Rhea Hughes is the little sister I never had. She was great from the first day, and then she only got better. She tolerated our obnoxious, sexist early years, taught us (mainly me) how to behave better and did so much behind the scenes that I'm hoping she will write her own book. How dedicated is Rhea? She reported for work the day she got labor pains with her awesome son, Clark. I sacrificed for WIP, but no more so than Rhea, who carried me to the finish line. In so many ways, she is the hero of this story.

Now that I'm really retired, I need to thank all of the other tolerant members of my family, which includes my own offspring, Neil and Meredith, plus Gail's sweet kids (now prospering adults), Caitlyn and Brendan, and the eight—and counting—grandchildren. Special mention goes out to my son-in-law, Nick D'Amico, who sold his Eagles season tickets right after the parade to spend more time with his amazing family. Nick knows what's important in life. And I can't forget my sister, Phyllis, and her husband, John, who were there for my mom when I wasn't. There's a special place in heaven for those two.

Gail (Autenrieth) Cataldi was with me for my last 27 years at WIP, and I mean really *with me.* She propped me up on the bad days, and she pricked the balloon when my head got too big. She was a partner like no one I ever could have imagined. Everyone who has ever met Gail loves her instantly. How she ended up with a grump like me is a mystery I have no desire to solve.

And last are the fans, the listeners, the callers who gave our show its personality. I will never be able to list them all, though I did dedicate a chapter to some of the most memorable. They made me want to do the best job I could every day, because they deserved it. They are the most misunderstood fan base in America, and will probably remain so because of the laziness of our national media.

No one inspired me as much as the fans. To Arnie and Shirley and Kenny and Jason and Rocco and SuperPhan, and Kim the Lesbian, and Marc from Mount Laurel and Levi from Overbrook Park, Tony from South Philly, Phil from the Northeast and Pretzel Bob, Pepper Bill, the two coma callers, Coma Tracey and Coma Jim, and the thousands of others who gave our show a true Philadelphia personality—thank you.

It was more than a privilege to share my sports life with you.

You all deserve a standing ovation.